IMAGINATION
and our world of
MAKE-BELIEVE

HOW ADULTS PLAY TOGETHER
IN THEIR MAKE-BELIEVE REALITIES

VINCENT SARGENTI

COPYRIGHT © 2018
by
Vincent Sargenti

Doug Offenbacher
Cover design and Art Director

No part of this publication may be reproduced, stored in a retrieval system, or transmitted in any form or by any means, electronic, mechanical, photocopying, recording, or otherwise, without written permission of the publisher. For information regarding permission, email: info@sargenti.org

DISCLAIMER: This is a work of autobiographical nonfiction. No names have been changed, no characters invented, no events fabricated. It reflects the author's present recollections of experiences over time. Some characteristics have been changed, some events have been compressed, and some dialogue has been recreated.

ACKNOWLEDGEMENTS

I would like to thank David Worrell for his invaluable assistance in the preparation of this manuscript, for helping me keep it real and for sharing his appreciation of great music.

Special thanks to Doug Offenbacher for his lifelong friendship and for his mentoring and guidance in the preparing of this manuscript and cover art. Both of these gentleman were there with me through a lot of the experiences in this book and helped me keep things in the right perspective.

I'd like to apologize publicly to my mom for all the dirty laundry I've aired here. This is the intensely personal story of my own life, not necessarily hers. Mom, you are a good person who's been through hell and you made it out alive, with your own lessons learned. I just want to you know that I care and I love you more than ever today. I am sorry if this is hard to read. It was equally difficult to write.

My wife Yolanda and my daughters, Pepper and Sienna, have been very patient with me in the year and half it has taken me to write this book. They've been loving and supportive the whole way. Our life together has been the greatest blessing, an unbroken circle of caring and consideration for what truly matters in each day.

There have been a number of good and decent people who have been role models to me, Fred Rogers and Arnold Palmer, the people in this book, like Al Jackson and brother Bill, and many who were never mentioned. Thank you for being excellent examples of fine character and the right way to live.

And above all, Yogi Tom Hess, who's presence has been seriously valuable, bringing about those crucial turning points in my life. Just by being there, he helped me see the wisdom this book revolves around. Thanks, Tom.

DEDICATION

To everyone who reads this: May you live with your whole self in the present moment, without resistance and find extraordinary joy in your most ordinary moments.

TABLE OF CONTENTS

Introduction	i
1) Genesis	1
2) Faith	13
3) Exposure	29
4) Healing	51
5) Work	71
6) Discovery	87
7) Knowledge	113
8) The Medicine People	145
9) Ceremony	163
10) Of Good And Decent Men	199
11) Dancing In the World Of Make-Believe	221
12) When All Is Lost	247
13) Imaginary Umbrellas	265
Epilogue: The Take-Away	281

*"I turned it off because I was the one letting it run.
I turned it all off because, now, I could see
through my own suffering to what was creating it.
I understood my imagination was the culprit,
it was something I was doing to myself."*

INTRODUCTION

It has been said the imagination is the most powerful force in the universe, but what is the imagination? Does anyone really study it, scientifically or otherwise? How do we even go about asking the big questions regarding the imagination's influence on all the qualities of life which mean so much to us: belief, faith, hope and love, morality, right and wrong? Imagination is deeply intertwined with the mystery of being alive, with human consciousness and, to be honest, science has not yet been able to answer the question of how consciousness occurs, what is causing it. We do not yet understand what makes a me: me. Though we are making tremendous strides forward in neuroscience, and cognitive studies, this is one great discovery, which still remains undiscovered.

As a layman, and general all-around suffering human being, I have always persevered in my attempt to understand what life has to teach mankind about itself. I have spent an entire lifetime learning how to distinguish between what the human imagination creates and what life actually is. What we believe it is, all too often, may be nothing more than nonsensical games of pretend that we play with ourselves and each other. As I faithfully listened to the adults in my life assuring me of what life actually is, what I must believe is true, their actions often contradicted what they outwardly professed. I loved all the adults in my life and I wanted to please them. I wanted to be like them and believe what they believed about the way life actually is. So I did exactly that. But as my life played itself out, as lifetimes often have a tendency to do, what I was taught to believe life actually is wasn't holding water out on life's high seas.

I found I had to toss a lot of my own deeply held convictions overboard just to stay afloat, both intellectually and spiritually. Even then, life's stormy seas had a hand in scuttling my dreams and washing me up onto the shipwrecked shores of my own human stupidity. Many times, I have had to start over, rebuilding all my hopes and dreams, so I could one day reset my sails for the sunnier skies of clearer understanding. Over the years, the insights came in unexpected places. They didn't come while I was in deep contemplation. They didn't come under the perfect conditions of expensive meditation retreats. They came while I was at work. They came while I was performing long hours of arduous labor on twelve-hour shifts, during seventy-plus hour weeks on my feet, while I was coercing a hundred-foot of seven-color, 57-inch offset printing press into running as fast as possible without stopping for long periods of time.

The mind, under these conditions of extended, highly focused concentration, can be pushed beyond its boundaries into elevated states of adrenaline and endorphin-charged awareness. Normally, a man would never choose to do this on his own, to go way out beyond the extremes of clinical exhaustion. He has to be forced into these feats of heroic productivity by the conditions of his miserable life, tricked into believing it will all be worth it. And at the end of the day, a man such as myself, can be more than a little resentful of the fact that I had to work so physically, while so many around me are doing next-to-nothing in regards to actual labor. Their job is to stand around bullshitting all day, walking off back to their desks in their air-conditioned offices, drinking coffee, staring at their computers from the comfort of a big leather office chair. What was the root of my cursed fate? What did I fail to grasp about staying in school?

How can we examine the contents of our minds, distinguishing accurately between what belongs to imagination and what belongs to the five senses, the natural world? I suffered from a tremendous amount of mental frustration and anguish, out at the far end of those unbearably long days, weeks, months, watching them all turn into years, into thirty years as a pressman in the printing industry. Over the years, the industry had grown worse and worse. The Internet killed the industry off and I was clinging to one of the last remaining holdout sectors left, printing packaging. The work kept getting harder. The hours kept getting longer. Companies were forcing the workers to do more with less people, treating men like farm animals, beasts of industrial burden. No one cared anymore. It was only about numbers. All the perks were gone now.

What was once an excellent family wage income had now turned into a sweatshop survival job. Jobs like these aren't there to serve human lives anymore, the humans are there to serve the dollar, to bow down and worship it, to sacrifice all to deliver more wealth to the wealthy. The more you give them, the more they figure you are capable of giving them. So, since you are allowing it, they will see how much more they can squeeze out of every man in their employ. No hard feelings, it's only business, they say.

I think over time, I finally broke. I reached a point where I probably should have had an aneurysm or a heart attack, but instead, as is my tendency, I broke within the guarded privacy of my own mind. I was way out beyond the extreme end of fatigue and exhaustion, suffering my horrible fate as a modern-day American worker. Suddenly, as if freed from a huge burden, my prison of self-manufactured feelings, all the anxiety and mental stress just suddenly disappeared. It was like opening an overstuffed closet of hardened ideas about what the world is, ideas which were controlling my feelings, when suddenly everything just fell out into the open light of day and evaporated as if awakening from a bad dream. The closet was empty the whole time. I only imagined the closet was overstuffed and slowly killing me. I came to a place where I could no longer deny it. I could no longer tolerate it. I had been living my life in denial. This endless dialogue I was having with myself inside my mind was definitely imaginary.

Very specific and powerful thoughts I had been having were backed by chest-clenching, heart wrenching conviction and the strain on my body was killing me. It all simply vanished, at once. I was so mad at people for things they said and so offended by the things they did, their disrespectful actions toward me, the way they expected me to accept and do what they demanded of me. All the people who ripped me off, all the people who had responsibilities they did not live up to and because they did not, I let it deeply affect me.

There were ongoing imaginary arguments I was continually having with my visualized images of family, friends and co-workers in my mind. The outrage! The indignity! I would imagine myself screaming at them with all the intensity I could possibly feel. My heart would race. My adrenaline would flow and my breathing would change. My blood pressure would redline. I would perspire and run my hands through my hair. It all simply vanished, once I asked myself the question, "Is this a product of my imagination?"

"Yes." I replied to myself, "Yes, it is, if I am being honest."

The final step was to quietly ask for the imagination to switch to the off position. So, I asked. "Can I just turn this shit off?" And it was indeed the final step. Square One realized.

The result, the real benefit, and the strike of gold that proved it all legitimate was when I realized I could truly relax and take a deep breath of infinite relief. Everything changed. My personal imagination could be disengaged and I could actually live in peace. It may have simply been the tipping of the scale in a long process of personal growth, but regardless of why, a whole new world opened up for me. It was not dramatic, or emotional, there was nothing powerful or earth shattering about it. I simply arrived an ordinary recognition of the way life is, the way I am and what the present moment actually contains.

I became present to the world that was actually surrounding me, without superimposing anything on it. It wasn't a perfect world but I had to take responsibility for where I had let myself run. If I wanted to improve my situation, a better job, a nicer house, a newer car for instance, I was going to have to make a fresh start from where I was, pull myself up by my bootstraps and let this newfound clarity become my guidance system toward a higher-quality life.

The mythical dragon of the mind, which millenniums of monks and spiritual warriors have fought since the dawn of time is only the human imagination in drag. I simply planted my sword in the dirt at my feet as I realized, "There is no dragon. This is all imaginary. I'm making it all up as I go." I simply came to understand that all this kicking and screaming going on in my head amounted to nothing more than me screaming at myself in an imaginary mirror. It was stupid. It was an idiotic waste of energy. I was angry inside. I was fighting with imaginary imagery. It isn't real. So, I shut it off. The dragon is purely imagined, I realized, both individually for myself and collectively for everyone. I shut it off with a single click because I finally understood what it was, what made it, what sustained it, what was driving it. The human imagination is powerful, yes, but it is not as powerful as a single moment of silent understanding. It wasn't an ordinary understanding. This came from a much deeper place in me.

"Turn it off." A still small voice whispered from within the depths of my soul. "Turn it off. Stop. Please. Just listen..." So, I listened. I turned it off. And I've been listening ever since.

I found life is far sweeter when I pause and listen. Occasionally, the whisper of the still small voice of silent understanding will speak to me. It speaks to everyone, so it says. It speaks without words in ways only sincerity of the heart can comprehend. It was sending messages that the voice in my head isn't real. "Listen deeper." I heard the whisper say. It was so hard to hear, so faint and soft. So, I shut off the turbulent movie in my mind. . . and I only listened. As I waited to hear it once more, silence was the only thing I heard. But the silence was enough. I could feel the still small voice was there.

I turned off the noise because I was the one letting it run. I turned it all off because, now, I could see through my own suffering to what was creating it. I understood my imagination was the culprit, it was something I was doing to myself. I was being negligent by letting my train of thought run down the mountain without brakes. I finally got it. Only I could make myself say, "No more." And I stopped. I had finally remembered to be here now. Fuck, what a long journey that was. This is the story of that journey.

My chronic relentless anxiety disorder could finally let go and come to peace, untying the knot in my stomach, it simply faded away. My mind was infested with thoughts and I was so sick and tired of it, it was like a disease that was slowly killing me. Why would I hold on to something so horribly painful? Imagination is powerful, but suddenly, I understood how I am more powerful, how my will to deactivate it is now clearer. The cruelty of mind games people tried to play on me to make themselves feel powerful at my expense: now powerless. That nauseating feeling in my guts of impending doom, the continual relentless grinding, the fear of getting fired because I wasn't working fast enough, or that I would make a big mistake, churning and rechurning, the intense vomiting of the contents of the sick and twisted torture chamber of my mind, just disappeared. As if I had been awakened from some horrible dream, the enflamed emotional wounds that just kept making it all worse are now left alone long enough for a lasting healing process to take hold. A stability and solidity returned as feelings of renewed self-confidence, the more I began taking responsibility for my own insanity. As time goes by, I just feel so much better. A lasting time of personal growth has returned. My life has improved. I don't work there anymore. I eventually moved on, of my own volition, as I chose to live more deliberately.

"Is this a product of my imagination?" It all just vanished. I am truly free of it all. Finally.

My entire demeanor changed overnight and it was noticeable enough that people were asking me, "What changed?" They would ask, "The expression on your face is so different." "You are so much more relaxed and approachable," they would say. "Your eyebrows are no longer all furled up," was one comment. Over time, I felt a healing process settle into my bones and a part of my personality began to experience mental health and personal growth in unexpected ways. For the time being, I was still stuck working ungodly hours at an awful job, but now I was looking at the world from a place of silent stillness as a man in a body, not a mind infested by a provocative frenzy.

I still worked impeccably but that was a matter of how I wanted to represent myself to others. It was about my own honor and dignity now, about being responsible for the agreements I'd made, holding up my end of the bargain. I began to see miserable suffering people, myself included, differently. I realized, if I could help myself, then I could help others, without them even knowing. I could sooth them. I could change the way they felt by declining each opportunity to be miserable with them, by lifting their mood with my own, by being friendly and making them laugh, if I could. It was a way of lifting their spirits when they were down, because I didn't give a fuck anymore, and yet, I truly cared more than ever. I just cared differently. I saved up enough money so if I ever got fired I would be ok. I wasn't running scared any more. I was more focused than ever on what was truly important in my life.

I came to accept how there is nothing threatening about being in the world with one less layer of subjective self-reflection. That layer is not protecting me from anything. Quite the contrary, it was actually inflammatory and terribly unhealthy. One day, I found I had gained the ability to let go of the anger, the rage against the indignities of life's demands. Because they weren't real. I completely forgot about them and became a different person inside. I had forgiven the world. Because there was nothing to forgive. I still got up and went to work every morning, but without all the misery and mental anguish. My sense of wonder had returned, I could resonate at a higher frequency, or greater amplitude, as the case may be, and more fully savor my time in the natural world.

It came with a sigh of relief that learning to distinguish what is imaginary from what is real isn't in any way threatening to our collective or individual identity. It had simply become apparent, to me anyway, what was purely imaginary and what was physically real. Simple. The imagination is not dead. It did not die in me. It is still a very powerful force in my life. I did not slay the dragon, but you could say, I made it lay at my feet and behave itself.

This was a turning point in my own life, which brought about a lasting calm the likes of which I'd never known. I would like to share this approach with you, this way I discovered to calm the run away train-of-thought and feel complete, right where we stand. I look at thought as purely an imaginary activity. Therefore, in my experience, it's not real. I am not encouraging mindlessness. Presence of mind is prerequisite. Simply deactivating the activity of being mindlessly lost in imaginary pursuits makes presence of mind become clearer than ever. It amplifies it. This is the story of how I learned to press the pause button.

Everyone, apparently, leaves their overly active imaginary activity running all the time, never shutting it off. Many don't want to admit all the crap going on between their ears has no value at all, most of the time. It's actually a liability. It is like a television in the other room that is always left on, even when no one is watching it. It's burning valuable energy for nothing. It's just distracting you from what you need to be doing to improve the quality of your life. It's contributing to the agitation and clutter in the valuable space between your ears. But this can all be changed, set right, made clear. We can easily return to our natural state and spend our time and energy experiencing deep inner-peace, presence of mind and greater wholeness of self.

Distinguishing between imagination and what actually exists is a constant process, it's an approach to living, to arriving at the most down-to-earth place one can come to. This approach involves an act of deep self-honesty, of taking responsibility for our own negligence, our failure to control where we let our minds run off to, our failure to admit to ourselves that we are the cause of most of what we let ourselves think about. This book reveals a new approach to being a calmer and more complete person. The endless suffering disappears like a mirage and I would like to share this approach with as many others as possible. I would like to see this mirage disappear for the entire world.

Chapter One
GENESIS

THIS COULD BE said to be an imaginary book about nothing.

It is imaginary because, at the time of writing, where I am sitting now, this book does not yet exist. I am simply imagining that I am going to write a book. The imaginary book I am going to be writing, I believe, is going to be about imagination and make-believe, which aren't actually real because they are merely made of thought, which has no corporeal reality. We cannot touch imagination, nor can we consider anything that is make-believe to be real. Since all of our thoughts are simply imaginary, theoretically, they don't exist. And in this sense, they are nothing.

So in this context, this is an imaginary book about nothing.

In that regard, you may simply put the book down now and say, "Fine! We're done with that then. Nice read!"

Ignition

In the beginning, there was stardust and gasses, gravity and electromagnetic forces. And there were no thoughts because there was no earth, no man to think them, no nature, as we would know it. No air. The earth was without form and time would simply flow into the void. There were stars in the distance, the Milky Way Galaxy, but where we are now there was just a big protoplanetary disc quietly forming. There were rocky materials and water ice. There were hydrogen clouds and a big thing called a solar nebula. And then there was accretion. Sweet, sweet accretion.

All-at-once, in the center of the disc, a spectacular phenomena! We had ignition! In a matter of minutes, where there was only darkness, an ever-increasing density of material crossed some critical physical threshold and collapsed inward on itself. Suddenly, there it was, a star erupted into life. Our star. Young and wild and intensely bright, the power coming off of the star as it burst into ignition sent a shockwave outward through the protoplanetary material causing it to vibrate and dance and sing songs of joy. Thus began one of the wildest parties in the history of our rocky, gassy solar system. Over hundreds of millions of years of time, all the matter set forever into motion by the initial blast of a solar wind began continually slamming into other matter in one endless cataclysmic event that would make Armageddon seem like Christmas morning.

And sweet accretion dealt the cards. It played its hand, as the chemical elements joined forming pairs, three-of-a-kind, a full house, and molecules began dancing into luminescent chemical arrays. These new molecules formed new compounds which reacted in the presence of everything as the protoplanetary disc formed into rings and the rings ordered the debris into spheres, in frequencies radiating outward, in orders of circulating magnitude. Sweeping, cleaning, these orders of magnitude unfolded in their cosmic design of pure physics. As this orderly chaos of matter struck into balance, it all convulsed in the presence of our powerful Sun. The spheres of accreting matter developed into orbital bodies. Yes. Accretion had dealt the cosmic hand, set the ante, raised the bet and doubled-down, calling all players then throwing down its royal flush. Life!

Then there was a cosmic order. Universal balance. Amazing grace. And it was beautiful. It was everything. It was us.

But overriding all of the commotion was some incomprehensible factor we call The Arrow of Time. And it pointed that-a-way. Time the great ruler, time the great healer, holding all things, all worlds in due course as we set sail past the point of no return, rising headlong across the face of the universal waters into the mysterious storms of a distant future evolution.

And evolution it would be... for this is the hand we were dealt.

Early Man

Early man was driven almost exclusively by direct experience perceived via the physical senses. As man evolved, the key development, which distinguished our new species of hominids from others, living around the same time, and what led to our unrivaled success as the dominant progenitor, was our ability to adapt by inventing new ways of approaching survival. Adaptation is forced on us by the pressures from the environment, the forces acting against us, the presence of resistance as we try to get through each day. Our ancient ancestors were survivors. They fought successfully. They went up against all the elements of their environment and continually came out on top. It wasn't easy, I'm sure. They had to kick some serious ass to keep things going. Our ancient ancestors were The Kings of Kicking-Ass. We owe them a great debt of gratitude. Three hundred thousand years ago, our 1.5×10^4-great-grandpa, must've been a real son-of-a-bitch when it came to adapting to his environment. I bet he took very little shit from anyone about anything.

At the dawn of man, in order to survive, we were forced to adapt to the challenges our environment presented. One of the ways we responded was our brains grew larger and larger. As this took place, our cognitive function increased and we were not only processing sensory data, but gradually, we developed the capacity to make more complex interpretations. We began envisioning possibilities and making decisions.

Before we could invent the first tools we had to perceive a resource with our senses. We'd see a rock, for instance, then envision ways we could use that rock to help us get food or build shelter. We slowly grew better and better at thinking about what we could do with what we had. For this to happen, you can bet there were a hell of a lot of days spent out in the hot sun staring at rocks, wondering what they might be useful for. But one day it happened. The idea appeared in the thinking brain of the first creature to start poking a stick down an ant hole, or bang a stone against some other stone to sharpen it. Where did the idea come from? Well, it came from a long process of evolution that gradually turned part of the protoplanetary disc into a lovely creature who had the presence of mind to imagine a new way to use a stick, or a rock. He or she was probably starving to death and driven by the will to survive.

In that environment, with its constant pressure to adapt or die trying, we began to develop the nascent spark that would ignite the power of human imagination. While our brain size slowly evolved, over countless generations, not only did it grow in size, researchers believe it changed in structure as well, in ways suitable for greater cognitive skills. We used our new creative skills to envision how the rock we were holding could be altered to extend our abilities to make tools, weapons, spark fire and eventually, one day, cook bacon. Now, that's progress. Imagine the first primal design studio, the first caveman engineering group. We began to invent new technology, which extended our reach and leveraged our advantage against the forces working against us. It was Stone Age technology but it set us on the road to where we are today.

The advent of imaginative cognition in a bunch of homininis gradually culminated into a whole new group of diverging species, capable not only of making tools, but of developing new ways of communicating, storytelling and collective conceptualization. There were many other species of the genus Homo, which in Latin means man. All these species, of which there were many, are considered human, several of which lived at the same time. All of these interesting folks are now extinct. The most recent human species, Homo floresiensis, was believed to have lived as recently as 12,000 years ago. However, new scientific data has pushed this dating back toward 50,000 years ago.

Over time, modern man, better known as Homo sapiens, survived long enough to become the only remaining human species. How much longer we'll survive is anyone's guess. We are not the longest living Homo species, nor did we evolve the largest brain. Homo erectus has us beat for timespan, having survived for long as two million years, possibly. That's a long time, considering we have only been around for about 250,000 years. Homo neanderthalensis is one of as many as seven other species which all developed brains larger than ours. Our developing intelligence and our increasing ability to imagine solutions to our problems may have set us apart, from other Homo species and other mammals. Maybe it was just dumb luck, who knows? While I could go on to speculate about the role of imagination in countless animal species, and the biological dependence of imagination on the physiology of the brain, in the interest of keeping this work focused and to avoid wandering into quagmires of tangential ideas, these subjects remain outside the scope of this present work. This is the story of imagination and our world of make-believe. This is an imaginary book about the invisible wonders, which have filled our minds for all these aeons of time since the dawn of man.

The emergence of the new improved, imaginative modern man, moved us along the slow evolutionary grind toward behavioral modernity, a gradually evolving genetic adaptation which required many, many thousands of years. I am satisfied with the story of evolution. So often, at the scene of big mistakes and accidents, I look at my fellow humans and see in their faces, the faint reflection of our ape-like hominid ancestors, still present as they scratch their heads and wonder how shit got so fucked up. There is still a bit of ape-like goon in all of us.

The Advent of Language

The origin of language likely did not occur in an instant. Very little is known of how human language evolved. We are left only with wide-open territory in which to speculate. When we had not yet invented language, how on earth would we go about recording its slow evolution into existence? Our ability to talk probably evolved over hundreds of thousands of years of time.

Once we developed simple ways of speaking verbally, it would still be many thousands of years before the earliest known forms of written language evolved.

In drawings, then by associating a sound with an image in the drawings, mankind first set foot down the path toward the languages we speak today. When an image drawn on the wall of a cave with the tip of a burned stick became a symbol for horse that was great day for mankind. The earliest known writing was the notation of numbers. Soft clay tokens would be marked, or notched, several times and then baked. They could then be strung together and held aside as a record used in trading.

As time went by, symbolic forms became associated with verbal sounds humans could make. Finally, they all decided on a vocalized sound for referring to a horse. This was probably something like, "Nayyyy!" or a snorting sound very similar what the horse would make. Proxy by proxy, things represented by sounds, sounds represented by symbols, symbols becoming letterforms, then letterforms carefully put together began to represent their vocal expressions. Through a long process of evolution, this all became spoken and written words.

Words!

They were just like tools, but unlike our sticks and bones, our spears and arrowheads, these tools were constructed entirely out of a more sophisticated use of imagination. These were the tools we used to fashion the earliest form of communications. Words are like imaginary little storage devices, containers, invisible boxes filled with little units of meaning. Words. Now we could give everything in our world an imaginary name and share that name with others, whether others were present at the time or not. When everyone kept forgetting what we named everything, we had to invent a way to remember. Like numbers before them on clay tokens, letterforms and words were now inscribed into soft clay and then baked. The first labels were invented when we wrote the name down and stuck it on the thing. Since paper wasn't invented yet, it appears to have been clay tokens and clay tablets which became the earliest known form of information storage. It was just one step removed from jamming a stick in the dirt but, hey. Who cares? It worked. Now everyone could speak the same language and share information. Because information could now be stored for use at a later time, learning and teaching a wide variety of skills filled the world with wonderful possibilities.

Within our minds, these little storage boxes began shuttling units of meaning back and forth between our ears and all around our brains, filling every corner of our minds with such wonderful thoughts. Slowly, we learned how to empty and fill, arrange and rearrange the tiny, invisible boxes, deepening each words's meaning. Every new generation developed the use of words in their our own unique way, to express the depths of how they felt. As groups went off into isolation, to develop in other parts of the world, languages continued to evolve.

Communicating through speech, we form puffs of air, each puff filling the air around us with imaginary boxes, words full of meaning. Words could now be openly shared. Non destructively, these invisible containers of meaning could be handed back and forth and used over and over again. Puffs of air in the wind could now carry the thoughts, like the pollen of knowledge spread over large populations of human beings, cultivating new ideas. It is as if we fill each box with meaning and place these tiny boxes on a conveyor belt of time, where they quietly move along until someone comes along to read them, or hear them. They become a little choo-choo train, tiny boxes all moving together along a track in sentences, a train of thought carrying all the little meanings safely to their destination. Throw in ten thousand years for good measure and time after time, year after year, generation after generation, the human ability to communicate our thoughts, both verbally and in writing began. Language evolved. Everything evolves. It's an evolution. It happens over time. Gradually. It's the hand we've been dealt by the universe. This is what is happening here. This imaginary invention of make-believe words made it a lot easier work together and this is when things really took off.

Mankind's ability to collectively imagine an entire detailed language, widely adopted by all the other hairless ape-like hominid creatures walking around the planetary surface, spawned the dawn of a new age. Sharing the same systems of thought and working cooperatively to develop them is the evolutionary master stroke that lifted us out of being ape-like animals, grunting and snorting our way to our next meal. Working together, developing systems of thought, is one of those remarkable make-believe activities that helped set mankind apart from other less successful hominid species alive around at the same time. Cooperative, organized effort of large human populations is a key factor in our evolutionary success story. Without the advent of this stunning gift of imagination, language could have never taken place.

Bottlenecks

Paleontologists have proposed theories of a big bang of human consciousness, which occurred over 50,000 years ago with the emergence of art and technology. Others say genetic bottlenecks occurred which affected the course of human evolution and brought man into the most modern form of our species. Scientists have proposed that 70,000 years ago cataclysmic events, possibly a meteor or a massive volcano eruption, such as the Toba catastrophe theory, created a population bottleneck that may have drove down human populations into the low thousands.

This theory states how those surviving Homo sapiens emerged from the bottleneck as a more homogenized, slenderized version of human gene pool. While this drop in the human population is supported by the weight of genetic evidence, there are many who doubt the theory on the grounds that it may not have been the primary cause for the near extinction of our kind. What caused our population to drop so precipitously is the subject of much debate. While we can speculate, these reasonable theories do offer explanations for how extreme conditions in the environment might have genetically cleaned house, killed off the last of our relative Homo species and drove the advent of the modern thinking man.

New, improved and equipped with our modern cognitive ability, we grew more intelligent, but above all else, became far better looking. The descendants of these handsome survivors pushed our ability to collectively imagine to new heights, working cooperatively in innovative ways never before seen.

It's believed they were no longer mere ordinary hunter-gatherers. They began developing fishing nets and specialized tools for hunting, arrowheads and various pointy things, giving themselves a big advantage over nature. What caused this ability? What made it possible for these awesome weapons of mass food production to suddenly spring into existence? Along our dimly lit path of human evolution, a light bulb finally switched on over somebody's head. All it took was for someone to imagine a possibility. These guys were all standing around looking at each other, and one guy's eyes grew really wide and his mouth fell open as he yelled out, "By Jobe, I think I've got it!" Next thing you know, all of these folks started banging rocks together, making obsidian spearheads, crafting bone into sharp tools. They really went nuts with the stuff. We know this because we're still finding these artifacts all over the world today. They're everywhere! It would take another 60,000 years, a long while, before we'd see the rise of more complex societies and the advent of civilization.

The ancient environment demanded that humans adapt to it or cease to exist. Our response to this demand brought about the advent of agriculture. With so much surplus food around, our numbers exploded even more rapidly, bringing forth denser populations far greater than ever seen before. We can only speculate about the social dynamics within early civilizations, which drove the development of our ability to cooperatively imagine more sophisticated political solutions. Necessity is a mother but creativity is her brother. When it all comes together, Bob's your uncle and everything is coming up roses. We actively invoked organizational unity across large groups numbering 10,000 and more, by collectively sharing, teaching and learning to adhere to a single system of thought, or else.

The Rule Of Law: Governing The Masses

The Code of Hammurabi is among the earliest known code of law, carved into a large basalt stele, which is currently housed at the Louvre in Paris, France. Drawn up by King Hammurabi (*c. 1792 BC*) in the Mesopotamian city of Babylon, there are hundreds of laws describing every manner of crime and punishment. You can bet there was a lot of flogging going on during this time. The system would be imposed by forcefully beating the offenders into submission, throwing them into the river, or killing them. This imaginary system of thought, along with The Code of Ur-Nammu (c. 2100), are the oldest known legal code surviving today. This grew out of the necessity to govern large populations.

When we consider this, a system of thought originates from within the world of make-believe, in this case, through King Hammurabi's imagination. It becomes a shared experience through his administrators and officials, when the governed populace learns about the laws and consent to be governed by them, or agree to adhere to the system of thought. In order to guide the entire population's behavior, even if some refused to agree, it's certain the king had some strong law enforcement officers ready to handle it. We can now see how ideas are able to reach out from the world of make-believe to issue forth, brutal real-world beatings in the interests of peer-pressure and social conformity. Here we have the early examples of adults using imaginary notions as justification for beating the hell out of someone. The words *make-believe realities take* on new significance when you think of one ancient man telling another, "I believe I am going to beat the living hell out of you!"

However, as time marches on, mankind refines and develops this unique proclivity for cooperative imagining through acts of planning, mapping and designing better ways to govern large populations for everyone's safety and survival all across this newly-minted idea of civilization. Through imagining the same vision together, we not only domesticate our environment, but our fellow man, bringing about a newly emerging law and order, enforced community tranquility.

Prior to these earliest civilizations, primal men, grunting, snorting, foul-smelling beasts that we were, had no such thing as the rule of law, nor were there writing, geopolitical borders or currency, as we know it today. There was no written rule of law or a court of law with which they could resolve their differences. None of the vital systems we have in place today were there to guide them. The world was a very different and far more unruly place. The idea of ownership of private property, of funding commercial enterprise or enforcing contractual agreements by a court of law had simply not been imagined yet. The idea of a corporate entity, the agency under which tens of thousands work harmoniously in-concert, had not yet been thought of, as these devices don't exist in nature. They exist only in the collective imagination of human beings. The Arrow Of Time was pointing toward them but the cosmic clock had yet to tick the opening tock when these intangible principles would begin to guide the everyday activity of humankind.

In the U.S., a court of law is intended to be a place where the human imagination is set aside while the facts of what actually happened are made clear. It doesn't always work this way but it is the clear intention of the court to get to the actual truth, the whole truth and nothing but the truth. This is a nice way of saying we want to know what actually happened, not what "make-believe" happened. Honestly presenting the truth of a matter, for the purpose of drawing completely reasonable conclusions from available evidence, is a hallmark of justice.

However, the scene of a trial, all-too-often, becomes centerstage for the most convincingly performed fictional theater mankind has ever produced. The imagination has never been so flamboyantly put on parade, by either the prosecution or the defense, as it often times is in a courtroom during a trial. It is as if the truth must outshine the most diabolically engineered attempts to drown it in the world of make-believe. I have never envied those who have a sworn duty to draw the crucial line of distinction between the real world of factual events and the world of make-believe on this stage. Especially, when so much is at stake.

I point to the court of law here to illustrate one of the points I want to make by writing this book: *what is actually happening versus what grown adults want to make-believe is happening.* Only one is actually occurring in real life. In regards to a past event, only one thing actually occurred. Any number of make-believe scenarios can seem equally convincing, equally plausible after the fact. How do we develop the ability to distinguish between fake news and real life when so much is on the line?

The rule of law as it is written, is a system of thought born out the collective imagination of the people who made it up and then it's agreed to by those who voted it into law. The law becomes a fact of life for all who live under the umbrella of its authority, whether it makes sense or not, they have no choice but to agree to be governed by it. Human law does not exist in the natural world. The laws of physics and the laws of nature allow for human behavior which would get a man arrested in all fifty states, and portions of South America, therefore, discussions of natural law will remain beyond the scope of this present work.

The idea of justice and the rule of law, as we know it in society, is a human-only device. It is a collectively imagined and agreed upon system of thought regarding ideal codes of behavioral conduct and ethics for large communities where it is not possible for all members to know one another. Our justice system has been ever changing, constantly evolving since the day it was first conceived. It has been said, in the United States, that our legal system may not be perfect but it is the best one we have and if we don't like it we can change it. Many believe it to be the finest, fairest rule of law in the history of mankind, even though there is always work going on to improve it.

The concept of law in the U.S. is very different from what is imposed upon those living, for example, under Sharia Law, Martial Law or the current set of laws governing North Korea, or Venezuela. The rule of law is a deep study of information stored in volumes of books filled with legal language, which remains open to interpretation on a case-by-case basis. The fact that it remains open to interpretation based on the composition of each 12-man jury exposes the imaginary nature of the law as a "whatever we can all actually agree on at the time," type of thing. Often, only a majority need to agree to make it function as law.

What one jury decides is worthy of sentencing to death, another jury may find excusable. What we may define as a misdemeanor in the U.S. could be a serious crime in Iran, or an accepted cultural rite in Somalia. The forms of human behavior that are punishable under the law vary greatly depending on where you go because the laws themselves are the ephemeral byproducts of the human imagination, which are limited by a society's ability to enforce them. By virtue of thousands of years of geographic isolation, similar to language itself, each society developed their own systems of thought regarding the rule of law, culturally diverging in regards to accepted and prohibited behavior. For example, while one culture would be accepting of same sex couples, treating them equally under the law, another society would find it fair and just to enact severe prison sentences. What is right is wrong and what is wrong is right. Many who've experienced culture shock, while traveling internationally, have struggled with the moral dilemma of this inversion in defining right and wrong.

What Is Real?

It is precisely because law is imaginary that the criminal mind can flourish. It is clear that the law applies equally to all, and yet we see instances where the wealthy, or the well-connected, get away with murder. Because the rule of law is collectively imagined, it has the weakness of being completely disregarded by criminals and courts alike, such as in the dismissal of charges, immunity or a plea deal. The court can decide which laws it choses to enforce, and which will simply vanish, in any specific case. The law comes down to whatever can be negotiated and agreed to in the context of the written law and the circumstances of each case. Some men walk away free while others go to jail for life, for similar crimes.

The laws of physics, however unforgiving they might be, supersede mankind's rule of law and allow for the possibility of criminals acting entirely outside of the laws of man, without ever being brought to justice. The laws of psychics can be much more difficult to negotiate with but are far less confining on human behavior than the laws of mankind. Journalists would have nothing to write about and police would have nothing to do, if law were to exist somewhere outside the human imagination and work with machine-like precision, in every instance. Society would operate like the clockwork of finely tuned instruments and yet it does not. The rule of law remains as a form of the honor system but the breaking the laws of physics will kick your ass.

The consequences of breaking the law, if caught by law enforcement, illustrates the power of the well-armed idea reaching out of the world of make-believe to issue serious, life-altering consequences, but only if caught. The man-made ideas of law and justice are among the most powerful implementations of control we have over men, to maintain the peace and provide public safety.

However, when we draw a line in the sand, call it a geopolitical border, then cross that line, the law vanishes, powerless, thanks to the collectively imagined idea of jurisdiction and borders. What is punishable by death on one side of the line is a celebrated act of heroic honor on the other. Birds can fly and animals can travel, without passports, back and forth across geopolitical borders all day long, as if they weren't even there. Because, for them, they aren't. Not that other creatures aren't territorial, but humans have the imaginative capacity to play with each other in the world of make-believe by setting up pretend check points with customs officials who have the authority to arrest and detain, who wear badges and neat little uniforms which empower them with the power of the human imagination to believe that things which aren't real, are. And while this system of thought is operating within the world of make-believe, we are under its spell. We agree to be governed by the way adults play together with imaginary things that aren't real. For mankind, borders, laws, justice, money, the ideas of what is heroic or horrific, right and wrong, exist only within the confines of the human imagination and nowhere else. There is a blank slate, a clean canvas underlying all of human activity, which is our natural world. We are merely painting the picture of our make-believe, man-made reality, a mirage that exists according to our own beliefs and the decisions we make about the kind of world we want to live in.

The law of the land will be interpreted in regards to your case in the place and time of your transgression and the hand of fate will deal your cards, hopefully not from the bottom of the imaginary deck and yet these underhanded dealings happen all-too-often based on race, religion or socio-economic status. The language we use in court, the intended meaning of each word, the glossary of terms we employ to articulate our story, the taxonomy with which we spin our tale, either twists the truth of our guilt or paints the picture of our innocence. The outcome of our fate suddenly relies on this ability to gain influence over the collective imagination of the human jury. You must convince them your tale tells the story of what actually happened. Even if they believe your story, they may differ with each other on what the wording of the written law actually means, how to interpret it, or how it should be applied in your case. The right to live, or a lengthy prison sentence, or the penalty of death, all swing on the hinge of worded speech, on how well we can control our world of make-believe. Our ability to articulate and persuade others convincingly becomes the only thing that matters. And this is all happening in an invisible world, which, through the wonders of imagination, we can collectively visualize. We can only hope the people listening, deciding our fate, are reasonable.

Exerting influence, imposing our will, shaping the shared experience of the collective imagination can determine the outcome of a fight for our lives. The consequences of the outcome are life altering. In everything from domestic violence, human rights abuses, trafficking and even corporations unfairly bullying and disempowering the worker, turning off our own imagination brings more of who we are into the present moment, amplifying clarity in situations which may otherwise start getting out-of-hand. By making clear distinctions between what is real and what is imagined, we can turn the tables and gain an advantage we may not have had otherwise. Bringing ourselves entirely into the present moment by setting ourselves on Square One offers us the ability to break the spell, see through lies and neutralize hate. It is to our advantage, if we make use of our underlying ability do so.

Chapter Two
FAITH

MASTER, HOW DO I reach enlightenment?
You must go beyond the beyond, my son...
And when you are done with that,
Go beyond that.
Then, when you reach there
Go beyond there...
Go beyond everything.
Only then will you finally be here now.

As a child, I was taught I simply must believe unquestioningly in the Bible, if I wanted to go to heaven and live forever after I was dead. I was told I must have faith in the Word of God and learn to rest in the knowledge that I am saved, because Christ was executed. This is a very beautiful story, if we take the time to fully hear it out. The Christian scriptures contain a wealth of meaningful parables and the accounts of historical figures whose stories offer a guiding light to billions. As I entered into adulthood, I would become a seeker of enlightenment and then go on to study the subject of World Religion in college, continuing my love affair with the scriptures and literary works of great significance. I spent the best years of my life studying how other cultures and civilizations maintained their own symbolic narratives of mankind's place in the universe. Through my studies, I would come into contact with countless beautiful creation ideologies originating throughout the richly storied course of human history.

Faith itself, like hope, seems to spring eternal throughout all of recorded human history. Faith is the bedrock of all religions, the medium which protects and nourishes the seeds of hope. Written into the DNA within each seed of hope is a call to bring out the very best in our earthly lives and live in alignment with our highest, most transcendent selves in order to please our creator. Our faith contains the higher calling of a supreme deity to live a good, clean, honest life, to learn and teach what is decent, moral, just and right. It is a common theme that to live justly on earth is prerequisite, in order that we may be proven worthy of our place in eternity. Faith also offers a path for sharing inspiration, community socializing and working to help fill the needs of the less fortunate, the poor, the sick, the displaced and the hungry.

Kindness, wisdom, hope, understanding, peace, joy, clarity of thought, the purest of intentions, sharing abundance out of love and concern for the health and well-being of our families and our fellow man, these qualities are among the best the human species has to offer in life. These are the qualities that we believe will bring our tiny individual selves into alignment with a higher will and unify our singular lives into oneness with our creator. These are among the elements of faith, the shared positivity identified across the spectrum of nearly all of the major world religions, as well as in native shamanic traditions and new age subcultures. Through our faith, we encourage our loved ones, families and friends to come together, dressed in our Sunday best, out of respect and honor for all that is good, for all we believe is just, the very finest qualities we are capable of aspiring to.

And, ya know, what the hell is wrong with that?

What is faith?

I was born into a Christian family and grew up attending services at St. John's Lutheran Church in Orange, California. When I reached the age of five, I was placed into the protective custody of the St. John's Lutheran School between the hours of 8:30am and 3:15 pm. I clearly remember being taught, very early in grade school, the definition of faith. They really drilled it into us. As children we were told, over and over, that faith means we believe in God, and all things unseen, without the luxury of proof of His existence.

I have a clear visual memory of my sixth grade teacher, Mr. Bode, explaining to our class for the umpteen-thousandth time that the definition of faith is choosing to believe in the Holy Trinity without the benefit of proof or absolute certainty. He bracketed his explanation of faith with his speculation that this is how God designed our world to be, in order to test the faithful, so he could separate the good eggs from the bad. It was meant to be this way. It was meant to make us stronger in our faith.

Although he was using circular logic to prove his point, he was reinforcing the idea that we are exercising own free will in choosing to believe in the Lutheran system of thought. He was inferring that we *had to believe* if we wanted to go to heaven and enjoy the afterlife. We had to choose to believe everything the Lutheran Church was telling us because God said so, and we had to believe no matter what. That's the precondition. That's why they call it a *leap* of faith. If all your friends jump off a cliff are you going jump off after them?

The not knowing is for a reason, they all said. Not knowing and believing anyway was the grand test itself, meant to galvanize the will and prove us worthy of living forever in this super-awesome place called heaven, with these really chill guys named Jesus and God. It was like a cosmic game of hide and seek. If Jesus and God were to stay in hiding and say absolutely nothing for thousands of years, then at the end of the game, when we never faltered in our belief in them, they would pop out of nowhere after we died and say it's all good. We're in. We get to be part of the club. We passed the test. But if we were to ever falter in our faith, forget it. It's the lake of fire for you, pal.

Suspension Of Disbelief

Cosmologist Carl Sagan, when asked about faith, replied by explaining, "It is belief in the absence of evidence." This is a very similar explanation to the one I was given as a child by the Lutheran Church. Faith is not absolute certainty in the absence of evidence, as many irrationally exuberant believers would one day demand I accept, it is simply choosing to believe though one has no verifiable way of being certain. I totally get that. Fair enough. Sign me up!

I have found, when asked, any reasonable person, from any religion, shares a similar definition for the meaning of the word faith. It's not just the Lutherans. 99% of the time I find we all agree on this definition. The one's who disagree are usually the emotional believers, who have strong feelings and mistake their powerful emotions for absolute proof of the existence of the unseen. Later in life, I would become one such person for many years.

Mr. Bode's contention of faith without proof hinged on the point that, although we cannot be certain, the moment at which we make the choice to believe anyway, is the precise point at which the Holy Spirit takes over and uplifts our souls into the unseen world of the faithful and it all comes alive for us. It is the classic principle of the *suspension of disbelief* acting as the pivotal point around which my entire Christian education revolved. Suspension of disbelief is simply the price of admission and it works at the movies, and in fairy tales, just as well as it does in religion and spiritual life. If you believe anything is possible, then certainly the Lutheran story is what you must believe is true. If you don't pay the price of admission, you can't see the show.

They were a loving and caring group of people as much as anyone could ever ask for. Our church was a community of nurturing families and quite often the line between families was blurred by extended families, cousins, and how we were taught that we are all children of God. They sincerely wanted to answer all my questions and help me understand that everything in the Lutheran creation story was spot-on accurate. And it worked just fine for me. For about the first eleven years of my life, I couldn't have been happier with the whole program. The whole Christian life is a beautiful way of living as long as nothing intervenes to corrupt your views and pop your little bubble. My great-grandparents lived during times when it was a lot easier to go through life, in a Christian society, where your bubble was in a lot less danger of suddenly disappearing from around you. But as I became curious of scientific discovery, as sure as the 1960's led into the 1970's, as sure as good old-fashioned common sense came to rear its ugly head, these wonderful souls were content to tell me they just didn't know. "We choose to believe what the Bible tells us." Over and over again, it just came back to this answer.

They were just being perfectly honest with me and to this day I truly appreciate them for that. Their honesty and sincerity is one of their central qualities that remain with me to this day. They never lied to me, even when I presented them with the wonderings of childlike doubt. They never tried to bullshit me that they knew with absolute certainty, they simply told me how and why they had faith, why they believed these are the actual conditions under which life is taking place. They told me the who, what, how, where, when and why of Lutheran belief in the Holy Trinity and they left it at that. Times were very different then. The world was a lot less interconnected than it is now. Not knowing the answers to life's big questions is just fine for a little kid. It leaves lots of room for just about anything to happen. The imagination is free to roam.

I never suspected, as a child, I would encounter leakage between the imaginary and what I was indoctrinated to believe was true. I loved the people who raised me, very deeply, but I found there was some slippage in the price of what they were selling me when I tried to realize a net return on my investment.

At first, I grew up happily within in the security they provided for me. We all lived together in a world where everything was carefully defined and very clear. I didn't have to question anything because everything worked quite well. It worked beautifully, as a matter of fact. The stories I was told as a child were magical and fulfilled all my wonderings with meaningful answers, which left me content and untroubled. Up to a certain point in my life, there wasn't any need to inquire further than the belief system I was originally equipped with. I had perfect faith that it would always explain all my experiences of life and for a long time, it did just that. It was only when my world came apart at the seams, and incongruity came to rule the day, and opposite terms became superimposed over each other, that the face of contradiction reared its ugly head.

Conflicting Systems

"I thought this was a book about imagination and make-believe? Why do we gotta talk about faith? That's a touchy subject!" Some would ask. Well, yes it is. It is a touchy subject. We have to discuss faith because, human evolution is happening in such a way now, where all over the world, we are beginning to come into daily contact with people of other faiths, other world religions and people who are not religious at all. Because of my background in the study of world religions, I may have a peacemaker's perspective to offer on the subject of global assimilation. Some aggressively try to convert us to their brand of faith or seek to convince us all religion is meaningless. We are coming into daily contact with people from many other walks of life, alien societies where individuals are taught a vastly different frame of reference, a way of thinking that is completely alien to us. People the world over are beginning to be force fed, for the first time, a conflicting new doctrine of tolerance for all walks of life and political correctness. And in case you have't noticed, it's not exactly going well.

The religions and worldviews of entire populations, entire cultural identities, which had once been evolving for centuries in the nearly complete isolation of their own geopolitical borders and demographics, are now being confronted by the cultural identities of the outside world. Both feel the moral dilemmas of being expected to accept another's culture, when they firmly believe each are doing things, which are very wrong. There is a glaring incongruity, which strikes at the heart of their cultural identity, and these wrongs will not be tolerated. When you have had what is right and what is wrong beaten into you, as a child, by generations of family members, who have had the same beaten into them and so on... and so on... you can see how ill-amused these folks are when, in the throes of the information age, they are expected to suddenly accept and condone alternative lifestyles and opposing beliefs. The world is presently a boiling pot of conflicting systems of thought. All-too-often we have seen the sad aftermath of religiously motivated conflict tipping past the point of no return and boiling over into eruptions of terror and violence on the streets of our own cities.

The loss of life is tragic and yet, it's happening everywhere.

Modern times have brought people from vastly different walks of life, from every region of the world, together for the first time. Internet discussion groups, university courses, corporate board rooms and production floors, trade and political dealings have placed each of us squarely into contact with people whose lifelong faith is born out of a belief system vastly different from our own. They are not simply different, they originate from within an entirely alien context to which we've had zero exposure. We have absolutely no experience with which we can even hope to understand how they think and how they feel. The simplest attempt at humor can either go by unnoticed, or be misunderstood as the most offensive slap in the face. It's difficult to avoid offending each other when we don't know each other's rules and values. However, I've noticed, if given a fair chance, we usually find that once we politely get to know each other, we often like each other anyway, if we are being honest, because we are all nice people. We find them interesting because they are so different from us, yet still so much just like us. It may be a clash of culture and yet, if we try, we can often find a deeply shared humanity which causes us to feel the same in many ways. This is where hope springs eternal.

Race Is Imagined

In regard to race, there is no biological basis, no scientific evidence of any kind, no DNA, no chromosomes, which can prove that race even exists. The same is true about religion. Religion and faith are not a biological trait. The scriptures have always been culturally based and largely the result of geography. Race, as we conceive of it today, is the result of where, on the planetary surface, in relation to the equator, our ancestors evolved. If they were closer to the equator, our ancestors evolved more melanin and pigment in their skin to protect them from the sun's stronger, more direct rays. Their hair was darker and their skin developed brown or black as an adaptation to the pressures of their surroundings.

This is purely biology's survival response, like developing bigger brains, for adapting to the conditions of our environment. If our ancestors lived closer to the poles, they didn't evolve as much pigment in their skin, their hair was lighter or blonde because the sun was weaker and their bodies were never pressured by the environment to develop it for their survival. Instead they developed in ways which helped them deal with frigid temperatures and weaker light. Eventually, after the ice age, the environment changed and people were able to move around the planetary surface more. As the human world became more geographically homogenized, racism became a problem. Religious faith, race, gender, sexual preference, you name it, we fight over it.

While humans are not the only animals which fight and kill our own kind, we contend our faith is about the very highest good in all of us and yet, we mercilessly slaughter innocent women and children, in terrorist attacks which seek to draw attention to some vague, collectively imagined ideology. We fight and kill and die for our religious ideologies. We kill each other, in our own communities, for our racial biases, though they amount to nothing more than eye color, hair color, or skin tone, features which are nothing more than shallow appearances that have nothing to do with how we are all profoundly human, the same within.

While it is believed nearly 40% of mammal species kill their own kind for whatever the reason, this leaves over 60%, which never do at all. While primate species are among the most violent in the animal kingdom, there are many other mammal species, which have far higher murder rates against their own kind than humans. We think of ourselves as more evolved than other primates, more evolved than any other animal, but this isn't exactly true, if non-violence were the measure of a more evolved mankind. Violence is illegal where I come from. Why is it still so pervasive in modern society, if it's against the law? We can build a less violent society, if that is what was intended when the law was initially imagined, but we would have to want to. We would have to care about it. It wouldn't be an impossible goal to work toward. Non-violence would have to be culturally elevated to the point where the male ego and pride shifted toward placing a much higher value on the non-violent man.

When we see a field of flowers, it is rare anyone would look on it with disgust or annoyance. It is rare to see any natural landscape without a diversity of colors, especially in greens. How wonderfully diverse is the color green in nature! The essence of what sustains our living world is a complex diversity of every kind. We are dependent on diversity. Without diversity a single species alone could not exist. The contrast of colors, creates a natural harmony and a landscape seems so much more vibrant when saturated with color and diversity. It is beautiful to the eye, to the point where it can move and inspire the heart, like for example, in a garden. Then, why would our human diversity not evoke the same response? Who would dare to perceive humanity as no different than a field of flowers, each person blossoming, each heart reaching upward and outward toward the light of their own transcendental sun? Why would this idea seem so threatening? How can humanity cross over into the other 60% of species who are non-violent toward their own kind?

Faith is our stately basket of tolerance in which we place all we imagine could be true, all we want to believe is true, the substance, the core, very heart of what defines us as a species. It is meant to be the antithesis of corruption. Faith is the umbrella under which entire communities come together to focus on what is pure, clean and sacred about living. Imagine every human being responding through an allegiance to our shared humanity and working together as a singular species to solve the world's greatest challenges, solving them all, one by one. Imagine what several billion people, or more, could do, if everyone cooperated in reaching our collective goals, if we could all agree on collective goals. Could it be humanity is moving in this direction, evolving toward a more homogenous, less violent and universally concerned global community? What would be required for all of us to join together to make this happen?

Through our faith in each other, our faith in mankind and all that connects us to the universal origin of life, our faith contains our hopes for the future and our dreams of what eternity might be. The most elevated ambitions of humanity, hinge on this one aspect of human not knowing. But, in modern times, we remain a deeply divided, segmented people, a puzzle to ourselves. One day, we may join all the puzzling pieces together and see the bigger picture of human possibility. But for now, as a world of many clashing faiths, we roll the dice and hope like hell our origin story is the one which will prove true in the end. We take the cards that the dealer dealt and hope like hell ours is the winning hand. We hope like hell.

And if not?

The Winning Hand

There was a woman I knew as coworker when I worked in a class-10 cleanroom of a semiconductor manufacturing fab. Anita was a very devoted Christian and mother of three young children. She had been born in the Philippines and was raised in what she called the Filipino Church. She invited me to come to her church on a Sunday morning and I went once. I wound up playing the electric guitar in their church worship band that day. She and I had been busily working side by side on twelve-hour shifts for almost two years. Needless to say, we had many interesting discussions about religious belief. She was never shy to profess her faith in conversation and challenge me as to how anyone would not believe the same, since the Bible implicitly states the points she would make are fact, circular logic at its best. She was the kind of person who would say, "The Bible says it. I believe it and that settles it!"

One of the most memorable conversations we had was in a group of coworkers, many hours into a long twelve-hour weekend shift. This workgroup we were part of contained the most internationally diverse group of cultures you could ever put into a confined space and force to get along. Out of ten of us total, we represented seven different countries and five different continents. I can't think of a racial profile that wasn't represented here. Asian, African, European, South and North American continents were all represented. And we all got along great!

We had casually been discussing faith while we worked, because Anita brought it up. Eventually, there was a lull in the workflow and we all collected in a big circle, some sitting, some standing, some leaning on desks and tables. All of us were covered from head-to-toe in white, cleanroom bunny suits and our faces were all covered with masks and safety glasses. This is how we had spent thousands of hours together. We had known each other as co-workers for years and were comfortable talking casually and freely about our beliefs. We came to a point in our conversation where we were talking about how, since we all believed in different religions, which one of us is right and what are the rest of us supposed to do if we're wrong? It was kind of a taboo thing to ask, an uncomfortable subject to breach. But of course, I did it anyway.

I boldly asked Anita if, after having lived with such moral constraint, adhering so strictly to everything the Bible described as true and just, denying herself simple pleasures, how she would feel if, at the moment of her death, she came to find she was wrong and nothing she believed was actually true? Mind you, her and I were in a friendly conversation with a Tibetan Buddhist, two Vietnamese who were a Taoist and a Confucian respectively, a Hindu from India, a Muslim from Ghana, a devout Catholic from Argentina, a Lithuanian Agnostic and a little Mormon girl from Utah.

Anita's answer really set me back and made me think about our human need for religion and spirituality.

She said, "It was 100% my own choice. I was true to myself, true to what I believed. I lived a good life." She said very matter-of-factly and with complete certainty of how she felt about it. "I would die without any regret, because I chose to live a good, moral way and above all, it was the right way to live for me and that's all that matters. Even if it turned out to be wrong, it's of no consequence. It was right for me."

And there you have it. She was true to herself and what she believed. She never sold out.

Faith runs through the core of our intensely personal sense of identity. It threads its way through the meaning we take in every aspect of life and the way we view our inmost selves, our relationships with others and the world surrounding us. But as this story illustrates, we have a number of other people sitting there also, questioning their own convictions, confronted by a moral and psychological dilemma. We all share the same shred of doubt, the same uncertainty, the same terror of not really knowing for sure. This is the wonder of faith. The intent of belief in the absence of evidence is to bring about a peace, which surpasses all understanding. It appears Anita, my coworker, had found this in her faith.

The Light And The God Window

St. John's Lutheran Church is a massive brick Church that was built in 1913. It was so big, that as a child, it was hard to believe how big it was. It was absolutely towering and still is, as a matter-of-fact. It was the kind of thing you didn't dare go to and not believe everything they were telling you to believe. It was a giant edifice of brick and mortar and religious thought.

We went there because my great-grandparents, Royal and Rose Mueller went there, and they went there because their parents, my great-greats, Dr. Charles and Emma Mueller, were among the earliest members of the church in the late nineteenth century and donated funds to help build the big brick behemoth. I never knew my great-great grandparents but just the thought of them and this towering brick abstraction was beyond my comprehension as a child and I was in awe. It was as if it all came from a land before time.

I did, however, know my great-grandparents very well and they went to St. John's from childhood. My grandmother on my mother's side also went there from childhood, and my mom grew up going there, so of course, my mom made us go. We were enlisted to school there from kindergarten through the eighth grade. My brother and I both, were forced to endure the slow, excruciating murder of our own ways of imagining as we were happily brainwashed into accepting the ways the faculty and parishioners of St. John's imagined life to be. But it was fun! They were really nice people and we grew to love them.

There is an enormous and beautiful circular stained-glass window, high above the main entrance on Center Street, in the shape of a giant mandala, a six-petal blossom form. It resembles a giant flower with an enormous oculus in its center. Within the oculus is the stained-glass image of Christ Jesus, through which the light would shine most resplendently. This sort of window is common in Christian religious architecture. Pastor Geisler told us it is called *the God window*, (also known as the Rose window or Catherine window.)

One late afternoon, we were having choir practice in the church. We were getting ready for our school's special Christmas music program. We were all nine, ten and eleven year-olds, in third thru fifth grades. Our Christmas music services had always been my favorite time of the year. There were three services on Christmas Eve. Beginning at 6pm, there was one every hour. As a child, I was so completely invested in the whole story of Christmas and I believed with my whole heart in the magical wonder of the birth of Christ. The memory of performing those hymns in the choir is among my warmest recollections of childhood. All the grades of schoolchildren gathered before a packed church and sang their little hearts out in front of the immaculate altar, with its multiple glowing, five and seven-light candelabra all around. The massive statue of Christ above the altar, towering over the world, His palms turned outward to reveal the scars of His crucifixion, an allusion to His triumph over death, was a formidable focal point, front and center in the great church. Hundreds of Christmas lights sparkling on the twenty-five foot tall, flocked Christmas trees sent the fragrance of spruce over countless rows of wooden pews, all filling the hopeful hearts of our faithful congregation, standing a thousand strong at each service.

The two towering trees on each side of the altar, and two more, even taller trees to the right of the pulpit, were all adorned with huge, spherical bulbs, some the size of soccer balls. These massive, dark blue orbs would refract vibrant colors and reflect the arcs of countless white bulbs, embedded in the architecture, throughout the ceiling beams. Copious amounts of tinsel everywhere would become shimmering glints of possibility, reflecting light into every corner of the church. The scent of the ancient, creaking wood throughout that old church, the sounds of the handbells and the sacred arresting melodies sent a loft on children's voices would enrapture the heart. Songs of holy nights and the star-of-Bethlehem, of three wise men, of virgins and mules, of frankincense, gold and myrrh... whatever myrrh is. I always thought it was an abbreviation of myrrhijuana.

As we practiced for that special night, in the choir box before the massive, towering pipes of our magnificent organ, on that late autumn afternoon, the sunlight was pouring in through that highest of windows at the back of the church. It was a bright, orange-tinged, sunlight passing through the multi-colored stained glass and as it came beaming through, the orange glow was filtered by blues and greens and reds of all values and tones. The church was flooded with a lustrous brilliance of the full visible spectrum of luminous color. A seemingly sacred eminence of purples and bright yellow-greens, with red casts of tinted orange autumnal hues, had entered the room like a forest of ancient light.

And the oculus! My Lord, the oculus of the God window was radiating the most powerful, focused shaft of clear, warm, Southern California light from so high up, straight through that sacred space and gently down onto the beautifully carpeted floor, in the front of the altar. I could see the shaft of sunlight illuminating a thin, amorphous haze of dust particles and candle smoke in the air, at an acute angle impossible to describe.

Pastor Geisler had been helping our teacher prepare us for our orderly travel between the choir section of the church, to the pews at the front, working out segue cues for during the services. He cued us to move to the pews and sat us down in the front rows. He wanted to tell our group of fidgety children about what was happening with the window, what it meant and how we should feel about it. With the patience of a saint, he quieted us all down and began telling us the story of the God window.

"The light is streaming through the God window!" he exclaimed. "Look at it! Isn't it remarkable?"

He continued to explain about how our church was built and what the God window is. "Way back before 1913, when the architect originally designed our church, the building itself..." he paused and gestured toward the roof, "Yes, there was an architect who had to make the blue prints and many men were involved in the construction of this building. It hasn't always been here, though, to us, it might seem so." He smiled broadly. "When they originally thought of the idea for our church, the founders decided to they wanted to design and build it in the shape of the cross." He paused and gestured toward the alcoves and corners of the church. "So the architect went to work and came up with this. This beautiful church we have today. What a precious gift they have given us all!"

"This in fact, is a traditional way in which many churches have been built, throughout the history of Christian religious architecture. If you were to look down on it, from the point-of-view of heaven, you would see the vague resemblance of the shape of the cross. This shape is very sacred to us." He told everyone.

"The Rose window specifically, was intended as a symbolic representation for the love of God. Not the window itself, mind you... but how the shape of it, how everything about its design, affects the light passing through. The Catherine window, a more common name for it, has been integrated into the design of churches and cathedrals for centuries. In our case, it is placed high on the west-facing wall, specifically to take advantage of just this sort of occasion, when the late afternoon sun passes through it just so. It's breathtaking!" He paused to appreciate the wonder of it all.

He explained to the children how God is without form and since He is so, it made Him difficult to describe. Pastor Geisler continued to enlighten us, "God Himself is impossible to talk about directly. To say, 'Our Father in heaven,' is a way we speak of God but the Bible says God is an unknowable mystery. He is beyond all description, beyond all words."

He continued advising us of the Lutheran view of the universe. He told us when religious scholars and monastic visionaries sought to describe God to the masses, which it has always been their sworn duty to do, the God window was about as close as they could come to representing how God might appear, should one be so fortunate to find themselves in the presence of His glory. He explained, all the while accurately citing scripture by book, chapter and verse.

"When religious visionaries, deep in prayer, experience the presence of God, the love of God, through Christ, the Holy Spirit comes upon them in this form, vaguely resembling the God window, at such a point when the light is blindingly bright at its center." He explained. "Those religious visionaries, the early Christian monks, were the ones who originally conceived of this design for the God window. For them, this form best represents and communicates, to the public, the truly sacred experience of communion with God. It is their way of conveying, to us, what they experience during their intensely personal visions within the presence of the Holy Spirit."

He told us that God's love is being shared with us, every time we experience moments such as these, we are reminded of the monks' message of divine communion." He told us, "The unspeakable quality of the light itself, what it does to us, it can bring about feelings of the presence of the divine." He explained as if breathlessly gasping for air, "These indescribable places of the heart contain divine sensations within which *you* may experience of the truth of God's love for yourselves." Some assumed he was rambling but I could follow what he was saying, kinda. The children were all just sitting there, taking in the impromptu sermon. Many weren't even paying attention to what he was saying anymore.

So, rather than sit in silence and enjoy communicating directly with God by receiving His love, pouring in as light through the God Window, rather than simply appreciate the experience of this holiest of moments, he chose to have us bow our heads in prayer, eyes closed, backs to the window, while he besieged God with words. Pastor Geisler plastered in the space, which contained this beautiful, silent, light-filled opening in the human universe. He went on for several minutes, beleaguering God with circuitous verbiage, with holy Lutheran speakings. We never had more than that little bit of time to appreciate this momentary opportunity to take-in the light, to bathe in the visionary experience of direct communion with God.

We found ourselves unable to drink-in the deep nourishment of pure sunlight, which I felt was a sadly wasteful crime against God, who was trying to speak to us and send us all His love through the window. It was as if God went to say something but was then rudely interrupted. If the still small voice of silent understanding was like a field of tiny flowers, then Pastor Geisler's sermon-delivering voice in prayer was like the blast of a monster truck bellowing to the back of the church. It was like a loud rush of sound from the powerful engine of over-rationalization. Monster mud tires, like a buzzsaw, went tearing through the flowers of our minds, throwing up debris as mud showering through the air, as he roared around the field, destroying the natural perfection, bouncing over hill and dale. His reverberating voice crashed into every corner of the massive church, until the last light through the love window had all but faded and gone.

All-things-being-equal, I enjoyed hearing everything he told us. As proof, I still remember it to this day. Though I always wanted to ask him how one applies for the job of religious scholar or monastic visionary, my childlike mind did wonder about his theory of how the monks' designed the window to convey a message concerning their extremely deep and powerful visionary experiences. I tried to wrap my young mind around how they might be communicating with us, through art in architecture, regarding an experience we might otherwise find difficult to comprehend. Thinking of it gave me a bit of a jolt, dislodging my ability to reason. I closed my eyes and imagined myself bathing in the sunlight of God's love and how it might feel to have this visionary experience of divinity and light.

Even considering an elementary school Christian education, as children, the story of the God window was extremely deep. It was a radical concept to attempt to wrap an average Lutheran schoolboy's mind around. It wasn't an astronomical stretch, because St. John's Lutheran School had prepared us, from early on, to deal with abstract religious concepts like this. I believe our Pastor felt he was making up a new Lutheran children's parable or Bible lesson. However, he was breaking some new ground there for me. To think our massive brick behemoth, which housed our tiny God worshipping souls in prayer, was actually constructed to be cosmic transceiver device, oriented in space, just so, to capture sunlight as a living thing and receive the messages of the heart which it contained, like a divine radio telescope? That was pretty heavy. But even deeper, for me, was the first mention, in my lifetime anyway, of a monk's direct visionary experience of a divine communion with an unknowable mystery. I really had wrestle with that one.

Was that even possible?

None of the children or the teachers knew what to make of it and at the end of the day everyone was left feeling awkward. It wasn't like anything he'd ever preached to us before or since. It was quite esoteric. Maybe, he had been drinking. I don't know for sure but I remember it like it was yesterday. I was trying to ascertain if he was speaking metaphorically, telling us a story in the world of make-believe, or was God really up there in the sky, sending us all His love in highly-encrypted waves of light, which only the God window, as an algorithm in architecture, could decipher for us.

"It requires we give the best of ourselves to each other, everyday, and that pays big dividends over time." He told me. *"It doesn't happen by itself. You have to make it happen. I want you to always remember this conversation."*

Chapter Three
EXPOSURE

In 1959, my mom became pregnant with my older brother when she was just fifteen. My Dad, a dashing football player at Tustin High School, just a year older, made an honest woman of her, then a few years later they had me. My young mother stayed at home and played the role of the dutiful housewife, just as her mother had before her.

My Dad had been self-employed for as long as I could remember, in his own pool service business. In Southern California in the early 1970's, this was a nice business to be in. There were plenty of pools to service and not a lot of competition. He was doing well for several years. Life was really great for us when I was growing up. My Dad had provided our family with a nice lifestyle, one where he could set up his own schedule. He had time to take us across town to school; to be at all our school sports games and even coach our little league teams.

We took fun vacations; we went to Disneyland several times a year and spent a lot of weekends at my great-grandparent's cabin in Lake Arrowhead. It was sweet. As a kid, I didn't know a lot about my Dad's business except that he cleaned pools. I had a good look at what he did when he built a full-sized swimming pool in our back yard when I was about six or seven. This was heaven for a kid, growing up under the Southern California sun in the late 60's, early 70's.

My Dad's largest account, the Tustin Meadows subdivision, amounted to over half his business. When this property, with three Olympic-sized swimming pools, was taken over by a new management, a retired Navy officer, he demanded my dad paint the inside of a large pump room or he would sever their business relationship. My Dad, as an independent contractor, was not about to take up the charitable vocation of being a painter and told the guy he wasn't going to do it. The account was pulled and my Dad suffered the loss of over half his business. It was a devastating blow, one the whole family felt.

In financial stirrups, he worked out a deal with a guy named Chuck Mackie, to roll the rest of his accounts into a franchise he would purchase from the larger pool service company, called Trigon. He believed it would not only save him, but possibly lift him to the next level of business success, a blessing in disguise. The man who sold my Dad the franchise, the outgoing franchisee, in spite of a no-compete clause in the contract, immediately started a new pool service company and was going around behind my Dad's back taking all his old clients back. California is a Right-To-Work state and from what I have been told it's hard to defend his specific situation in court. Lacking money, he chose not to get involved in expensive litigation he couldn't afford. My Dad's new franchise failed and, by no real fault of his own, he went bankrupt. (I don't believe he ever regretted not painting the pump room.)

Ever resourceful and determined to remain self-employed, he tried to move on and start a new company, this time outside of the pool service business, which was now becoming a lot more competitive, obviously. My mom later told me she felt he may have been suffering from burn out, after building up his businesses and suffering such harsh financial setbacks. Since his parents were in the restaurant business, they had a line on a guy who cleaned the overhead grease traps in restaurant kitchens using a new chemical bath process. He thought this would be another undeveloped market he could get in early on, so he worked out a deal to buy him out. His plan was to provide a grease trap cleaning service, from the back of a truck, with a chemical bath process which degreased the traps in a few minutes. He called it Chem-Dip Filter Service. He thought the name was funny and went into it with a good attitude, telling us he was sure he could build a big company out of it someday, with lots of trucks.

All I remember is that he brought home this nasty, filthy, old, rusted red, 1964 Chevy C-30 pickup truck with these two big, disgusting greasy box-tanks in the back of it. The rinse tank, which took up the entire area behind the cab, to the wheel wells, had a big heavy, greasy lid he would lift up and lean against the cab. He would set the big stainless steel restaurant grease trap filters in there to rinse them off and hold the yucky water. After each stop he would drive down the road a little ways to a roadside storm drain and, when nobody was looking, he would reach under the truck and throw the lever on a valve and all the yucky water would dump in to the roadside drain. He told me not to tell anybody because he was a small businessman and couldn't afford to truck it off and dispose of it properly. He told me, even if he did pay to have it properly disposed of, the people he paid would probably just get rid of it the same way he did.

"At the end of the day, it probably all winds up in the same place anyway." He hollered over the roar of the engine, as he'd grind his three on the tree, column shifter through the gears. "Out there!" He pointed out my window as we drove across a bridge over one of the massive spillways, which run through the Los Angeles area. "So, I am just beating them at their own game." His truck was loud and rattled like a motherfucker. It swayed and rocked on the over-burdened suspension with every bump and pothole in the road.

The other tank was the heart and soul of his new venture, the chemical bath tank, a big cubic meter of off-center toxicity, hanging over the left side of the rear axle. It made the truck lean horribly off to the driver's side. It looked awful. It smelled awful and the thing was oozing with nasty, rancid, foaming green, restaurant grease. But off he went to seek his fortune, or maybe just try to recover from losing one.

My parents had overspent on credit and were constantly stressing each other out over money in those days. Their arguments erupted into throwing things and blaming each other for fact that all the money was gone. It wasn't good, at all. They were in bankruptcy and we were going to lose the house, the cars, everything. I remember having a complete inability to understand why we were going to lose our house. My grandfather and my dad built that house together when my dad was fourteen. How do you lose a house your grandpa built? I had no understanding of finance at this age. I never even knew there was a bank involved in how we came to live in that house. I always thought Grandma and Grandpa just gave it to us.

Seeing your parents scream at each other in anger is extremely unsettling for a child. I couldn't understand why they were so upset. My parents were an easy-going young couple. They were never prone to fits of anger or rage. So, when my Dad's company went under and my parents ran out of money, in order to keep paying for everything we had, while he was trying to get Chem-Dip off the ground, my mom went out and found a job working as a receptionist in a medical clinic. This angered my dad further, because as a product of the 1940's white suburban America, as he did not approve of his wife working outside the home. It reflected poorly on his male image as the provider of the family. It was extra money, and although my mom had never been employed in an actual job before, she used the office skills she had to try to help make the money they needed.

I remember riding home from St. John's with my Dad after school in his big ugly, disgusting truck that all my friends laughed at. The whole situation was giving me horrible feelings of anxiety in the pit of my stomach and I just couldn't shake the doom and gloom. I was scared; I was sad and just sick about it. He was talking about what was going to happen, how we weren't going to be able to live in our house anymore, complaining about money and not knowing where we were going to go, telling me our nice new cars were being repossessed. As we rounded the last corner toward home, he told me not to worry, that everything was going to start getting better now.

"Really?" I asked. Feeling an overwhelming sense of relief and hope in his words. "How do you know?" I asked him hoping he had some good news to report, hoping he had somehow called off the dogs of financial ruin.

He said, "You know how I know everything is going to start getting better now, Son?" I just looked at him shaking my head. I was crestfallen when all he said was, "Because it can't get any worse."

Making It Count: The Gift Of Al Jackson

My friend Eric's dad, Al Jackson, who had been my Dad's assistant coach for our little league team that year, took me aside when I had been coming to their house and wanting to go with them on their family outings just a little too often. They used to take me everywhere with them, when Eric and I were great friends. I probably went to the beach with Eric, his mom and dad a dozen times over that one Summer alone. They took me to dinner with them, lunch, shopping, wherever they went I would ride along with Eric and we had a great time. I was just all over them. They were the nicest people in the world.

Mr. Jackson alluded to the fact that he knew my mom and dad were having problems. He took me aside one afternoon after we had returned from the beach and said he wanted to speak with me privately for a moment. He told me he and my Dad had spent a lot of time together, during the last season, while they were coaching our little league team. He said they got to know each other quite well and my Dad confided in him about the trouble he had been having all-around. I honestly didn't know what he was talking about other than my Dad's business troubles. He assured me that I knew, on some level and he was going share with me something that I should always remember.

Al was a real winner of man, the nicest guy in the world and yet, he could be quite firm as a coach and a parent. He was tall, handsome with jet black hair, striking features and a polished, elegant personality. He was a very friendly, conservative gentleman with a quick sense of humor and strong sense of right and wrong. I liked him more than I could ever say. I looked up to him. He had asked Eric and his mom to give us a moment alone. We stood in the late afternoon sun at the entry way in front of his beautiful, sharply maintained two-story house, which stood along a clean, wide neighborhood street of similarly well-kept homes of the highest quality. He said to me, "You know, Vince, what we have here." He said to me referring to his family's overall situation. "You are a good kid and I see you reaching out for something our family has, that you're not finding at home." He looked at me knowingly. It wasn't an accusatory glance. He was exuding a sense of wisdom and empathy.

"Eric's mom and I have built a healthy, stable marriage and along with Eric we are all very happy together. You feel our comfort, an easiness in our home. It has required that a lot of things go right in order to have this happen. We've had to build all of this together over time and do things the right way." He looked at me as if to gauge the impact of his words. "We have been through a lot together, some things have been very difficult but the love we have is very strong and I know you feel it and want it in your own life. Sadly, what we have is a lot more rare than you might imagine."

Only a few years earlier, their house had burned down to the ground. All the families in the neighborhood were heartbroken for them but they rebuilt it as if it had never happened, though they lost their family dog, a beautiful Irish Setter, in the fire. "Aside from the trauma of losing our family pet, we came through it. All the other stuff is only material." He told me, "Even though we shed a lot of tears, almost all of it was easily replaced. What you see in us, what you seem to want to so badly to be a part of, has nothing to do with anything material, or going to the beach, or out to dinner or the movies or whatever. That stuff is nice and it's an important part of why we're happy but it's not that. All of this stuff is just the icing on the cake. You want to be here with us as much as you do because you feel our family bond, the underlying stability, the honesty and love we have in our home." I could only lower my head to him. I didn't know what to say. I felt awkward, as if I had somehow been exposed. As an eleven year old kid, it was all a bit beyond me, but he continued anyway because he knew what he had to say was going to stick. He knew I respected him and that his words were going to stay with me.

I felt vulnerable and yet, as he delivered his final words to me, he knew he had me in a learning opportunity and he was fully prepared to make it count. "No matter what happens to you, or what happens in your family life, I want you to always remember the comforting warmth of this family bond you've experienced in our home. We have a rare and beautiful thing here and we know it. I know you recognize what it is. Now, I am not a religious man and I know you have been brought up in the church, so you will understand what I am referring to when I tell you, regardless of how you think about it, there are basic qualities of honesty, moral decency, caring and personal integrity everyone has to live up to if they want to enjoy a higher quality of life, like what you see us enjoying here."

As we came to the close of our conversation, he stressed each word every carefully. "We are enjoying an exceptional *quality* of family life *because* of this bond we share. Not because of all of this..." he waved his hand in the air referring to his property, his cars and his large family home.

"When you're with us, Vince, I feel you reaching out for the warmth of this strong bonding experience because I know you're not getting this at home." I tried to protest, saying that everything at home was okay, that I didn't know why he kept referring to this, that it would all be fine, but he stopped me without accepting my denial. "We had to build all of this, over time, through a lot of honesty and hard work, because we feel it's worth it. We place a very high value on each other and on the time we spend together. We have worked very hard for what we have and it's very important to us. Do you understand?" He asked me and I nodded. "It requires we give the best of ourselves to each other, everyday, and that pays big dividends over time." He told me. "It doesn't happen by itself. You have to make it happen. I want you to always remember this conversation."

He put his arm around my shoulder and I could feel the assuring grip of his strong hand, "We haven't minded you coming along with us, at all. You're a fun kid to have around. I understand it was our place to play a role in your life, for some inexplicable reason, that you recognize this says a lot about you." He smiled. "I know you'll remember everything you've experienced with our family when the time comes for you to settle down and build your own." And he let it rest right there.

He never mentioned it again, but he was right. He stood up and went in the house. I gathered up my beach gear and rode my bike home. Everything I experienced with the Jackson family, during those warm, wonderful summers, has stayed with me for a lifetime. They were an ideal family that I could never live up to, but even still, they were like a guiding light to me. Even Eric, who grew up to be a fine person, was an example of excellence for me. He became our class president in high school and went on to college and a career as an airline pilot, the Captain of the ship, flying enormous Airbus jets all over the world. I should have known. He never went to St. John's Lutheran, or any private school. He never went to church, that I know of. He never even mentioned it, if he did. But he still grew up to become an exceptionally high-quality person. As you can tell, I've always admired people like that.

Al became a role model, in my memory, all through my adult life, a fine example of a good and decent man. He had done all the right things, lived the right way, worked hard, worked smart in order to build a rewarding life for himself and for his family. I would spend the rest of my life trying unsuccessfully to become half the man he was. But even half, for me, is something I hoped he would have taken pride in seeing.

The Broken Circle

Though I believed my dad when he told me, it couldn't get any worse. Sadly, it could. And it did.

One evening, my mom and my Dad had been arguing. It had something to do with his drinking, which had never been an issue before. He had told her he was going to the liquor store and she started giving him shit about it, which just pissed him off even more. He asked her why having a drink after work was now suddenly a big deal and asked her why she was acting so different lately. My brother wanted to ride along with him and maybe get some gum or candy while they were out. My dad said he was stressed out and just needed to relax. I was standing in the garage as they loaded in the car and drove off, the tires screeching in anger. The air was palpable with stress and animosity. I had a lot of anxiety about all the bad vibes in our home.

I clearly remember, standing there at the edge of a February night, looking out across the driveway from the empty garage at the street. My mom said, "Vince," Suddenly, I was hearing the words that came falling from her mouth, "I'm divorcing your father." Hearing her tell me, it just turned me inside out. She said it in anger. Her words contained complete finality, as if she had cursed our family unit for all time.

All at once, so unexpectedly, I felt as if my heart was breaking, it frightened me and I became enraged. I remember the fear and the horror welling up out of me as I ran past her, exploding into tears, the only way an eleven year-old boy can deal with feeling at this depth and of this magnitude. Screaming, I ran across the house to my room and throwing myself onto my bed in a puddle of tears. It seems a child's natural flight response is to run for the safety of their bed when they feel overwhelmed and are freaking out. She came following behind to comfort me but I was inconsolable.

She tried to explain how my dad's financial collapse was a humiliation, a dereliction of duty. Things were getting messy and all of it was just beneath her dignity. She had options. She said she was going to leave in the morning and she would take me with her. She said we would go somewhere new and we would live there together. I began thinking that it might not be so awful, to go off and live in an apartment, in a nearby neighborhood, just me and my mom, the same as my friend, Chris Peltzer, had done when his parents divorced a year earlier. Chris had been on my little league team and because our two families had become close, meeting up for family barbecues and so on, and because Chris had been my best friend at the time, I had a front row seat to that one. That divorce was difficult for Chris. He had a tough time but he got through it and we stayed friends through it all. All of this came to mind for me right then and I thought maybe, I should listen to what my mom was saying, maybe it wouldn't be so bad. My dad had always been my disciplinarian and my mom the nurturer.

I remember her telling me, "If he can't make enough money to keep me in the lifestyle I am accustomed to, then there is plenty of fish in the sea, someone else certainly will." It was then when she started to break the news to me of someone else, another man already waiting in the wings. My hopes for a life with just me and my nurturer turned to ash. I was truly put off by the idea of another man. I remember that part being tremendously hard to accept.

I was just turning eleven when, unbeknownst to anyone, after fifteen years of marriage, my mom started having an affair with her new boss at the medical clinic. After a single month of infidelity with a total stranger, she hatched up a plan to leave my Dad and run off to live in sin with this man, right as my dad filed for bankruptcy and our family home fell into foreclosure.

When she broke the news to me that she was leaving, it was completely unexpected. I never saw it coming and something in the way it all went down hurt very deeply. It took my already sick feeling of anxiety and drove it off the deep end of panic. There was no, "Hey, let's sit down and talk. Your dad and I have something we want to tell you and your brother." Then, carefully break the news. There was none of that gentle, levelheaded approach to telling the children, in my case. It was like an axe in my chest.

I believe that, as the daughter of a prominent physician, she obviously felt a strong entitlement to a certain lifestyle that my dad just wasn't going to be able to provide for her. Her voice exposed the fact that she had completely given up on him. My dad was not a doctor, or a professional of any kind. For all he was able to provide, he never had anything that could be construed as wealth, although as a business owner, he certainly dreamed of it. He was a fat guy, who drank, smoked, swore and drove a slimy truck to work everyday. But all in all he was a good man, an honest man with a great sense of humor. Although he could be very grumpy at times, there was nothing seriously wrong with him that couldn't be remedied given a little time and few stiff drinks. The whole thing just made me sick to my stomach. I didn't understand why she would commit these horrible sins. She would never get into heaven now.

She put it to me this way. "Your brother is going to want to stay with your Dad. I just know it, because he identifies so strongly with him." She wanted me to go with her and she really laid it on about how wonderful it was all going to be. I couldn't imagine anything wonderful would ever come of this. Then, completely out of left field she gave me an ultimatum, and here it is again, the classic, "I needed to decide for myself" thing. This time, it was that I needed to decide for myself who I wanted to live with, her or my dad. She reasserted that she was giving me the choice of staying with my dad or going with her. She told me it was not her decision, it was mine to make for myself. Then, she laid down one condition, she told me if I did not choose to go with her, she would call the whole thing off because she could not bear to go without me. Then, she just sat there quietly looking at me, while I sat there sniffling back tears.

So, at that moment, she put it all on me, at eleven years old, to choose between her options, *for* her. If I chose to go with her, I'd be the Judas, the one deciding to betray my father's love, stab him in the back and set in motion the sad fate of a family's broken circle. I had this one chance to make her call it all off and I could tell her, "No, don't do it." If I chose to stay with my dad, it would stop her from leaving and she would call it all off and stay with my dad, too, as if this discussion had never happened.

I had that fateful moment of standing at the crossroad waiting for the devil to show. Which way was I going to go? All through my early childhood, as a second child, I had always identified with my mom more than I had with my dad. She was my mom. She was my champion, my protector, the nurturer of my little existence. I spent the most time with her because my dad was always at work. My dad was the heavy, the one who disciplined us. The one who issued my spankings as a child, when I probably full-well deserved them. He was the one who smoked and drank and kind of smelled bad once in a while. But I loved my dad. I couldn't fathom the immensity of the impact this moment, this decision would have on the outcome of the rest of my life.

I could only feel the raw exposure to the harshness of the adult world and see the burning bridges of the only life I'd ever known. She was proposing hardcore betrayal, adultery, dishonor and certain, infinite, searing shame. The shame I felt in the idea of betraying my dad knew no boundaries. After a time of pregnant silence, with her waiting for me to acquiesce, I caved and said I would go with her. I said it because it was what she wanted me to say, it was the emotional undercurrent, the rip tide, the unspoken inevitability which had already been decided before I even got the news. For the rest of my life, I would hate myself for not standing up for what I believed in, at such a critical moment in my life. Even while everything in me was screaming to stay, I acquiesced and chose to betray my dad. I had decided this, an eleven year-old boy.

I felt as if my decision to go with my mom was the worst thing I had ever done but that it was what she wanted me to say. The net result, however incorrect, was that I came to blame myself for betraying my father and destroying not only my family, but the life we had together. I felt like I should have fought harder and made a stand for what I wanted, what I believed in. But I realized I was nothing more than a coward. At eleven years old, we aren't accustomed to standing up to the authority figures in our lives. I would have to leave St. John's. No more little league, which had been a centerpiece of our social lives for years, at a time when I was just starting to come into my own. All my friends, everything I knew, shattered in an instant. It would be all over now and it would be all my fault, because I did not have the guts to say, "No! You can't leave and I am staying here with my dad!" It was what I wanted to say but I couldn't say it.

After my dad and brother came back from the liquor store, she told me not to say anything. She said she would tell them tomorrow. He asked my mom, "What's wrong with him?" She made up some lie to tell him and I suffered through that night alone in my room. In the morning, my mom explained to my brother what was about to happen. I don't imagine he took it very well. Then, she placed a Dear John letter on the dresser and left. It was a Friday and she told me she was taking me out of school for the day. She already had me all loaded in the car with a bunch of things, brother Bill got in the car and she promptly drove to the high school and dumped him off. I couldn't imagine how it must have felt for him to be forced to go to school within an hour of getting that news. Personally, I may have only been eleven but I had a strong sense of disgust with the way this was happening. Everything about what she was doing, for me personally, was extremely harsh. It was incomprehensible to me that she would treat the people who have always loved her like this. It was cold as ice.

Under the overall circumstances of their marriage, if she wasn't happy, her decision to leave my dad might have been considered reasonable in the 1970's, but not like this. This was cut and run. She was running away while ducking her responsibility to neatly and fairly resolve her circumstances. Sneaking off like this was a dishonor to herself, to the dignity she professed the night before. This was a cowardly act and I was also guilty by complicity. This went against the steadfast standards, which all the adults in my life had painstakingly engrained into my brother and I since birth. It went against everything we were indoctrinated with at St. John's. It broke the core ethical code of honor and virtue in our ultraconservative Lutheran morality, the sacredness of family bonding, the purity of eternal love and unbreakable vows of holy matrimony in the eyes of Almighty God. Adultery was a sin. The idea of deliberately and knowingly choosing to go against the Will of God disturbed me at a deep level. It frightened me. It hurt me in ways I couldn't understand and brought forth a looming tidal wave of eternal uncertainty.

Divorce, that marriage could end, was unthinkable to my eleven year-old Lutheran schoolboy mind. But what began in sin, as teen pregnancy, would end in sin, as adultery. The members of her ultra-conservative, extended family would, once again, suffer embarrassment in the eyes of their friends and the local community. There would be nothing I could do about it but suffer the fallout and learn to accept my fate. News like this would spread like wildfire through all the folks that knew our family or knew *of* us. This was unnerving for me, as I felt the embarrassment encroaching on my reputation as a good and decent person. Now I would forever be the product of a broken home.

She didn't even have the dignity to face my dad and be honest about what she was doing. The whole thing felt like a criminal act to me. She was absconding, with me as her accomplice, and we were going into hiding. Leaving only a note to inform her high school sweetheart and husband of fifteen years, the father of her children. In the absence of any abuse or danger, this is deeply disrespectful by most anyone's standards. Her shame must have been far greater than my own. I was even more dumbfounded when, after dropping my brother off at the high school, she simply drove straight up to Glendale and dumped me off at her sister's house for the weekend. As she left me there, I protested that I didn't realize I was staying and she was leaving. She was trying to explain that because she was starting a new relationship with this other guy, as adults, they needed time to be alone together and bond, to sort things out. That's when part of me realized she felt no shame at all. She didn't care about anyone but herself.

Maranatha Breakdown

Once my parents divorced and the tragic events had unfolded, the pieces fell where they lay. Time marched relentlessly forward, no matter how much my thoughts and feelings tried desperately to turn it back. My mom was excommunicated from St. John's for being a sinful, lecherous, cheating woman. Confirmed members of a Lutheran congregation are taught that divorce is an unforgivable sin. Until death do us part is the sacred vow one has made in the house of the Lord. Unrepentant, she was cast out.

In my fifth grade year alone, we lived in four different locations. I was moved between four different schools and along the way, I broke a bone in my hand, was bullied horribly, got beat up a few times and tormented for being the new kid. Tired of seeing me get beat on, my mom pulled me out of the public school and enrolled me in the last of the four schools for that year, what was supposed to be a safe place, Maranatha Christian Academy in Costa Mesa, California.

I wasn't settling into this new life situation well at all, though I had no choice but to sincerely try. Getting beat up at the apartments we moved to and bullied by street kids was all new to me and it couldn't have come at a worse time. I had no concept of the myriad forms of bullying present throughout society. That one could be bullied, and even beaten down, spiritually was something that I couldn't even conceive of.

Calvary Chapel was championed by a charismatic leader, Pastor Chuck Smith. By the time I came along, he was wildly popular and his name was known far and wide as the leader of an Evangelical offshoot ministry with an innovative new approach to converting the masses to Christianity. They called it *being saved*. He was instrumental in the rise of a craze called the Jesus movement, in California in the late 60's. Calvary became ground zero for a mid-70's explosion known as the born again Christian movement. This was a Jesus-based counter-culture of young hipster's rebelling against traditional church-type conservatism. Individuals who joined this movement underwent an intense conversion experience they called being born again. They were practicing what was fast becoming a popular new form of Christianity we were taught to fear at St. John's.

It was about as far from conservative protestant thought as anyone could imagine. By Lutheran standards, they could be considered Christian radicals based on the version of the Bible they used, their baptism by fire style of worship and the emotional outbursts of praise all throughout their services. Their beliefs centered on the book of Revelations and the Apocrypha. For Lutherans, the book of Revelations was practically deprecated and the Apocrypha, which have always been considered deprecated, I had never even heard of them. Born again Christianity was an apocalyptic belief system that warned of an imminent second coming.

To be certain, they were convinced that their powerful emotional feelings were all the absolute proof they needed of the Holy Spirit's immediately presence. These folks believed there was something each individual had to do, an act every human being *must* perform before could become eligible to receive salvation. Besides just believing in Jesus, we had to be born again. If we weren't born again, if we weren't baptized by the Holy Spirit itself, forget it. Lake of fire.

When Martin Luther nailed his now-famous 95 Thesis to the door of the Catholic Church in 1517, there were two central ideas that sparked the Protestant Reformation. These ideas centered around the belief that the Bible is the sole religious authority, not man, and that salvation is bestowed by faith alone and not by one's deeds.

Both the church and the school at Calvary practiced an emotionally charged religious experience which was not a good thing for me during this emotionally-charged time in my life. The church itself seated three thousand people at a time. The congregation as a whole was easily five times larger than St. John's. This was Christianity for the masses. They had the passing of offering baskets down to a science. They would pass them several times during a single service and the congregation was already tithing their asses off. Shameless. It was an industrial-scale, for-profit, albeit tax-free religious operation,

It was the opposite of St. John's Lutheranism, where instead of being lobotomized and behaving like a zombie with a hymnal, born-again Christianity was about acting really excited about everything. It was as if the more revved up and intense they were outwardly emoting about Jesus, the closer they were to the presence of God somehow. It was far more active and participation oriented. They had rock bands inside the church! Christian Rock music was practically unheard of in 1974. Calvary celebrated it. It became part of the magnetism that drew in large crowds from all over the region.

It wasn't the Lutheranism I was taught where you sit around waiting for the God window to light up like some holy Hot Light at a Krispy Kreme Doughnut factory. They believed the human heart was where the light of God's love would live in you, shine from within you. Every person was called to be a witness because, as in a court of law, you saw what actually happened. Now that you are born again you know the whole truth and nothing but the truth. They believe this intense spiritual experience means they are now divinely ordained and it is now their sworn duty to persuade and convert everyone they possibly can to this system of thought.

So, I really didn't have any choice. I was dropped off at the school and for better or worse, I had to act like I accepted what they wanted me to accept, even though a lot of it went against much of the doctrine I was brought up to believe at St. John's. That is the way these church schools work, you either go with the accepted program or you are a bad kid and deserve to be punished. You learn to blend in.

At the very end of the school year, before lunch recess in my fifth grade class, our teacher said we were invited to join in a special prayer session asking to receive the Holy Spirit, directly through the gift of tongues. They had talked about this a number of times during school but now it was going to happen. It was time. Some of the kids in my class were really excited about it and had done it before. I had a lot of anxiety about it. It wasn't required of me and I felt it would be embarrassing for me. It seemed really awkward for a kid to speak in some weird language. Since I had arrived later in the school year, I hadn't been given the opportunity to do this yet and they wanted me to understand this was a really big deal. I told them no.

At recess, four of the boys from my class came up to me on the playground and, not forcibly, but very formally told me they wanted to talk to me about something very important. They sat me down and told me I really needed to experience the gift of tongues. They weren't demanding that I go, they told me that I had to go for Jesus. They told me not to be afraid of it. They said whatever it was that I feared, I needed to let go of it and accept this wonderful gift from the Holy Spirit. There was far more peer pressure in this than the first time I smoked a joint, which I had already done that weekend my mom dropped me off in Glendale.

They were witnessing, either on their own, or the teacher put them up to it. They said they would help me through it and we would receive the Holy Spirit together. They firmly believed were doing me a favor by convincing me to go. I agreed, or was heavily pressured by my peers to agree, that I would go to see what it was. Once again, it was my decision to make if I wanted to participate, but there was a lot of pressure. It was a lot like being bullied on the playground, but by nice Christian boys. I had been involved, indoctrinated in Bible study since before I was able to read, so I knew the story of The Tower of Babel and the story of the gift of tongues.

The teacher of my class, Mr. Ken, it was all first names here, was the one initiating the spiritual practice, which was a prayer session designed to become something akin to a hypnotic trance. He asked for the Holy Spirit to come upon us that we may receive the gift of tongues. I sincerely tried to do everything they said I should do to receive the Holy Spirit. This is the last thing I remember.

The next thing I knew, my arms were draped around the shoulders of the two biggest boys in the class, two of the four who had pressured me to go, and they were dragging me to the office to see Pastor Chuck, who was waiting there with a concerned look on his faith. What actually happened before this moment was something that had to be related to me later in the day. Evidently, I went into the trance and started singing in the unknown language of the gift of tongues. Then, I began shaking and convulsing violently as if I were having yogic Kriyas. When that stopped, I began crying, bawling my eyes out. It appeared was having a nervous breakdown.

The teacher believed I was enraptured by the Holy Spirit and tried to calm me but couldn't. That's when he got on the phone to pastor Chuck and had the boys drag me over to the office. I started to come back down to earth on my way to the office. I have no recollection of any of that, even to this day. I just remember being dragged across the courtyard to the office.

I eventually realized I was in a red leather chair in a waiting room and being told I needed to sit here quietly with Pastor Chuck.

Pastor Chuck Smith was as highly regarded of a human being as anyone will ever meet. He possessed a very strong presence of friendly spiritual authority, calmness and a surety, and here I was awash in a sea of the most powerful feelings I have ever felt. I was a mess. Whatever I had bottled up inside me had completely overwhelmed me. He had my hand in his and was quietly praying. Pastor Chuck was simply concerned and helping me come back from my ordeal. I was only just now beginning to realize I was having an ordeal. I felt as if I had been unconscious and was just coming to, wondering what happened. I was a newcomer to him and they all weren't sure what to make of me. They placed me into the gift of tongues and got an ear full of holy shit all over themselves.

This experience, as it turned out, was merely a precursor to episodes of a similar nature I would continue having throughout my life. I would repeatedly be persuaded to confuse these psychiatric breaks with religious visionary experience. Advanced spiritual practices were often precursors to these traumatic events, whenever they were suddenly, or spontaneously, administered to me by others who believed they had in my best interests in mind.

In this case, since my parents had recently divorced, everything I knew was ripped away, I had suffered an emotional trauma that I was repeatedly being told I was not suffering from. Whatever forces erupted out of my emotional depths this time, fractured my personality for good. I took a really hard beating, a direct hit to my soul this time and it really hurt at a very deep level. After the fact, I felt this event like I'd never felt anything. It stayed with me for several days as a cloud of desolate melancholy. Whatever psychiatric problems I might have had a potential toward, were now set firmly into my development. My psychotic inner-child was now free to move about the cabin.

Pastor Chuck, though warm and kind, was not my Pastor Geisler, who along with Pastor Hilmer were the only spiritual authorities I had ever known. Pastor Chuck was one of those spiritual celebrities we tend to meet in life who have the gift of people power, charisma, a real charmer. His persona is the reason why the Calvary Chapel brand became the highly recognizable, nationally franchised, religious corporation it is today. Who calls a pastor by their first name? It's unheard of! It's just wrong. He smiled knowingly as he carefully explained to me that I had received the gift of tongues and that I was immersed in the power of the Holy Spirit. I just sat there sniffling back tears. I was extremely distraught and the more I came back to earth, the more I realized how intense the anguish going through my body actually felt.

Their highly-emotional way of receiving the Holy Spirit did nothing more than to place me directly into a torrent of emotion I could not bear to feel, that needed time still, to heal from. I was heartsick and heartbroken and I had it all stuffed away has best as I could. What they had just done was to rip me out of a relatively safe place and position me directly into a wound of love so deep, an aguish so intense, that I was unable to work through it in any healthy way. I was so poor at dealing with how I felt that I wound up being overwhelmed and blacked out into a psychotic break. I don't remember anything. I was defenseless against what I was feeling, all the grieving I had not been allowed to mourn, it all came welling up at once, and they were encouraging me to feel all of it and dance in the joy of Christ's salvation.

I shook my head as Pastor Chuck made the hard sell on the precious gift I had been given. "It didn't feel good." I told him, "I just feel really upset right now." I explained how my parents had recently divorced and how my mom was living in sin with this extremely volatile man and I just felt sick about it. In all honesty, I needed to use him as a child psychotherapist but he just wasn't having it. I told him this experience felt as if I had simply been pushed into a deep trance, through a form of evocative hypnosis, and spoon fed suggestions, encouraged by everyone around me become very emotional and to speak in gibberish. Pastor Chuck didn't want to hear that at all. It seemed to actually piss him off. I had the sense that he realized I wasn't one of them. I wasn't buying what he was selling today. I felt him dismiss me in his mind and then, as was his duty, I then witnessed a modern-day master of religious conversion seek yet again to force my soul into his make-believe reality.

He was convinced he was in my life at the moment by divine right, to teach me about the power of the Holy Spirit and I was refusing to learn from my experience. Maybe so, but I was pretty spent by then. I really wasn't all there. I was eleven years old and just going with my instincts on this. He felt that whatever problems I might be having, the Holy Spirit was there to take them from me, if I would only hand them over.

He could not comprehend the non-imaginary reality of my life situation. He was talking about my place in eternity. I was talking about my state in the here and now. He had probably enjoyed a perfect life and never felt this kind of harsh exposure. I was being subjected to a continual stream of emotional violations, which I wasn't handling well and as a result; it felt like I was being forced past the point of nervous breakdown and into a full psychotic break. My home had been broken, my mom and I had been captured and were being held by a psychopathic predator, the man she ran off with. This is the man who is waiting for me after school. I was left with the feeling that Pastor Chuck lived in another world. He couldn't even conceive of what the world I lived in might be like.

Imaginary Thing

By the summer of 1974, we were living in a beautiful apartment with a view of the ocean, at the top of Golden Lantern Street in Dana Point. My mom suddenly developed cold feet and wanted to get out of the mess she'd made. The guy she'd tried to run off with, (I reluctantly introduce this character by name into my life's story, this character's name is Jack,) turned out to be an angry menace. Once again, she tried to pull the old, leave-a-Dear-John-on-the-dresser-and-bail thing again. I think she had realized, as she entered the working world at the medical clinic, she had the misfortune of falling under the controlling power of a textbook corporate psychopath, a predator in a suit and tie.

Jack took advantage of my mom's weakened state and seduced her with romantic passion. Then, he very directly led her to immediately break the bond of her family situation, before his charming spell had time to wear off. It was actually quite sinister, when you think about it. But it takes two to tango, so maybe it's not my place to judge others. In any case, he immediately and aggressively moved on her, using the chemistry of romance and threats of exposing their affair, to control her, so he could keep her for himself. He used his anger to dominate her. He would yo-yo back and forth between charming and explosive outbursts of bad temper, as a way to control her.

In some sick way, they both kind of suited each other. She was an emotional basket case, a masochist for punishment and he was a vicious sadist. The odd thing was, I had never seen my mother act emotionally before. She had always been a very levelheaded, intelligent woman with a strong interest in scientific discovery. I don't remember ever having seen her cry. Only in the context of this relationship with Jack, and throughout the divorce, had I ever seen her become so emotional and cry so often.

They hardly knew each other when she ran off with him. Jack turned out to be a hyper-controlling, emotionally unstable nightmare of anger and rage whenever she would commit the slightest infraction against his complete control. What are the odds? At first, this didn't raise any red flags with my mom. For whatever the reason, her primal dysfunction needed to feel deeply humiliated before she could feign her mock dignity again. So, these two cycled off of each other in mutual desperation through one emotional apocalypse after another.

Finally, she realized this was simply passion gone awry and she loaded me in the car once more and this time, we went back home, to the house I grew up in, to my dad's, as if life would go on, same as it ever was. But it didn't last. My dad wasn't going to simply take her back, even though she probably hoped she could "just come home." She could not just click her heels together and repeat, "There's no place like home." We weren't in Kansas anymore.

Years later, my dad told me he thought she was going to get her own place, stand on her own two feet and if things worked out long term, and she proved she was really devoted to staying together, they would work it out over time. Any reasonable person would agree this is a fair approach to handling this situation. However, the problems my parents had between them, by now, were extremely complex and had only compounded during this horrible time.

And they weren't psychologists, or relationship geniuses. No one had the capacity to explore the possibility, except maybe her father, the physician, that from a certain point-of-view, she had been taken, victimized in a very difficult way to justify. If this consideration did enter anyone's mind, they were all in denial and wouldn't admit it, except for her father, my grandfather, the good Dr. Sanday, who understood the situation very clearly, but had the good sense stay out of other people's business, especially his own headstrong daughter's.

My mom was led to believe the blame was solely her own and that Jack was the victim of a mixed up woman who didn't know what she wanted. In his mind, he wanted everyone to make-believe he only became angry because she was victimizing him. However, now she knew the situation was out of control and she was just looking for a way out of the mess she'd made. But for her, there was no way out. There was no one coming to rescue her.

Without any reasonable explanation for why she did it, everyone else, myself included, came to see ourselves as her victim. She was the one who made all her own decisions and she made them against her own family. No one really stopped to think that she was the victim of a psychopathic salesman running around loose, that he was the one making all the decisions for her and we were all survivors of a horrible tragedy. She was taken over by a master manipulator and spirited away. No one, myself included, not even my mom, ever considered the possibility that none of this was her fault. However, even if all that were true, she was still complicit, she was allowing this to happen and therefore she was equally guilty of these horrible crimes of the heart by association. These are other spins to the story. You can either buy one or not.

Either way, I landed back at my childhood home with my Dad who wanted nothing more than to shield me from all that crap. And I wanted nothing more to do with any of that mess she'd made. I wanted for my nightmare to be over. When it was all said and done, I got tired of transferring schools and getting beaten up for being the unproven, new kid in town. I was burnt out on religious zealots and people fucking with me in ways I couldn't even imagine. There was no way I could go back to that, not in any way, shape or form. As an eleven year-old kid, my Dad could and did protect me from that, given the slightest opportunity to step in, he did so, right then. My mom, however, was now her own person, a woman set adrift, and, for the first time in her life, she had to make her own decisions about who she would become and what she was going to make of herself in the world.

I wasn't old enough to understand why she couldn't stay with us. I'll never forget the day we stood alone together in the driveway and she was leaving, in her little car, by herself. It was so incredibly sad. I asked her why she had to go. Why couldn't she just stay here with us? She told me that, right now, Jack was her meal ticket and she had no other way to get by, so she had to go back with him. She told me she had never stood on her own two feet and she couldn't make it on her own. That was incomprehensible to me. I couldn't understand why other arrangements couldn't be made. However, she had no real, marketable skills by which to pay her own way through life, let alone rent an apartment for the two of us. She wouldn't be capable of getting anything but the most menial, entry-level of jobs.

She had made her bed and now she had to lie in it. If she was a victim, she had to live with the damage this kind of horrible accident inflicts on one's life. Yet that kind of thing was way over my head then. I couldn't make sense of it, the child I was then. I couldn't comprehend why our home was being broken. I only knew that I didn't want any of this to happen. It not only went against everything I had ever been taught, it went against every fiber of my being.

That moment when she drove off and left me standing alone in the driveway, for the first time in my life, there was nothing left to distract me from it, I had no protection against the unbearable exposure of my heart breaking. My uncontainable anguish simply poured out of me, screaming into the sky. I couldn't black out, I had no one there to turn to. The feelings of despair and uncertainty were more than I could bear and there was absolutely not a god damned thing I could do about it.

I was suddenly left exposed to the harshest actuality I had ever had to face. Standing alone in that driveway, I was entirely unshielded from a severe and merciless torrent of sadness, which at that very moment completely overwhelmed me. My mom just left our family for good and she was never coming back. I felt betrayed by the one person I trusted more than anyone in life. At the same time, I felt ripped off by a merciless, home-wrecking psychopath and the worst part was, at the end of the day, my mom abandon her own children, her own family, over money. She abandoned me, she abandoned us, the people who genuinely loved her. To this day, I don't think she could even begin to imagine what that felt like.

Imaginary Thing

I promised I would love you in the summer
But I had come to need you then by spring
And when the autumn leaves gave way to winter
As if in slumber, two hearts waken from a dream

And it seems to me that it was all for nothing
When feelings turned so cold inside my being
Our love, our time, forgotten, some vague
memory... Everything we were
now vanishing

Can it be?
Love is an imaginary thing
Only real as long as one believes
Seasons approach only to pass
Recede into forever
I felt the autumn leave
As fell the autumn leaves
And if our love were such a thing
Then why so deep this suffering

I always brought you roses on your birthday
And candy on our anniversary
Even seasons fade in time
The fire warming our home is dying
The taste of bitter fruit grown wicked on the vine
In vain, we've built together
    the hopes and dreams we worked for...

Was our love just an imaginary thing?

"Howard became like a Search & Rescue of the heart type person for me. He had that very rare set of skills, like Al Jackson, to know when and how he had something of importance to offer someone, emotionally."

Chapter Four
HEALING

As TIME MOVED on, we would finally begin to settle into another new living arrangement, living with my brother Bill, my Dad and his new wife, Pamela in a large rented house in on Breezy Way, in the southwest corner of the city of Orange. Living with my dad offered the stability I needed and I was able to return to St. John's Lutheran School, which my great-grandmother, my mom's grandmother, had always paid the steep tuition for. Even after the divorce, she was still my grandma and she was happy to keep paying the tuition for me. My brother had already moved on to Foothill High the year before. St. John's became my unfaltering bedrock, the unchanging foundation of stability through it all, a moral touchstone. It was a huge relief to be able to return to familiar ground for sixth grade, a place where everybody knew me, not having to change schools for the entire year. Attending four different schools in fifth grade, three different family arrangements, in a total of five different locations was too much, a real nightmare. It kind of freaked me out. But now it had all calmed down.

My great-grandparent's side of the family, the Muellers, were ultra-conservative Orange County citrus ranchers, very salt of the earth German folk and deeply Lutheran. They did not drink or smoke at all. They did not swear. None of them. Divorce was out of the question. You could probably go back hundreds of years on the family tree and find there had never been a divorce anywhere on this side of the family, nor a baby out of wedlock. They would rather live in complete misery than commit such a heinous crime against God. They could be very harsh and judgmental, like many of the Lutheran conformists I knew. They had a strict, but pleasantly humorless quality to them and when the family gathered it was usually after church. Straight-laced, clean-cut and behaving socially proper were the qualities of basic dignity on the Mueller side of the family. Anything less and it was open season for contempt and talking behind your back in disgust. You can imagine how well it went over when my mother became pregnant at fifteen only to divorce fifteen years after and wind up with this Jack guy. They were a very contemptuous bunch.

It wasn't like my dad's Italian side of the family where gatherings were far looser and the liquor, the food and the laughter all flowed freely. My dad's family gatherings were loud and filled with roars of laughter. By stark contrast, the Mueller's were quiet, polite and subdued, with only immediate family. We always gathered at my great-grandmother's house, which was, after all, a great-grandmother's house. The homes of the elderly are never really great places to cut loose and party. I always felt like I had to appear to be a certain way that was acceptable to them. It was more strict, like being at St. John's, you had to appear in your Sunday-best behavior at all times.

On the outside, I had to appear like I was a great-grandmother's house, but on the inside I was coming into my own as a wild party house late into Saturday night.

Disownment

The Muellers and the Sargentis were as different from each other as Germans are from Italians. There was no sense of shame or blame anywhere on the Sargenti side of the family, unless you failed to get up and go to work in the morning. They were some grumpy ass bitches on occasion, but that was usually because they worked so hard, stayed out too late drinking and had to suffer the recovery from hangovers. Their grumpiness had no lasting impact because as soon as drinking would resume, there were always ample hangover cures to be deployed.

To talk about the Sargenti family without a reference to my grandmother Hazel would be a crime. As a young woman, she found herself divorced with a five year-old boy, my dad. Between working to support herself and caring for her five year-old son, she couldn't get out much. At the urging of friends, she attended a Marine Corp social event where she met the handsome young, Al Sargenti.

After suffering the divorce from my Dad's biological father, Arthur Neighbors, she told me she had a very difficult time, that it was nearly impossible to meet someone new in a small town like Taft, California in the mid-1940's. Divorce was unheard of in those days, but he had cheated on her and, being the powerful woman that she was, she wasn't having it, to hell with whatever people might think.

Hazel was as beautiful outside as she was strong inside. She took my dad, then five-year old Billy, and gladly made her own way in the world. Al Sargenti was a handsome young Italian immigrant, who had come to the U.S.

with his mother Lisa and his father Humberto before he was age ten. He retained the thick Italian accent through his lifetime. He entered the marines where he rose to the rank of Master Sergeant and stayed in the service for a total of twenty-five years. As Sergeant Sargenti, he commanded the mess hall, endearing him to countless soldiers over the years by virtue of his association with being in charge of the food. Some might speculate this is why he grew to be so dearly loved by so many over the years: he served marines food.

Upon meeting my grandmother, they became inseparable and my dad instantly bonded very deeply with Al. Five year old Billy simply loved Al Sargenti to death and the two became very close. Within a year or two, Al married Hazel and legally adopted my dad, hence the name. He would only have very rare, occasional contact with his birth father after that. My dad disowned his father, Art Neighbors, and in his mind, he was even a full-blooded Italian named Bill Sargenti, who retained some Cherokee blood on his mother's side.

My dad introduced me to his birth father once, when we visited his paternal grandmother, my great-grandmother, Grandma Neighbors, in Maricopa, California in the 1960's, when I was about five. My dad was very adamant when he told me he did not respect Art Neighbors and did not regard him as his father. When he spoke to him, at least in my presence, he addressed him by his first name. He never called him dad. He would not carry on his name and he regarded Al Sargenti as his only father. He told my brother and I that we should always respect our family as descendants of Al Sargenti, that Art Neighbors was not worthy of any respect in our family.

So, here we are on another side of the family with Art Neighbors playing the role of villain. Cheating and womanizing was his most vicious crime, worthy of complete and total disownment and abandonment by all of his descendants. I find this difficult to fathom but that is the way it worked out in the long run. My dad had not chosen for himself as a child, so he only knew what they told him. I was never sure how much weight the opinions of other's held in influencing his decision to write off his birth father and how much actually knowing him as a person had to do with it. I can't remember if Grandma Hazel told me there was domestic violence involved, but if there was, I would think Art would have been the victim. Grandma Hazel, as loving and kind as she was, would be the least likely person I have ever known, to take shit off of anyone. Art Neighbors was completely and totally replaced by the greatly loved Al Sargenti, a truly good and decent man, honest hardworking and very, very loyal. I would come to know Al Sargenti as my grandfather and would never know Art Neighbors other than as a man I met once, at the age of five, in passing through the extremely remote Central

California oil field town of Maricopa.

Sargenti's

Sargenti's was an Italian restaurant owned by my paternal grandparents. All total, there was about six various locations, through the years, if you count the two locations my dad would one day open on his own. Each had a full bar, a lounge area and each restaurant was a fine dining establishment with candlelight and five to seven course dinners. Sargenti's II, however, was just a small bar that served a limited menu of sandwiches and fries.

My Dad's side of the family was all very down-to-earth, hard working people. They just drank a lot, smoked and cussed. I liked that about them because we all laughed a lot. Even as a small child, I wanted to drink and smoke and cuss, too. They never, ever said the word fuck, but I did. I used it a lot! I never used it in front of adults but I used the word all the time with my friends. Adults are never supposed to swear in front of kids, but they do anyway. It's funny how kids know better than to swear in front of adults. My dad's family used words like shit, god damn, asshole and son-of-a-bitch a lot but never the word fuck. It was the damnedest thing. Adult jokes were funny on this side of my family and I remember Playboy magazines could be found here and there, though like alcohol, they were only for adults, but there was no sense of shame attached to them.

If I asked an adult why they had Playboy magazine on the coffee table, it would always be said in a thick Italian accent, "It's not for kidsa. Get away from there, eh! Gimmie dat! They have very interesting articles. What's a matta wid you, eh?? It's good reading. Good interviews!" They would tell me.

The freedoms of being an adult were celebrated on the Sargenti side of my family. Mario Puzo's, The Godfather was a fair representation of the culture on this side but my family had zero criminal element. They were honest and hardworking to the core. My grandfather's business was legitimate the whole way through. Al Sargenti, my dad's adopted stepfather was an honest, hardworking restaurant owner and I have never heard anyone say a bad thing about him. He was his own man and friend to all.

He was the celebrated figure at the epicenter of my family and a large community of restaurant goers. He was like a respected celebrity, truly and deeply loved by all who knew him. He was not the Godfather, but in our family, and at each of his restaurants, he was treated like The Don. Rumor had it that he knew people who knew people. He had frequent customers who were thought to be Made Men but nobody really knew for sure because this sort of thing is never spoken of. Never. But it's understood.

Later in life, I would run up against a newly emerging epidemic of The Bloods and The Crips, Mexican gang members and the Gangsta Rap explosion, a world occupied by brothers and sisters of friends I had grown up with. I would run into them at clubs and various bars around town. They would try to intimidate me, a dirty white boy and I would set them back. "You think I don't understand this shit? Huh? My last name is Sargenti. I'm Italian! You get that? My family invented this shit. You don't want to fuck with me. My people will put your entire family in the grave! *Capisce*?"

Marina

Al and Hazel Sargenti had a daughter together, my Dad's half-sister, Marina. As fate would have it, she had become a highly regarded psychic healer who gave readings and offered counseling to quite a wide array of people. I had no idea. They told me a lot of people would come to her for help and that she could work wonders. My aunt was involved in the world of psychic energies, seeing into the unknown, warning of impending darkness and shining her healing light in the form of well-intended psychic readings, for thirty-five dollars apiece. That was good money back then.

She was kind of like a non-religious, universal prayer warrior, calling upon the forces that be, opening channels of clear light to help heal the infirm. She was a seer and a lot of people, including my father respected her for her abilities to foretell and heal with psychic power. She wasn't fly by night and there wasn't anything magical about doing it, for her, it appeared to be an explored area of human discovery. She took it very seriously and, like her mother, could be an extremely focused and confident person. To say she believed in personal excellence would be a serious understatement. She was a bright, wonderful person to be around.

When I was twelve years old in the spring of 1975, my Dad, his new wife, Pamela, my brother and I, were comfortably living a very stable life on a well-manicured, suburban street in sunny Southern California. At Marina's behest, were going to be attending a four-day workshop in Silva Mind Control. This was a training program she had taken and was very excited about it. She felt mind control was a good influence on anyone and that we should all take it. She even got her parents to take it. Since we had just come through a horrible time in life, I believe she wanted us to go out of concern for our well-being, because it would help us heal our wounds.

Silva was a meditation-based, psychic healing program based on gaining control of one's thoughts in order to enter into the alpha brainwave state. Mind Control involved slowing the brain waves, measured in cycles per second, to the alpha range between 14Hz-7Hz, which allowed one to enter a state of enhanced awareness. This highly receptive state allegedly enabled the student to begin projecting the mind to remote locations, for the purpose of practicing healing work, visualizing people who were not immediately present, utilizing psychic energy to do healing work on them.

While I could not take her to St. John's and introduce her to Pastor Geisler as my psychic aunt, nothing about her practices would have conflicted with my family's Lutheran beliefs in the slightest. It was a non-religious view, but it was the same the unseen mysteries of the human condition. It was the same, *make up your own mind and decide for yourself what you want to believe* kind of thing.

My dad believed in his sister, he had respect for her reputation as a psychic counselor and thought it might be good for us to do as a family. They felt it would be good for me, as it had been found that children were especially adept at utilizing the alpha brainwave state. There was some evidence to suggest that a child's young brain never operated faster than 12Hz until after the age of fourteen or so. Brainwaves become faster with age and children naturally remain in the alpha brain wave state all the time, which explains why kids are so imaginative and adept at playing in the world of make-believe and lose it with age. (Or do they?) After the last especially difficult year, it would be good for our souls to learn about meditation and how to practice healing with psychic energy. I didn't like the idea of going to this weird meditation thing, at first, I was gun-shy after the Maranatha breakdown, but like all the years of church and Lutheran school before, they were going to make me go.

Howard Britton

Silva was taught by a man named Howard Britton, in an event room, just off the lobby of a big hotel in Santa Ana. Howard was a man of slight build. His head was bald on top but he retained the ring of hair over his ears and around the back, which he let grow a little long, shoulder length. It was the balding intellectual male hairstyle of the 70's. He had round wire-rimmed glasses and spoke quietly with the air of a true intellectual. He was an erudite man who always wore plaid button-down shirts with a silver gemstone string tie and khaki pants. He had a very friendly, approachable way about him. Howard was a learned man in the field of hypnosis, parapsychology and things like clairvoyance, contemporary metaphysics and psychic healing. His personality was serious, quiet and kind. He possessed an easy sense of humor and could always get a laugh out of you.

Howard was a very consistent man, not in the least bit boastful or full of himself. He was quite the opposite, the kind of man everyone could only speak good of. I never met anyone who felt any other way about him, other than he was just the most lovable little man you could ever hope to know. And that's the way I came to feel about him as well. He was a very sweet and gentle soul. It simply takes just this long to describe what a wonderful person he was. He came into my life at just the right time, in just the right way to provide a comforting, healing positivity that was at the core of the self-help movement. Howard became like a Search & Rescue of the heart type person for me. He had that very rare set of skills, like Al Jackson, to know when and how he had something of importance to offer someone, emotionally. He could go to and stand at the edge of the abyss with a troubled, tortured soul and have them laughing it off in no time. This was a very special gift. He was an excellent teacher.

He opened my mind to ways of thinking I had suspected as a child but would have been reluctant to venture into otherwise. He introduced me to the idea that it was perfectly virtuous to use the mind as a vehicle of intentional visualization, and he believed anyone could become very adept at controlling the focus of their mind, in order to put visual thought-energy to use in ways that could bring healing to others. On the downside, as was often the case in my life, here is another adult teaching a form of what some might call magical thinking to child who had the misfortune of one day becoming a maladaptive daydreamer.

Howard believed and taught about a metaphysical principle called The Universal Mind. For him, all minds were united through visual and verbal thought to a universal mind and through this route, we could instigate intentional change by visualizing the result we wanted and taking practical action to reach this result. Silva was a self-empowerment approach to using thought in reprogramming the world according to one's own will. For me, the mind became a place to escape the discomforts and disappointments of life. Howard taught me about my *ideal place of relaxation* and *setting up my laboratory* where I could begin my psychic work. That was *it* for me. This became my ultimate place of escape.

I was free to imagine anything I possibly could. It was encouraged, considered perfectly okay, to just lay back and daydream out loud, in all it's Technicolor glory. I could live right there in the visualization space for the rest of my life and be perfectly happy. It was the equivalent of being a fiction writer without the hassle of having to write anything down. I could dream up scenario after scenario about how I would like my life to be and then simply sit back and imagine it was so. The rest of my life could be going to hell in a hand basket but I would just stay right there in my ideal place of relaxation and forget the actual world in favor of my inner one. I was happy there. Not exactly a good idea to teach such a fertile form of escapism to a maladaptive daydreamer but, who knew I would come to use it for such narcissistic purposes?

In teaching us Silva Mind Control, Howard firmly believed in everything he covered in the class and had a complete command of the material. As far as teaching the class went, he had been teaching it every other weekend for years, so he had the whole spiel down pat. There was a lot of turning off the lights and going into guided meditations. He would lecture and carefully answer questions about each new section of the class and then down went the lights, on came the strange relaxation audio track and we were off into another guided meditation intended to invoke the alpha brainwave state.

Silva Mind Control

As, the class progressed over two-weekends, the first Saturday was the 101 level training and Sunday was the 202 level. The next weekend was off and the following weekend was 303 and 404 level trainings. These were the different ways the material was broken up and made more readily digestible. It was very important to Howard that everything he taught us stay very clearly organized in our minds. The class stressed a relaxation of the body first, and then a focusing of the mind, in order to induce alpha, beta, theta and delta brainwave states. In each successive level, one was said to be capable of deeper and deeper states of mind. Each respective state was said to offer deeper and deeper benefits for the mind control practitioner, yielding more effective results.

My big brother was skeptical the entire way. He didn't believe in any of it. He was not subject to magical thinking in any way, shape or form. It was either practical and rational or he wasn't interested. He felt ridiculous and awkward and it just wasn't for him. He was born with the reasonable mind of an electrical engineer and his interests lie there and there alone. He had a talk with my Dad about it and was able to get out of going to the second weekend. He possessed the ability to stand up for himself and be honest about what he believed. I on the other hand, had to go and even wound up taking the entire course a second time for free a few months later, with my step-mom, who got really into it, maybe even more than my Dad did.

Howard had his rap down tight. He had a set opening he would run through every time he started into one of his patented guided meditations. The lights were dimmed down and the strange new age relaxation audio track would come up. It was a mixture of white noise, random clicking, like beach sounds recorded from a scratched up old vinyl record. In an especially deep and relaxing voice he would lead the session, "Take a deep breath and visualize your ideal place of relaxation. 10 . . . 9 . . . Feel going deeper. 8 . . .

7 . . . Deeper and deeper." His voice was so smooth and trustworthy. It would take him a full minute, it seemed, to finish his opening countdown. It was a long, slow ride, with Howard. He was an infinitely patient man. "Feel your body begin to completely relax as all the stress and tensions of the outside world begin to melt away. 6 . . . 5 . . . Feel going deeper now. 4 . . . 3 . . . Deeper and deeper."

He used the same opening statements every single time, intending to induce the slowing of brain cycles per second. Slowing them into the alpha state. He spoke slowly and steadily, "2 . . . 1. You are now in your ideal place of relaxation. All thoughts and tensions have melted away. Your mind and body are now completely relaxed. You can feel yourself becoming open to the sensations and intuition the universal mind."

Howard was preparing us for an uninterrupted state of focused meditation at a deeper level of consciousness, similar to a light hypnotic trance state where his instructions could be more readily suggested. He would reintroduce the concepts he had talked about in his lecture just before, but now offering them in a more active process, suggesting you might try to visualize certain things, like placing your self into other locations for instance, in the company of a specific person. He would suggest ways you could notice your surroundings in these visualized locations. It was all headed toward the notion, "You might even consider you have the ability to visualize the energy surrounding the person you are now visiting. You may find yourself sensing some silent intuition of their medical condition, for instance. What do you instinctively feel about this person or their state of health? Is there a disease there? Are they troubled or at peace? You may wish to visualize yourself removing health issues from them by breathing in clear light and exhaling all negativity, cancelling it out, rendering it null and void." Howard would suggest how doing so is completely natural and easy, guiding us in the process of visualizing.

"Breath in clear, fresh, healing energy and exhale all that is unhealthy and negative." He would suggest, "All bad thoughts and bad intentions, both in ourselves and from others are now leaving your body. If a negative thought or intention should appear at any time, in any place, you may simply cancel that thought by telling yourself the word 'Cancel' two times. Cancel, Cancel. There is nothing which remains and there is only clear light and healing energy present now. Breathe in and out . . . In . . . and out . . ."

Howard had complete mastery of the material and he really believed it was something worth spreading around in the world.

We were exposed to a lot of Edgar Cayce, Carl Jung and Kahlil Gibran type thinking during this time, the latter of which was refreshing.

Immediately before each meditation session, Howard would read a short paragraph or anecdote, often referring to Gibran's writings, such as *The Prophet*. We heard about peculiar states called lucid dreaming and out-of-body experience. It meant that you could wake up in a dream and know you were dreaming, or you could slow down your brainwaves while you were awake, relaxing below the alpha state, into states known as theta, or even a delta state, and your psychic perception would 'leave your body' and travel, also called *astral projection*.

I remember being told these are more advanced skills, which one should never try without extensive training and guidance from an experienced teacher. I was admonished that there was danger of getting lost and not being able to find one's way back to the body. In those cases, they told me, "Someone would have to spoon-feed you the rest of your life or you could die."

I remember being really intrigued by the ideas, by being able to float of above your body and look down and see yourself on the bed. I had a strong desire to find out for myself if this is how the universe actually works. I simply had to know more about this. I had been steeped in religion my entire life and I just knew it was going to be a secret key to unlock the unspoken mysteries of life. I was a curious young lad. I had powerful experiences in meditation during this class and Howard was well aware of my proclivity for it. He gave me special guidance and encouraged my family to allow me to take the class a second time for free. Even going as far as to say he would take responsibility for watching over me, if they wanted to drop me off in the morning and pick me up after. As it turns out they didn't have to send me alone. Pam was more than happy to take the class again.

Howard was a knowing soul and he just wanted to make sure I had proper training. Silva would become like a confirmation, and even a level-up, of my childhood daydream fantasy world. I wound up having a great time. For me, it was like I was coming home and they all knew it. I kept having the experience of seeing a light in my meditation, though it was only a pinhole of light in the darkness behind my closed eyes, something told me that I would spend many years learning to bring this light closer and closer, until one day when I might finally reach it. I even told Howard about it because I had the same experience several times. He didn't have any answers on that one.

The intention of the Silva curriculum was to be able to find people through the universal mind and read them. This ability to do psychic reading of people by just being given their name and the town in which they live was the focus of the final day of the class. They had index cards with a real person's name and city. He'd pair us all up with a class partner who, once we'd reach the alpha state, would take turns telling the other the name and city of the person. Then we'd would have to visualize them and read anything we could about their medical history and any issues they might have. If we wanted, we could visualize working on them in our laboratory, making their medical conditions disappear.

There was information on the cards about each person's condition and more details about age, eye and hair color, height, weight, etc. They said I was reading off the information on the cards with 100% accuracy. I would picture the person and tell them what was medically wrong with them. I would only say what I felt very strongly about and if I couldn't get anything I would tell them that. I was correct about things like hair color, eye color, if they had a hysterectomy or cancer, heart ailments and everything else too. It was all on the index card and I just read it out of the air. I would tell them things which weren't on the cards but nothing I said contradicted the details on any of them. Psychic stuff is like that. The more general you are, the more accurate you seem to be. Even Howard, my dad and Pamela were excited about it and they all took turns picking a random index card and asking me to read the person. They were all thrilled with how I did in the class. I was a natural at that stuff. Who knew?

It was all a big surprise to me. I just felt like I was a kid having fun playing a game of cards, or a game of make-believe. I felt that I was imagining what was on the index cards and it was just dumb luck that what I happened to say matched the details on the cards. But they were convinced there was more to it than that. So, I took it with some seriousness and whenever my parents asked me to "go in and do some work" on someone they knew who was having health problems, or serious troubles, I wanted to oblige and be helpful, so I would sit down and have a go. I sincerely believed I could help, in some small way, if I really tried. They felt every little bit could only help, if it was meant to be. But mostly, I just toddled off into my own world of make-believe and lived in my maladaptive daydreams where I could be anything I wanted to be.

Our time with Howard in the Silva courses had the effect of reshaping our family dynamic in a way, which was emotionally healthy, positive, and life affirming. Howard gave us a new glossary of terms to use as we went up against life's future problems and challenges. It affected the way we would communicate with each other and yet it did not interfere with the religious aspect of anyone's life. It could be likened to an add-on software, a plug-in, used to extend the abilities of an application. From then on, any time I would say anything negative or self-defeating, my Dad would always knock it back with, "Don't say that, son! Cancel, Cancel!" The idea of saying it twice was that once set up the mind to focus, and the second time would smash the very thought from the universe for all time.

The Story of Fred Gomez

We were living on Breezy Way in Orange. We had been there for over a year by now. It was an idyllic little neighborhood in the shadow of where the 55 and the 22 freeways meet. Our house backed up against the huge sweeping ramp from the 22 west onto the 55 north. The sound of big trucks slowing, by laying heavy on the Jake break, was a constant theme here, at all hours of the day and night. In Southern California, the sun has a life of its own. There is a brightness about the sun. The angle at which the light shine is more direct, especially so in finely manicured suburbs such as Orange. It shines most resplendently in the afternoon and everything glistens in the warm rays of the Southern California sun. As the afternoons linger, the sun begins slowly descending and the cool springtime shadows lay longer and longer across the deep green, well-fertilized lawns. The asphalt streets are all neatly edged with the sharp, tight lines of cement curbs, with green strips of grass, or colorful flowerbeds bursting along brightly lit sidewalks, and driveways. The driveways seem to go on forever, entry ways to home after home in what seems like a world of endless subdivided, single-family neighborhoods.

On one such afternoon, my dad was working in the garage sorting engine parts for a car he and my brother were rebuilding together. It was later in the day on a Sunday afternoon. It was a beautiful, stunning day. The sun was perfection and the air was cool and warm at the same time. You simply could not have asked for a nicer day. Our front lawn was one big, continuous space which included the next door neighbor's lawn. It ran from our driveway, all the way across both lots, to their driveway.

The family next door was named Gomez. I instantly liked them because my dad's sister, Marina, married a man named Javier Gomez, my uncle. I have cousins whose family name is Gomez. The family next door had two boys and I used to joke that we were practically cousins. The youngest was Carlos and he was eight. The oldest was twelve, the same age as me at the time. His name was Fred. We used to play catch on our front lawns. He would stand over by his driveway and I would stand way over by mine and we'd throw the baseball or football back and forth while we talked about everything under the sun.

Fred Gomez was a very nice kid. He was honest. Not the kind of kid to get into trouble at all. He was polite and friendly. He was a clean-cut, good-looking boy. He wasn't tall or imposing at all, moreover, he was slight and would tend to blend in to a crowd of kids and not stick out. His family was Catholic and he was raised in a rather conservative household. His dad wore a suit and tie to work every day and his mom stayed home. I remember the inside of their house was always immaculate. His mother kept the house very clean and her boys were always nicely dressed and well groomed. He was a soft spoken boy and not very aggressive at all. A lot of the other kids in the neighborhood were louder and had more dominant personalities. Fred would just hang back and go with the flow of whatever was happening in the neighborhood. He wasn't the kind of kid that instigated action, but he was all-in if something fun was going on.

I had been riding my bike around in the street in front of our houses earlier that day, like I always did for hours on end everyday, working on tricks I liked to do. I was into bicycle motocross, which was a new sport back in 1975. I was getting pretty good at it. My dad bought me a special bike for racing and it was helping a lot. I was breaking through and starting to win races, at the local racetracks, for the first time. Fred was interested in my bike and the tricks I could do on it and he would ask me to show him how I made the back wheel kick up in the air, how to ride wheelies and hop up curbs. That was all new stuff back then. Fred and I had spent the morning hopping curbs on our bikes with his little brother in-tow.

I liked Fred. Being my next-door neighbor, it seemed like he was always around, always ready to play ball or ride bikes or run around. He was a willing participant. His little brother was a fun kid and was always out on the street following his big brother around or playing with the kids his age. I think he idolized his big brother and looked up to him because he always wanted to do whatever Fred was doing. Fred was a great big brother, too. He catered to little Carlos and looked out for him in the neighborhood. Fred would usually choose to do what his little brother wanted to do, over the rest of us and they would go off to do their own thing, more often than not.

I remember someone, down the street a ways, put an empty box from a new refrigerator out on the curb for the trash truck to take. Some of the younger kids got a hold of it and dragged it over to the curb at the front of a little cul-de-sac that came off Breezy Way, and they were playing with it. There was about eight or ten kids in a group right there. Fred and his little brother were messing around with the enormous box. Two or three guys in the group were my age, they were just hanging' back, standing around talking while the rest of the younger kids were getting really into this huge box. I had been over there on my bike about ten minutes earlier, checking it out, talking to Fred and the older kids. The younger kids where playing make-believe games with the box, like it was a bus or a truck or a starship. They were getting in and out of it and kicking the flaps open, closing them up and dragging it around. They were having fun with it. It was still up on the curb, on the strip of grass between the sidewalk and the street when I saw my Dad out in the driveway at our house and rode back down there, about five houses away, to see what he was up to.

We were talking about something mundane when all of a sudden a car came flying around the corner onto Breezy Way. It was a couple of teens hot rodding in an old Ford or Chrysler sedan around through the neighborhoods. My dad was pissed and he yelled at them to slow down. I might not have even paid much attention to the fact they were hot rodding, had my dad not been so outraged by them squealing the tires loudly, as they careened around the corner in front of our house. I dismissed it as a relatively ordinary moment. He watched the car rush away down the street and turned around in disgust. "Damn kids!" He growled, "They're gonna kill somebody if they don't do it to themselves first." He hated that kind of stuff.

We went back to what we were doing. It was all quiet in the neighborhood, it seemed. But then it wasn't. Suddenly, it dawned on us that there was a big commotion down by where the kids were. My Dad and I were wondering what was going on. Fred's little brother came running down the street in tears, white as a sheet, he ran into his house. Not one-second later, his mom and dad were at the curb looking down to where the kids were, in shock. I noticed the box was in the street now, busted open and laying flat. Fred's parents ran full speed, not something adults normally do, with little Carlos right with them. When they got to the box, both parents, their hands on their heads, fell to their knees.

My Dad said, "Son, just stay here." He told me. "We don't know what's going on. Just let them handle it." We began hearing sirens approaching in the distance.

A fews minute later, as my Dad and I stared down the street in horror, my friend Danny came walking past our house. The paramedics and the ambulance were pulling up on the scene already. They showed up within three or four minutes. We lived close, less a half-mile away from the fire station. As they arrived, all the neighbors began coming out of their houses to see what was happening. We could hear more sirens start in the distance and grow nearer. Danny had been standing right there when it happened and he told us the whole story. My stepmother Pam came out of the house and asked what was going on.

My Dad was visibly upset. He yelled, "Some asshole kids came flying around the corner! ...And I yelled at them to slow down." He was overcome with tears.

Danny explained, "The kids were playing in the refrigerator box next to the curb down there. Fred's little brother was really having fun with it and he wanted Fred to get into it." He told Pam. A look of horror overcame her as she realized what he might be about to say. "Fred just was humoring the little guy, he really wasn't playing with the box at all. He was just hanging out talking with us. It just was the little kids doing it." Danny was shaken up and just trying to stay calm.

"Fred got into the box and Carlos closed the flaps up on him." Danny recounted. "They were laughing and just having fun. Fred was completely closed up in the box and wouldn't have been able to see what was going on. That's when the car came squealing around the corner and the little kids all ran back up on the sidewalk. Fred's brother stood in front of the box waving his arms, screaming for them to not run over the box, but it was no use. The car sped up and turned right for it. "

"Oh, My God!" we all said in unison, my dad, Pam and I.

"Fred..." I whispered.

"But the box was on the curb!" I pleaded, "Did he drive up onto the grass?" I asked

"No, the kids had knocked it down along the curb. It was in the gutter by then, along side of the street." He explained. "It wasn't out "in" the street." He said, "It was just, well... where it is now." He pointed toward the box and the crowd gathering around it. "I think the driver thought it was empty and just wanted to scare the kids. I don't think he realized Fred was inside."

"Oh my dear Lord..." I said in shock. "Didn't they stop?"

"No!" He said, tears streaming down his cheeks. "They never even slowed down. They just ran him down and just kept on going." I asked if anyone got the license number. He just shook his head. He described what he had witnessed. "It all happened so fast. There wasn't time. One minute it was all quiet and the next thing you know this car is barreling down the street aiming right for the box! There was a loud crack and some horrible sounds as the car ran over the box. Fred was sitting in the box facing the direction car was coming from. Carlos dove out of the way at the last second. Fred got hit really hard." He mentioned, shaking his head in disbelief. "Really hard."

He started to describe the scene in hideous detail. "His head would have been right where the front bumper was. I mean the car just nailed the box. The guy was just on the pipe. He had it floored. You could just hear it hit him. I mean, there was a loud cracking sound as he went under the car and the box was just shredded. I don't know, man. Fred's in really bad shape. I am going over to tell Steven what happened." His eyes were like saucers. He walked over to Steven's house at the end of our street.

My parents were both emotional, overcome with tears and sadness. They could only shake their heads and pace around on the lawn, glancing every so often, with parental concern, down the street toward the crowd at the scene. I eventually rolled down the driveway and slowly rode my motocross bike over to where the crowd was. I wasn't there to gawk. I felt so awkward. I didn't want to appear as if I was there only looking out of morbid curiosity. There was simply a lot of very concerned people standing there. It was hard to take in what was happening. There was an ambulance and a fire truck parked in the street with their lights flashing. The police cars were starting to show up. The paramedics had Fred wired up to monitors and were working with his lifeless body as they were speaking into radios.

As I craned my head around some of the onlookers, there was cardboard everywhere. I saw Fred. He was on his back, surrounded by a large pool of deep, red crimson blood, just flowing from his head out onto the asphalt street. He had lost a lot of blood and his body was mangled really bad. His skull was misshapen. His arms and legs were going directions arms and legs should never go. His body was completely limp, like a rag doll. He looked very bad but the paramedics were reporting into their radio's handheld microphone that he was still alive, reading his vital signs to a doctor on the other end. I don't think he was conscious. It was hard to tell if he was aware of his situation. If he was, he appeared to be in a deep state of shock... as were we all, right about then.

I only looked for what amounted to one full second, but in that second something in me changed for a lifetime. I had to look away. It was that bad. I slowly rolled away from the unimaginable scene to make my way back home. As I did I noticed Fred's parents and his little brother kneeling over him with the paramedics working, desperately, over him. I was more deeply affected by the look of such infinitely deep concern on his mother's and father's faces than anything else. Carlos appeared to be in a deep state of accelerated fear and anxiety. He was five miles past panic and on to a place none of us would ever want to know. They were 100% focused on Fred, in caring for him. There was nothing anyone could do, just try to get him moved to the hospital as quickly as possible.

At home, it was very quiet. I closed the front door behind me. As I did my Dad said, "See? See? That's why I worry about you out there?" He said, "Come here." And he pulled me close to him and hugged me. He told me he loved me and asked me what I saw down there.

All I could say is, "It looks really bad, Dad. I don't know if, Fred is going to make it," my voice breaking as the words left my lips.

Pam came closer and hugged us both and we just stood together for a long time, holding each other close.

"We'll just pray for him. For his family." Pam sighed. "God, I can't imagine. We'll all just do healing work on him tonight, the way Howard showed us."

The Aftermath

The next day was a school day. I had trouble sleeping that night, agonizing about what Fred and his family must've been going through. I prayed a thousand prayers asking God to save his life and let him survive it. I visualized doing round after round of psychic healing work on Fred the way Howard taught us but in my readings, my visualizing of Fred, I could only see massive injuries sustained in every area of his body. I didn't know where to begin. Deep down, I knew he wouldn't make it. How could he?

When I came downstairs, first thing in the morning, my dad and Pam were there waiting for me.

"Have you heard anything?" I asked hesitantly.

My dad looked at me, "Fred didn't make it, honey," he said softly. "His injuries were just too great. He died late last night at the hospital. I'm so sorry."

I was in complete shock. I sat down at the breakfast table and my face went white. I was overwhelmed by not knowing what death even was... let alone how my twelve year-old friend could have met his death overnight. I felt a wave sadness and a cold shiver come over me.

My dad explained to me what happened. "We called the nurse's desk at the hospital periodically throughout the night to get updates on Fred's condition. Just after midnight they told us he had passed," he told me. "There is an article in the newspaper this morning."

He gave me the paper. There was a short, single paragraph about Fred, describing his injuries and the car the police were looking for. There was no license plate number. There was no definite make, or model, or color. No definite description of the driver. Fred had multiple broken ribs which collapsed his lungs and severe head and brain injuries, as well as numerous other broken bones, it said. He passed at 12:11 am at UCI medical center. I was stunned. Speechless. Even though, I had never expected he would survive it, I was still quite horrified by the finality of his death. I was unable to comprehend how he could be absent from this earth.

My dad asked me how I was doing with it. I told him I would be okay. "It's just shocking," I said.

He said I could stay home from school, if I wanted, but he and Pam still had to go to work. I told him it would be better for me if I just kept my normal routine going. It kept my mind busy.

Before I left for school, I stood on the sidewalk in front of Fred's house, just looking at it. The morning air was fresh and cool, damp with morning dew. The sun was up and beginning to cast its golden glow through the spaces between the trees and rows of houses. Everything was stone silent except for the birds and the freeway sounds. It seemed as if there were no sound at all. I couldn't imagine what Fred's family must've been going through. I had no thoughts. I could only stand there, staring. I could only feel the overwhelming sadness of a child stolen away from his family by death. It was unimaginable, the thought of how this family was going to be able to go on in life without Fred. The entire thing was simply unthinkable. The house was absolutely silent. It was eerily still at that moment. I don't think they ever came home.

I arrived at St. John's just before the bell rang. We always started the day with morning prayers. Before beginning, our teacher, Mr. Bodie, asked if any one had anything they wanted to pray for specifically.

I remember telling him, "I would like to pray for my friend and next-door neighbor, Fred and his family." I told him Fred was killed yesterday on the street were I lived. "He was the same age as all of us in this class." I told him, "He was run over by a car while playing in a refrigerator box in the street. The driver never even stopped. He just kept driving."

"That was your neighbor?" He asked me, shocked. "I heard about it on the news and on the radio last night."

"I was there when it happened," I told him. He looked horrified. "Fred was my friend. We played together all the time. He lived in the house right next to mine." I could feel myself starting to lose my composure. Some of the other kids in class, knew about the incident and were just as horrified. Other students kept asking the teacher what happened.

"I heard all of this in the news," Mr. Bodie repeated to the class, "Both last night and this morning, they were reporting a child being run over by a hit and run driver. All I could think of was, thank God it's not one of our kids here at St. John's. And then here you are this morning," He said looking at me with great concern. "It's gut-wrenching. It's too close to home. I pray they find that guy."

He explained to the class what he had heard in the news. He had read this morning that the boy was "taken home by the Lord." Then he turned to me and got down on one knee and looked at me, eye-to-eye, "Son, are you going to be okay? Is there anything I can do?" he asked. "Would you like to talk to Pastor Geisler?"

I told him, "No. I'll be fine. All we can do now is pray for him, and for his parents and brother, especially. It must be very hard for them."

Mr. Bodie gave the morning prayers and focused on Fred and his family. He prayed for understanding, "...though we may never understand why things like this are part of His great plan," he said. When he finished the prayer, he dismissed himself from the class for minute. We could see him through the windows as he walked across the street to the office and then returned immediately.

It wasn't long after, Pastor Geisler was standing in our door. He came into our class in his full white robes, with his black pants and black shirt with the clerical collar underneath. He kneeled down next to my desk and asked me, "Would you please walk with me to my office? I would like to talk with you. If it's okay?" He looked at me with the deepest kindness and honest concern. His eyes were wet with tears.

He was there to offer me bereavement counseling I didn't even know I needed. Until we had sat together and talked for a while, in his little office, just off to one side of the altar, in the big church, I didn't realize the shock I was feeling was a state of mourning I was entering into for the loss of my friend. And that terrible state did stay with me for quite a while, for a few days, at least. He wanted to help me prepare for the feelings that were coming my way. It was his duty, caring for one of his flock by sharing his Lutheran perspective on how to suffer loss.

"When the Lord takes a child, it's impossible for us to grasp how such a thing could happen. How can we ever accept that this is God's Will?" And like Pastor Geisler always did. He asked me to bow my head and pray with him. It was soothing and comforting to have that one-on-one time with Pastor Geisler. He was such a good and decent man. I don't know that he ever realized how disconnected and three-layers removed he was from the tragic events he would counsel people on. I had been to funerals of loved ones where I was amazed at how unfazed and emotionless he could be in dispatching the standard ecumenical fare to his Lutheran constituency and their extended families. The fact remains though, the teachers and clergy at

St. John's caring enough to take me aside and comfort me that day helped me, a twelve year-old boy, get through yet another glaring exposure to an extremely harsh fact of life.

It seemed as if they were as deeply impacted by what happened as I was. It felt as if we all needed each other to get through that. What I found most comforting was that we did have one another, that we were each and all together right then. We had built and nurtured these strong relationships in our lives and they would come to support us in an hour of need. They would never leave me twisting in the wind, nor would I fail to be there for one of them, if anyone needed me. This was matter of the heart and everyone could feel it. I think the whole community was in shock over how Fred was senselessly killed that Sunday afternoon. The two teens driving in that car were never caught. Nobody ever saw the license plate and they were never reported to the police by anyone.

Whoever they were, if they knew what they did, probably thought it was funny and got a laugh out of it. They had no idea what a beautiful young boy they subtracted from this earth and how devastating the event was for everyone who had to go on living without Fred Gomez. These young men, whoever they were, had no idea what kind of a hole they ripped in the fabric of the universe on that Sunday afternoon and how many hearts were left defenseless against an unimaginable emptiness, which remains to this day.

Chapter Five
WORK

After my mom had moved out of state with her new husband, the psychopathic control freak, she would call me from time to time, wanting to talk, trying to stay in touch. This was always very difficult for me, when she would call. She would tell me how much she missed me and wanted me to come live with her. All it did was tear me up inside. It would take time for me to recover from those calls. It was clear she didn't understand how painful hearing her voice was for me. I'd been nailed by a few hard hits of emotional trauma during these awkward, preteen years and I wasn't taking it well. There was no way to heal fully. The more distance I could get on it all, the better I felt, in the long run. However, her calls would serve as a constant reminder of my emotional distress and unresolvable anguish. St. John's Lutheran School was the best place in the world for me to be through all of this. It's where I had grown up and it was where I felt a sense of belonging.

She moved around a lot with her new husband. It was part of his plan to completely isolate her from her family and keep her all for himself, keep her off-balance, so he could verbally abuse her and treat her horribly, to make her deeply subservient to him. They never stayed in one place. At the time, they were living in Vail, Colorado and she was undoubtedly playing it up about how this was one of the trendiest ski resorts in the country. I'd never heard of it. I'd heard of Aspen but knew nothing about Vail.

She convinced my dad to let her schedule a visit for Thanksgiving. I was supposed to fly alone from LAX to Denver and they would meet me there and then we'd drive to Vail. I was in seventh grade by then. She had been coercing me, plying me every time we talked, about coming to live with her permanently. I felt sick to my stomach when she would do that. I didn't like being put in that position but, just as the night she told me she was leaving my dad, I was too weak to shut her down. I was too nice. I didn't want to hurt her feelings.

I was perfectly happy living with my dad in sunny Southern California. I had a stable life again and I needed that structure and stability. She cared only about what she wanted because she, too, was hurting over all of this. She had made several bad choices by now and she was stuck with the consequences of her actions. Her controller had taken her away from everything she knew, gone to great lengths to create distance and was perfectly content keeping her to himself. I really didn't want to be a part of that. I'd seen, all-too-well what their world was all about.

As Thanksgiving approached, my dad knew my mom had been talking to me about coming to live there. I think maybe my brother told him, or he had asked me and I told him. I don't remember. He was open to discussing whatever I wanted to talk about. He let me know he wanted me to stay with him, that it was best for me if I stayed with him, but I was free to do whatever I wanted to do. I honestly wanted to stay. I didn't have mixed emotions. I felt like I was being pressured into it and knew I would not speak up for myself. I knew, once I was there, I would be at an extreme disadvantage. For whatever reason, I still felt torn between my two parents.

I wish it hadn't been my decision to make. This was probably the one time in my life I wished I wasn't free to do whatever I wanted to do because what I honestly wanted to do wasn't always what I would actually wind up doing. I have spent a disproportionate amount of my life being my own worst enemy and I regret my own myopic vision at that time. Once again, I was caught in the middle and it was stressing me out terribly. My brother noticed and he took me aside before I left for Colorado and he implored me not to do it. I promised him I wouldn't but I told him I felt resigned to the fact that I wouldn't be able to break my mom's heart. I knew she would cry and carry on if I refused her invitation, her temptation and enticements from the start, once I arrived there. It wasn't the bent of my twelve year-old personality to coldly refuse her, to see my mother upset like that and know I was causing her anguish, even though I knew it would mean certain torment for me. It was a horrible situation to be in, after all I'd just been through.

Brother Bill told me how it might seem fun for a little bit, "But you know how Jack is He can seem like a nice guy but you and I both know what an asshole he really is." And big brother was right about that. I was caught between missing my mom, my nurturer, caught between something new and exciting, yet wanting to stay with my dad at the same time, remain within all that was familiar and ordinary. It's hard to appreciate the mundane and the ordinary until it is harshly snatched from your life. You would think I would have understood this by now. These were very powerful life lessons I had to repeat several times before I could learn how to pass these kind of tests. To value the comfort of the ordinary and avoid exposure to the harshness of gut-wrenching life-changers, like going broke and losing everything, or the uncertainty of moving away from everything we know, only to end-up living with miserable people, these are difficult lessons to have well-in-hand before the age of thirteen. The problems lie in the fact that I was a coward. I had not learned how to tell people no and deal with their displeasure.

I had not yet learned how to state with absolute certainty, "This is who I am. This is how I feel, and this is what I am doing." Trusting myself like this was a jewel of understanding I had yet to claim. That was going to be a hard-earned lesson for this little guy and I was about to get schooled, at the good ol' Academy of Hard Knocks.

The day before I had to get on that plane to fly to Denver was a fateful day that tipped the scale and probably fucked up the rest of my life forever. I know it had a nefarious effect on my personality as a whole, if I could blame my personality on someone beside my own self. Let's just say this didn't help.

My homeroom teacher at St. John's that year was this guy named Mr. Senne. What a Fucker! I had heard he made a habit out of being unreasonably strict with his students. I mean, I get it. I was going to a private school. There is structure there and it's serious business. They don't take crap off of kids there. Okay! We were there to learn, not BS with the other kids or flip shit on the teachers.

Well, Mr. Senne had said something in class about schoolwork we were going to have to do and I groaned quietly to myself, then shook my head. I may have made a gesture to one of the kids next to me in the classroom. I honestly didn't think I had barely whispered a sound. Mr. Senne's head swung around and he just laid into me.

"Mr. Sargenti!" He yelled, "That's going to be one hundred sentences! I will not talk in class and I want them the day you return from Thanksgiving vacation!"

I remember trying to defend myself, "I didn't even say..."

"Two hundred sentences!!" he yelled

"But I..."

"Three hundred sentences, Mr. Sargenti! Would you like more?" He looked a me.

"But Sir..."

"Five hundred sentences, Mr. Sargenti!"

"This is outrageous!" I stood up and screamed. I wanted to kick his fucking ass now and he knew it. He was purposely inciting me at this point. He was emotionally charged and releasing his anger and his ego, like attack dogs, basically, on a child. We was being a bully.

"Seven-hundred sentences! And you better sit back down and not say another darn thing or your going to the Principal's office right now." He stared me down. "Don't challenge me, Son," he warned me. I just shook my head and stared at him with my mouth open. Now, it was all about a game of chicken with our egos and who was going to swerve first. Being a kid, I just lowered my head. I was so pissed I just wanted to scream.

He gave the class a series of short instructions and dismissed us.

"By Monday, Mr. Sargenti." He said sternly as I exited the room.

"What a fucking asshole." I said to my friends as we made our way down the hall toward our lockers. They were as shocked as I was.

Denise Leseberg, the biggest goodie-good on earth, said to me, "See, I told you. You gotta watch out for him. He is super, super strict." She was being a know-it-all again. But then, when I looked at her with a frown, she became sympathetic, "I'm sorry he did that to you."

With a little pixie hair cut and big tortoise shell glasses, lenses thick as the bottoms of coke bottles. She was kind of like a tiny schoolgirl version of Bubbles from television series *The Trailer Park Boys*. I had coined the nickname 'The Bookworm" for her. It stuck because it fit her to a T. She would never admit it but I think she kinda liked me. She stayed with me at my locker until I had calmed down a bit and was finally ready to go to my next class. I was really pissed. I wanted to kick the locker and throw things.

"Don't say anything, Don't do anything. Just go to your next class and forget about it." Denise warned me. "You can't win against him. He's just that way."

"Forget it?" I whispered, "How in the hell am I supposed to forget seven-hundred sentences by Monday? Are you going to write them for me?"

She just looked at me. "Uh, no." She smirked, "I think he would notice the handwriting."

Make The Call

When I arrived in Denver, of course, it was a big celebration. I had not seen my mom in almost a year. She was really happy to see me and I was glad to see her again. I missed her because she was my mom, but she had this guy with her now and there was always something about him I didn't like, at all. No one did. To be honest, I constantly visualized ways in which I could murder him and get away with it.

As we made our way out of the airport, Jack was his usual charming self, on his best behavior. It was a two-hour drive, from the old Stapleton Airport of 1975, to the ski slopes of Vail, we slowly made our way up into the Rocky Mountains in the late afternoon. The light coming over the mountaintops, beaming down into the valleys, through storm clouds as we past Breckenridge, was stunning. I had never been to Colorado or seen the Rockies before. The grandeur was spectacular! It looked like a storm was coming in.

My mom was convinced I actually wanted to come stay with her but I really did not and I didn't know how to tell her, to deeply disappoint her, to see her cry. I knew it was all about pressure and I was very uncomfortable about it. Of all the people I would never want to disappoint, she would be one of them. She said they had my room all set up and a big surprise for me when "we get home." She was laying it on thick, never stopping to think I was a twelve year-old boy with a whole, full life somewhere else. Running off and leaving a note on the dresser was her style. Why shouldn't it be mine, too? As we drove she talked about how I could call my dad and tell him I was going to stay and live with her permanently.

When we arrived in Vail, the mountain itself and ski resort was extremely impressive. The main village with it's clock tower and little stores had a quaint architectural style all its own. It was a very elegant place, very unique. It was like a winter Disneyland for skiers. The mountain seemed to go up and on forever. It looked like the funnest place you could ever turn a kid loose and say, "Go have fun." Which is exactly what they planned to do. I was eagerly looking forward to hitting the slopes. As we walked into their little apartment, she said, "Wait till you see your room! We have it all fixed up for you and a big surprise is waiting in it."

When we went upstairs to the room, she threw the door open and inside was a huge sign on the wall that said, "Welcome Home, Vince!" And there was a real motorcycle in there. I don't know how they got it up the stairs but it was in there. A Hodaka Ace-100 with the big chrome gas tank. They were so excited over what they had done. My mom never even considered the possibility that I would go back home to California, but if I knew then, what I know now...

I mean, I knew what was happening and I knew I was becoming an accessory to murder, so-to-speak. Though deeply torn, I knew I had a shared responsibility for the crime about to be committed. I also knew how wrong what they were doing was. If I could only tell them how I really felt, which I was never invited to actually do, nor did I feel safe exposing my true feelings to these two, even if I did, I knew they would hit back hard with a counter-barrage of blame and finger pointing, if I said, "Sorry. I don't want this." They would stop at nothing until I acquiesced. They had already gone to great lengths to place me into this high-pressure sales situation, to close the deal. They were just that type of people.

But this was my mom and I was twelve years-old. Until you find yourself in a situation like this you can never appreciate how horrible it actually is to be torn between two totally separate identities, to have your personality ripped in half like this. Now, you tell me how you are going to look at that sign and a new motorcycle, your mother's loving, smiling face, pleading for your acceptance, after all we both had been through, and at 12 years-old, look them in the eye and tell them, "No, thank you," knowing the emotional blowback you would receive from her, and especially from Jack. I was just not that strong of a person, then. I certainly am now, precisely because of situations like this, but not then.

They took me skiing. Or rather, they sent me skiing by myself, because they didn't actually ski. They just lived in a ski resort. They told me all about how great everything was in Vail and how life was going to be so good here. We went out to dinner and shopping. They took me on a little tour around the local area and showed me all the sights.

And here is the thing about Jack, what none of us could have possibly known yet. In the years that would lie ahead, he would go on to win national sales awards and take over command of vast regions of corporate territory in his climb up a future company ladder. He was about to go from a route-driving salesman, to a branch manager, to a regional manager, then a district manager, to a vice-president of a chemical company within the span of the next decade. All by brute force of his ability to persuade others to buy, to sign on the dotted line. This guy had a way of making people do whatever he wanted them to do. In the world of corporate appearances, if the numbers weren't going his way, he had no trouble cooking the books, or altering sales report numbers, until he could devise a plan to cash out and move on, leaving the real numbers to fall on the next guy. He was a textbook corporate psychopath and I don't use this term lightly. He would fuck over anyone, including the company he worked for, if it served to get him what he wanted. This kid was a total pushover in his hands.

I was in over my head. My mom wanted me and he was going to get her what she wanted, so, I never stood a chance. I could blame myself six ways to

Sunday but the fact remains, every hardcore sales technique in the book was about to be deployed out until the pen came out and the deal was closed. The pen was a phone and it was time for the power close, "Make the call, Vince."

How was I supposed to make a clear decision about the rest of my life with no help from anyone else, when they are putting this all in my face and then handing me a phone saying, "Make the call, Vince." She was asking me to betray my dad's love, the way she had, but now for a second time, in far harsher terms. Seven hundred sentences was simply grease on the ball bearings of the wheels of change. There was a lot more going on here than seven hundred sentences. There was a lot more, on so many different levels, it was overwhelming.

Bad Decisions

As I heard my dad's voice crackle across the phone, I didn't have to say a word. He knew why I was calling. The first thing my dad said to me was, "I had a feeling. Silva mind control and all, ya know." But he wished me well and told me, "No matter what they tell you, you can come back to live here any time you want. You know that, right?" he said. "Just pick up the phone and I will always be here for you," he told me. "I don't want you to live with them, but if it's what you want, and I don't think it is..." he suggested to me and he was right. He was an excellent judge of character and he knew me better than anyone else ever could, "I think they are pressuring you into it." There was silence on the phone, "They are. Aren't they?" I didn't say anything. "It's up to you, Son. I don't know what to say about this one. I just have a feeling this isn't what you want and they are making you think it is. Just remember what I said. I love you and take care of yourself. Okay?"

"I will." And I hung up the phone. He always knew me inside and out. There was never any bullshitting him. He could read people better than his sister could. My mom threw her hands up in the air and celebrated by giving me a big hug and telling me how much she loved me and how much fun we were going have together with our new family.

It wasn't but a few minutes later, I went up to my room and quietly cried my eyes out. I knew I had made the wrong decision. I felt a kind of despair I had never known before. This is one of the most memorable moments of my life, one of the most negatively powerful moments. I experienced a kind of helplessness I will never be able to describe. I felt like I had not only betrayed my dad's love again but that I had betrayed myself.

I had buyer's remorse, big time. But I felt there was no going back now. I felt I had done something that my dad would never forgive me for, that somehow he would be devastated and always be mad at me because of this. I felt that he would now write me off in his emotions, the way he had written off his father, Art Neighbors. I believed he would feel this way because this was the way I now felt about myself, for the crime of disloyalty to the people who love me. I entered into a very dark place of self-loathing over this event.

I thought about Denise Leseberg, my little bookworm, and wondered what she was going to think of me, doing this. She would, of course, know partly why I did it. She could not know everything I was dealing with, but she would think it was all about flipping the bird to Senne. And it was, but not entirely. As much as I'd like to think it really came down to that, the situation was far more complex than I could comprehend. Senne drove the last nail into my coffin to be sure. I was going to miss my little bookworm. I was only twelve, but over the years we had grown up together, I had suddenly come to have quite a warm feeling of calmness in her presence. At the age of thirteen, this natural evolution of a life-long friendship would be one more of the sweeter things in life I was losing the chance to explore for the first time.

I felt remorse when I thought of her, like should I have stayed near her, that she may have been a very good person to have kept in my life. She had a stabilizing affect on me. She made me feel like I needed to be a good person, a goodie good, like she was. She had a way of making everything seem okay, even when it wasn't, she had been there and was always kind to me, friendly, very, very nice, all the time. And my dad had the same effect on me. So why would I leave all that love and support and stability? It was like waking up and realizing I was right back the same nightmare again. And I was. There was no waking up this time.

If it had not been for that singular event, the seven hundred sentences of Mr. Senne, I always wanted to believe I could have grown a set of balls, told my mom I wasn't interested in staying with her in Colorado. Whether it was true or not, it was the sticking point in my head for many years, a place to avert the blame, the sting of my own guilty feelings. But as fate would have it, like anyone who hates their sucky job, I now had an out. Before I left California, I never told my dad about what Mr. Senne did. I found out later, but far too late, that when my dad learned of it, he was completely outraged by the seven hundred sentences situation and would have gotten me out of it. He told me he would have had me change homerooms, if he had to.

My great-grandmother had a lot of pull down there at the school because she donated so much money to the church each year, as her family had since the place was first built. I may have stood a chance. But because I didn't talk to my dad about it, I never knew they would have helped me.

Leaving the way I did had a tremendous impact on both Mr. Senne and my dad. Classmates would tell me later in life that Mr. Senne was never the same after that. So for whatever the reason, we both impacted each other's lives very deeply that day.

I had wished I had the guts to just go back to Mr. Senne's room that next Monday and say, "What sentences? I taught you was jus' fokkin' around, eh?!" and just not do them, make them kick me out of St. John's. That kind of thing just wasn't my style. I was afraid, yet loathsome. I did not have that kind of temperament. The pleasure of staying in Vail, Colorado at the start of the ski season versus the pain associated with going back to Senne's room made it a slam dunk, fuck you to Senne. But the cost to me came on credit. I still had to pay full price for making this decision, and it came with an ungodly interest rate that I paid for many years, if I'm being honest.

Being impressionable, vulnerable to suggestion and unable to bear hurting my mother's feelings was who I was. I would put other people's feelings before my own and often just go along with the prevailing course of action. If I didn't like a kid but that kid really liked me, I would try to be nice but avoid them. When avoiding them didn't work I would wind up involved with people and things I didn't like because I didn't want to hurt their feelings or tell them I wasn't interested and deal with their anger or disappointment. I let a lot of bad influences and toxic people into my adult life, too, over the years, before I figured that one out. And it would be more than 30 years before that kind of clarity came to visit my mind.

I spent the next year and half in six different cities around the U.S., from Denver to Honolulu. I and attended a total of seven different schools during my seventh and eighth grade years. Add-in the four different schools for fifth grade, for a total of twelve distinctly different schools under my mom's watch. Most of the schools were in cities quite distant to each other, from Vail, to Denver, to San Jose, to Honolulu, Hawaii. We just never stopped moving.

The Corporate Psychopath

By the end of January, we had left Vail suddenly. Bait and switch. Now that I was locked-in on the contract, suddenly we couldn't afford the ski resort life, so we were moving to Aurora, Colorado. Ski paradise lasted two good months. And what a two months it was. I was told we would be moving late the next night and I could not tell anyone we were moving. None of my friends could know where we were going. Not even Mary Jane, a pretty young girl I had begun having a very warm relationship with. That one would also now be taken away from me. To this day, she would never know where I went, why I was suddenly just gone.

It was the same when we left Denver at the end of the school year. I had made some wonderful new friends during the seventh grade. Each time, in Vail and in Denver, I was just starting to get my feet back under me, as a kid making new friends, starting a new life. I was told I could not, under any circumstances tell anyone we were moving. If I did, I was going to be in super big trouble and it would be very injurious to my parents for some reason. So, too often, I had to leave my friends under cover of darkness and not tell them. Vince just disappeared and all of his best friends never knew where he went. This was just more of the same heart breaking shit, which occurred over and over again for me during those years. I honestly had no choice but to ride along, no matter what they did. I very much hated their lifestyle. I hated moving.

For some reason, it never occurred to me that I could call my dad, beg for mercy and get out of that nightmare. I don't know why that didn't dawn on me. I think my mom and Jack had led me to believe it was not an option. Somehow, I believed my Dad wouldn't want me anymore, that because of my disloyalty, he had written me off like he wrote off his birth father, and I was deeply ashamed of that. For whatever the reason, my dad and I never talked on the phone. I never called him and he never called me. I am not sure why it was but this is how it played out. He probably didn't have a current phone number and I was never encouraged to make contact with him.

After I finished seventh grade, we moved to Palo Alto and then to San Jose where I started eighth grade. My mom had become pregnant before we left Denver and was overjoyed about having my little sister, 13 years younger than I. I did really understand all that, I was focused on the great friendships I had started making with kids I'd met at John Steinbeck Jr. High, friendships which could have lasted a lifetime but by Thanksgiving, my little sister Heather was about to be born and then, I was also informed we were moving to Hawaii, January 1.

This time the moving thing wasn't so secretive, because Jack was being promoted in the company he worked for and he was on a big ego trip. I had to sell this awesome drum set I had just built out of various kits because they couldn't afford to ship it, and it was too noisy for the baby. Every time I started having my life feel good again, building new relationships, it was always shattered. Now I was off to two more schools in Honolulu and I had heard legendary stories of how brutal it was for white kids to go to school in Hawaii. I bought an electric guitar with the money from the drum set, but no amplifier, just a very quiet electric guitar. It required a lot of practice but eventually, I learned how to play *Stairway To Heaven*.

I wound up working for Jack as his little helper while he made his corporate climb. I witnessed firsthand, his psychotic tactics, the way he used and squeezed people, the way he held the power of firing them over their heads. He berated and verbally abused his employees into doing everything he demanded, to get the exact number he needed, which would trigger his own bonus check. He treated them the same way he treated my mom and me. All of them, the office employees, the sales staff, the company itself, it was all there for the sole purpose of triggering that bonus check. None of the people were even human to him anymore. They were chess pieces in a game of power. He got off on the feeling of squeezing them and controlling them, using people as resources, making them do whatever it required to bring him that goal number. He had to have a number and it was there job to get that number for him or else they were done. For a kid, it was terrifying to watch him fuck people's minds again and again, the screaming I'd hear coming from the office as he laid into his staff, then turn around and be perfectly charming when he got what he wanted.

In Hawaii, I had actually missed the entire third quarter of eighth grade because Jack kept me out of school longer than expected. They never put me back in school after we had moved there. I just wound up going to work with him everyday to help him at this first branch manager gig, in Honolulu. They delayed putting me back in school so I could work in the warehouse, clean, organize, rebuild the equipment and, of course, help him make deliveries. This freed him up so he could focus on making the sales numbers, the one thing that would bring him the recognition he craved, as well as the commissions and bonus checks he believed he was entitled to.

I was of immense value to him in getting the odd little things done. It just went on and on and when they finally put me back in school, my grades had suffered horribly. I was lost when it came to the math. And the wicked Kona Gold I was smoking with all the island kids wasn't helping matters any, in regards to the studies.

Of course, Jack blamed me and the abuse elevated when the notices came home from the school saying I was failing. I still had to work in the warehouse after school, so Jack could succeed, and double up on my studies at night amid the horrible blame that I was a total fuck up.

One day after school, I brought home a notice of some kind about my grades and Jack grabbed me, pushed me up against a wall, in front of my mom and wrapped his hands around my throat, threatening to choke me out if I failed a single one of my classes, or if he got one more notice. It was the most absurd moment of crossing the line with me. I will never forget it. I'm still pissed about it. The whole situation was completely out of hand and yet they acted, both my mom and he, like I was a total fuck up and needed to get my shit together. My mom did nothing to defend me. She just stood there watching.

When I worked for Jack, I had to load the trucks and, once on site, do the delivering and changeover of solvent drums, while he drove the truck and made sales. Anyone else who did that same job worked alone and had to do everything themselves. At each stop, he went in and schmoozed his way to the next sale and to the top of the sales charts. Every weekday and on Saturdays, Jack would wake me up well before first light, make me get ready, then we would drive to his work, before anyone else was there. I would have to get the delivery trucks ready for day's routing, collecting all the paperwork and marking all the stops on our map, in order, and they'd better be right or I'd catch holy hell. I got some of the worst brow beatings you can imagine when I fucked up out on the road. Jack had the worst sense of direction and the worst temper of anyone I'd ever met.

To be fair, we had a lot of fun sometimes with the customers and had some great laughs out there, too. It wasn't always totally fucked. That was when Jack was at his best, when the customers were around and the sales were rolling in. There was some net benefit in the long run. Along with learning to take a ton of shit off people, I learned to overcome any resistance I had, as a kid, to hard work. Looking back, I respect the fact that I learned to work hard at an early age, but it doesn't change the fact that I did so at the hands of a corporate psychopath who was bending anyone at his disposal to his wishes, twisting the world according what he wanted to get out of the deal. It was unfortunate, yes, but I learned the ugly truth about the dog-eat-dog corporate world from the inside, all while I had barely become a teen.

He would continuously get the best sales figures in his region. Astonishingly, he'd take whatever branch they'd give him, from last place in the region, the real dog of the company, to number one, every single time. He became a corporate branch resuscitation specialist and the higher-ups, at the national headquarters, swiveled around in their big leather chairs, eyebrows raised, taking notice. He did this primarily by being a cutthroat asshole to his employees and one charming son of a bitch to his customers. He did it by pure intimidation and psychological force, but most of all, by example. He showed them it was possible first, by doing it himself. This guy could demonstrate how to post sales on the board like nobody's business. His employees either got the results he was able to get, they either made the sales, or they got fired. Period. Well, they got yelled-at a lot and then they got fired.

I got paid for my work and this was actually the point in my life when I got my first face full of working forty-or-more, hours a week, at the age of thirteen. I worked hard during this period of my life, eight to twelve hours a day, six days a week, harder than I would have to in many of my later years. I really learned the meaning of hard work, firsthand. I saw the benefits and the glory. I observed the pain of failure and what it meant, emotionally, to get fired and for a man to lose his family's sole income. We would hit the ground running early and wouldn't stop until bed time. It was horrible, as far as I was concerned because I was supposed to be in school. I hated every minute of it, but I learned to survive and not get yelled at by working hard and doing what I was supposed to.

There was always something that had to be done. At thirteen, I am certain child labor laws were flagrantly broken, but I did everything I was told. I had to do it or I'd be yelled at until I did. Jack clearly took full-advantage of my availability and youth when he needed to get sales done. It was brutal. No matter what happened, I had no choice in the matter, it was completely forced on me. At thirteen, I never would have chosen to do any of that on my own.

Looking back, it was really hard but I was forced to learn the value of hard work. I got paid. I had my own money. That part felt really good. It was my bootcamp for a lifetime of survival as an American Worker. I was trained and conditioned for a life of hard work like none of the other kids my age had been. Jack didn't fuck around when it came to making other people work.

Even on our days off, there were projects around the house that had to get done. Drywall to be hung, painting, appliances to be moved, furniture, you name it. It was exhausting and it was never ending. He made you get shit done and he wouldn't let you do it wrong. If you did it wrong you would catch total hell but he would carefully teach you how to do it right, then he would make sure you did it right. Then, he'd expect you to do it right every single time from then on. If it wasn't done in time, he'd ride your ass until it was. The guy was a total motherfucker but he was number one and he knew it. And he made sure you knew it too. "This is how Number One gets done, Son!"

Brother Bill To The Rescue

Within a week or so after eighth grade ended, Jack was transferred from Honolulu to his next set of victims in Portland, Oregon. The work never stopped. The cycle of screaming, firing and the relentless effort of hard work simply began all over again. All summer long.

My mom and Jack had been planning a road trip to Southern California, before I was to start high school, god-knows-where, in whatever high school there was in Beaverton in the fall. I assumed we were going to visit my great-grandmother, and I would get to see my brother Bill and my dad, finally. As fate would have it, my mom let me know, one day in mid-August, my brother and his friend Tom Moses were driving up from Southern California. Since it was summer, and they'd just graduated high school, they decided to make the eighteen hour drive, a pre-college road trip, in brother's Chevy luv pickup, to come visit us, first.

All summer I had been working my ass off with Jack in those sweltering fucking trucks, delivering solvent drums all over hell's half acre and now finally, I was being informed, I would be able to take a little break. Once brother Bill and Tom made it to our place, fate smiled on me. After almost eighteen months of living hell with my mom and Jack, they told me I was going to ride back to Orange County with my brother and Tom. They would pick me up in two weeks when they came down. I think brother Bill saw the writing on the wall and went to bat for me, trying to negotiate an opportunity for me to see the forest from the trees. I was off the hook for the rest of the summer. You can't imagine my relief. It was time for me to be a kid again, to go visit my dad and a just spend some time not having to work from first light until dark.

That was my big break. Off I went on a road trip with brother Bill and Tom Moses. Man, it was a godsend. It was a totally unexpected break of sunlight in a shit storm of total bullshit.

Once I was back in So Cal for about a week, enjoying the swimming pool, laying in the sun, sipping iced tea, I remember saying to Pam and my dad how much I dreaded going back. I had been telling them the whole story I have written in this chapter. They were just hearing it for the first time. They had no idea what I'd been doing all this time. I couldn't imagine what life was going to be like going to high school in yet another new school. They just looked at me like I was from outer space. They couldn't have imagined what I had been through, how I had been programmed to think and why I believed I had no choice other than to live with my mom and Jack. This was all news to them.

But they just started laughing, "You know you don't have to go back, right?"

I looked at them like, "Are you fucking kidding me? Really?"

My dad said, "I don't even know why you stayed there in the first place!

Or why you stayed this long! You could have come back any time you wanted to. I told you that. You can stay right here and go to foothill high with everyone you know. It's always been your decision. You can spend the next 4 years in the same school. Wouldn't you rather just go to one high school instead of sixteen?"

I just looked a him like, "Are you fucking kidding me?"

It was like the weight of the world had been lifted off my shoulders and I felt also relieved. My sense of relief at the thought of being back home, of by-passing St. John's and going directly to Foothill High, with all of the kids I had grown up with, was limitless and complete. I had come out of the isolationist hell, a nightmare within a nightmare and, now at fourteen years old, I had made it back from the single worst decisions I had ever made in my life. The debt I incurred by not writing those seven hundred sentences for Senne was now marked paid in full and I was back in the Southern California sun. It would have been easier just to write them. Nevertheless, now it was summer time... and the livin' was easy again. I could just go ride my bike around all day and be a kid. I could go hang out with friends I had known all my life, friends who were all like, "Heyyyyy man, where ya been?"

Even after eighteen months of hell, telling my mom I was staying with my dad was extremely difficult thing to do. My dad sat me down before I went over to grandma Mueller's house and explained to me how serious this would be for her and although I was excited to stay, even vengeful against the two of them, he admonished me to be considerate of my mom's feelings. Even though my mom had burned him over and over, he still loved her and wanted me to think of her feelings in all of this. It was true that not everything during the eighteen months was hell. There were many memorable events but they were greatly outweighed by all the wailing and gnashing of teeth.

When I pulled up and great-grandma's house and got out of the car, my mom was there and she was so happy to see both me and my brother. But she took one look at my face and broke down crying. I never had to say a word.

I would go on to spend the rest of my teenage years living in the town where I grew up. No more transferring schools four times every year. No more being around a hardcore, workaholic, psychopathic control freak. No more of the shell shock of not knowing when you are going to get screamed at again, on any given day, by a raging asshole of a man who was not in control of his own faculties. That was all behind me now. And I was glad to see it gone. However, it was not going to be a perfect world. While I enjoyed my teen years in So Cal, now much more than ever before, even as I was learning to cherish my life in the hometown I had been born into, darkness would return to visit me, again and again.

Any reprieve I was ever granted, in this regard, would always prove to be short-lived.

Chapter Six
DISCOVERY

I Went Down To The Crossroad

While I was at the Guitar Institute we were told about the legend of the crossroad. For Guitarists, the crossroad is the mythical place we go to wait for the devil to show. When he shows, we make a deal with the devil, along a remote Spanish highway. We sell him our soul in exchange for all our dreams to come true, our dreams of possessing wicked playing ability. When the devil agrees, we sign what the industry calls a Standard Contract. It's a record company contract, which gives the devil 88% while the whole band splits 12%. The devil advances your band a few hundred grand to make your record and cover living expenses, which you have to pay back to the devil from your 12% of gross sales, before you see any royalties. The devil banks 100% from the first sale, until you pay back every penny of the advance out of your 12%. Then, once you've paid the devil back his several hundred grand, he keeps taking his 88% for the rest of eternity. Sound like a good deal? Sign here.

The teachers at G.I.T. told us that we would individually arrive at the mythical crossroad in our own time, whenever it was meant to be. At that moment, we would make our own personal toss of the dice. The decision of the toss would be final. The decision would determine the course of our career from that day forward. They told us we had to decide on what our specialization would be. They said it would be necessary to specialize in a focused area of the guitar playing field in order to develop the exceptional playing ability needed to get noticed, or attract any interest whatsoever. Guitarists, artists of all kinds, live and die by their ability to move people, to excite audiences to come out of their homes and watch them do their thing. That highly specialized thing, whatever it is, has to be extremely professional in order to make the general public decide to plunk down their money to buy a concert ticket, or a record album for instance. For this reason, we needed to make a choice down at the crossroad: what, precisely, are we going to specialize in doing?

When my day came, I grabbed the dice and blew on 'em as I rattled them around in my hands. I threw those fuckers into an empty guitar case with all the spin I could muster. The decision said: Songwriter. I had given it deep contemplation but I realized the decision had already been made years before. It's true that the main thing people care about when they listen to music is whether or not they like the song. For me, the music business was all about the art of writing number one hit singles, all-time classics and all-around great songs. Writing songs, for me, is what separates the men from the boys. An artist is nothing but for that one great song they play, the one audiences wait for and want to hear any time they buy a ticket to see them perform. Many of my classmates at G.I.T. chose to become jazz improvisors, some focused on developing the ability to sightread from sheet music, so they could work for the union as studio musicians, some became arrangers of musical scores, working in television and film. Of course, I took the one-in-a-million route, I decided to be a recording artist and a songwriter. I needed to write a ton of songs first and I believed the rest would come of its own, once the undeniably great material was made real.

I looked the devil right square in the eye and I winked at him. I never signed the 88/12 contract, but from that day on, my whole world became about the chord changes and what would sound good over them. I became completely immersed in the world of writing songs and performing them for audiences. I dove headlong into the world of imagination and melodic improvisation. The muse running through my world of ideas became the latest new songs as soon as I wrote them down and played them into a little cassette-tape recorder. My practice was a daily nurturing of a garden of ideas, enticing the mysterious imagination to fork over the good stuff. I was fascinated, completely in love with music. Music was my love and my songs were our children. There was nothing else in life I would have been content to become. This was it. This is the man I wanted to become.

My entire consciousness would be completely absorbed and safely lifted into trance states by the songs of Van Morrison, James Taylor, the bands Rush and Yes. Cat Stevens was the artist who I naturally sounded most like and whose songs I adored more than any other. I had to discover my own unique sound, my own original voice. I had Cat's anthology songbook and I dissected every chord change, every phrase, every nuance of his vocal inflection. I did the same with James Taylor and with other artist's catalogs. I bought each artist's every record and pored over every chord and melody, every harmony. I listened to every artist I could and made learning the craft my sacred quest. At 18 years of age, I left G.I.T. a changed man and knew what I had to do. I had to post original material equal to that of my heroes. I had to prove myself as a songwriter. For me, it became a higher calling and everything in me screamed out to answer the call.

I ran out of money part of the way through the year and had to leave The Guitar Institute without completing the entire program. A friend had offered me a place to live and a job at a print shop. So rather than starve and sleep on the street, or find some other way to work and go to school, to scrape my way by in a very expensive part of town, I took the easy way out and folded up shop and moved back to Tustin. The road to success in Hollywood was beyond my ability, flying solo. I would have needed more support, at eighteen, to successfully complete the program and find career opportunities there. Hollywood is a tough town. I was going to have to find another route. I continued to be a very prolific songwriter, albeit, one with a day job and bed to sleep in.

I Went Down To The Crossroad

While I was at the Guitar Institute we were told about the legend of the crossroad. For Guitarists, the crossroad is the mythical place we go to wait for the devil to show. When he shows, we make a deal with the devil, along a remote Spanish highway. We sell him our soul in exchange for all our dreams to come true, our dreams of possessing wicked playing ability. When the devil agrees, we sign what the industry calls a Standard Contract. It's a record company contract, which gives the devil 88% while the whole band splits 12%. The devil advances your band a few hundred grand to make your record and cover living expenses, which you have to pay back to the devil from your 12% of gross sales, before you see any royalties. The devil banks 100% from the first sale, until you pay back every penny of the advance out of your 12%. Then, once you've paid the devil back his several hundred grand, he keeps taking his 88% for the rest of eternity. Sound like a good deal? Sign here.

The teachers at G.I.T. told us that we would individually arrive at the mythical crossroad in our own time, whenever it was meant to be. At that moment, we would make our own personal toss of the dice. The decision of the toss would be final. The decision would determine the course of our career from that day forward. They told us we had to decide on what our specialization would be. They said it would be necessary to specialize in a focused area of the guitar playing field in order to develop the exceptional playing ability needed to get noticed, or attract any interest whatsoever. Guitarists, artists of all kinds, live and die by their ability to move people, to excite audiences to come out of their homes and watch them do their thing.

That highly specialized thing, whatever it is, has to be extremely professional in order to make the general public decide to plunk down their money to buy a concert ticket, or a record album for instance. For this reason, we needed to make a choice down at the crossroad: what, precisely, are we going to specialize in doing?

When my day came, I grabbed the dice and blew on 'em as I rattled them around in my hands. I threw those fuckers into an empty guitar case with all the spin I could muster. The decision said: Songwriter. I had given it deep contemplation but I realized the decision had already been made years before. It's true that the main thing people care about when they listen to music is whether or not they like the song. For me, the music business was all about the art of writing number one hit singles, all-time classics and all-around great songs. Writing songs, for me, is what separates the men from the boys. An artist is nothing but for that one great song they play, the one audiences wait for and want to hear any time they buy a ticket to see them perform. Many of my classmates at G.I.T. chose to become jazz improvisors, some focused on developing the ability to sightread from sheet music, so they could work for the union as studio musicians, some became arrangers of musical scores, working in television and film. Of course, I took the one-in-a-million route, I decided to be a recording artist and a songwriter. I needed to write a ton of songs first and I believed the rest would come of its own, once the undeniably great material was made real.

I looked the devil right square in the eye and I winked at him. I never signed the 88/12 contract, but from that day on, my whole world became about the chord changes and what would sound good over them. I became completely immersed in the world of writing songs and performing them for audiences. I dove headlong into the world of imagination and melodic improvisation. The muse running through my world of ideas became the latest new songs as soon as I wrote them down and played them into a little cassette-tape recorder. My practice was a daily nurturing of a garden of ideas, enticing the mysterious imagination to fork over the good stuff. I was fascinated, completely in love with music. Music was my love and my songs were our children. There was nothing else in life I would have been content to become. This was it. This is the man I wanted to become.

My entire consciousness would be completely absorbed and safely lifted into trance states by the songs of Van Morrison, James Taylor, the bands Rush and Yes. Cat Stevens was the artist who I naturally sounded most like and whose songs I adored more than any other. I had to discover my own unique sound, my own original voice. I had Cat's anthology songbook and I dissected every chord change, every phrase, every nuance of his vocal inflection. I did the same with James Taylor and with other artist's catalogs. I bought each artist's every record and pored over every chord and melody, every harmony. I listened to every artist I could and made learning the craft my sacred quest. At 18 years of age, I left G.I.T. a changed man and knew what I had to do. I had to post original material equal to that of my heroes. I had to prove myself as a songwriter. For me, it became a higher calling and everything in me screamed out to answer the call.

I ran out of money part of the way through the year and had to leave The Guitar Institute without completing the entire program. A friend had offered me a place to live and a job at a print shop. So rather than starve and sleep on the street, or find some other way to work and go to school, to scrape my way by in a very expensive part of town, I took the easy way out and folded up shop and moved back to Tustin. The road to success in Hollywood was beyond my ability, flying solo. I would have needed more support, at eighteen, to successfully complete the program and find career opportunities there. Hollywood is a tough town. I was going to have to find another route. I continued to be a very prolific songwriter, albeit, one with a day job and bed to sleep in.

Discovery

Just before I turned 20, I was out with a friend one Sunday afternoon and we wound up dropping by to visit my aunt Marina, at her home. We had a nice visit with my uncle and all my cousins and while we were sitting talking I remembered to ask her about out-of-body experience. I told her I had always been curious about it and wondered what it was, if it was for real. If it was possible, this would have a big impact on my world view. Her and I had never actually spoken, one-on-one, about meditation or her psychic abilities before this. Our family talked about mind control or similar subjects, here and there, over the years, but her and I never had a conversation on any of these subjects before.

Her answer was unexpected. She began talking to me about a traditional yoga teaching I had no knowledge of, referring to seven energy centers in the body, or the chakra system. I had never heard of it, or anything like it before. I had no clue. For me, this was something straight out of the blue. She said if I was interested in learning about out-of-body experience, I needed to learn to control my energy and attention, more specifically how energy collected and moved through these seven centers. She explained how people have a given amount of personal energy, in and around our bodies, whether a lot or a little, and it is distributed through each of the seven energy centers, these chakras. She said personal energy is often collecting more into one location than others, depending on our personality and disposition at any given time.

She told me that handling the flow of personal energy through the chakra system and being able to focus attention on specific centers as needed, was a prerequisite for out-of-body experience. Then came a very quick description of each of the seven centers. I found it all very intriguing.

Long story short, she had just introduced me to the practice of yoga meditation, which I had no idea even existed. I only knew what Howard had shown us during the Silva classes, which was a more scientific, western approach. In the 1970's there was not a Yoga class on every street corner, the way there is today. Yoga was associated with eastern mysticism, strange body poses and little understood spiritual traditions taught by men wearing turbans and robes. When you spoke about yoga, you were talking about India, the land of Gurus, Maharajis and ashrams, which are little monasteries, where Hindu and Buddhist monks pray and meditate in isolation. The emergence of the cosmic consciousness counterculture in America happened around the time of the hippies, during the Summer of Love period in the mid 60's. Interest in eastern yoga mediations and cosmic consciousness followed along with the electric guitar's rise to glory in the popular culture of the day. The rock concert scene was fertile ground for those interested in exploring traditional eastern meditation because it blended the LSD movement with all of the imagery of mysticism creating a muse of intoxicating and colorful theater, which sparked the advent of the psychedelic era.

As an ardent student of the rock concert profession, I listened attentively as Auntie explained to me a little about each of the seven energy centers and then told me a specific exercise I should try. She explained how I should focus my attention. She said I should place it on a specific center in the body, a specific chakra, it could be any of the seven, then through breathing and concentration, bring energy toward that center. Then, she went into more precise detail, carefully explaining an exercise I could practice to enhance concentration. As she went on, I was taking it all in, as anyone would a casual conversation about any intellectual subject. I was actually broken of that spell when her eyes grew quite bright and she said, "Try it!"

I felt awkward and hesitant because, up until this moment, everything she was speaking of had all safely existed only in the realm of words. Suddenly, I was being asked to act on what she had just told me. I felt myself having to shift gears in the context of this conversation and think for a second. I had to reach back into my now neglected Silva Mind Control training and have a go at this meditation exercise. For me, meditation with Howard had always been about visualizing, imagining, seeing with the mind's eye. What she was now proposing was raw focus, for the sake of concentration, not only of attention, but rallying all my personal energy toward a single point. At least, this is how I understood it. So, that's what I tried to do. Bring all of the energy, in all of my chakras, to a singular point, at the sixth chakra. Easy peasy, lemon squeezy and BANG! I never in a million years expected what happened next.

As I closed my eyes and tuned my peripheral awareness onto this chakra idea, I also moved my direct attention to the specified location, the sixth chakra. Immediately, I saw the shape of the seven centers of energy as if I were reading it all, like the index cards during the Silva class. I heard Marina say, "Now, breathe and focus. Bring all your energy to this one point." It all felt very natural and easy. I took a breath and as I focused, I became clearly aware of all the energy throughout my body and where it was. I felt it. I was entirely capable of bringing it all together, to focus everything on this single point, so I did.

As I brought my full-attention to bear on the place between my eyebrows, I experienced a jolt, as a current came flowing in from all around me, driving into the point of my concentration. I gripped the arms of the chair I was sitting in, as I felt a rush of speed as all the energy around me flowed toward the area between my eyes. It was startling. I had a brief instant of the spins, but it was a very balanced and powerful sensation of light vertigo. I had to shake my head and pull out of it. That jolt startled me and my concentration was interrupted by it. It was all very unexpected.

My eyes instantly popped wide open. In that one instant, my breathing had changed involuntarily as adrenaline went surging through my blood. My senses came alive like I had never felt before. The only word out of my mouth was, "Whoa."

Marina laughed and said, "See! It works really well!"

I think everyone, myself included, had forgotten that I had always been a natural at this kind of stuff. Something about it had always come very easily for me.

*[The exercise she asked me to try is traditionally known as the Ajna meditation. It should only be learned under the guidance of a professional yoga or meditation instructor after first learning to practice more fundamental exercises.]

For most folks, this moment would be shrugged off as a note-to-self kind of insight, devoid of any earth shattering excitement. But for me, my breathing and adrenaline had changed involuntarily, and I did not yet know it, but my life had changed with it. My switch had been thrown into the on position and there was no going back. This was a moment of discovery, a life-event. Everything about the experience I'd just had was a huge turn on for me.

Marina told me she had given that exercise to a number of her clients and they found it very beneficial. I asked her why I hadn't heard of these seven centers in the body before. She told me Western civilization isn't interested in these subjects. "We are mostly Christian people in the West," she said, "and we tend to deny what isn't in the Bible." She explained how these kind of yoga teachings have been around for thousands of years, predating the Bible and are common throughout India and Buddhist countries. She told me I could find books on the subject at most bookstores. Then he handed me a little book called *The Lazy Man's Guide To Enlightenment*, by Thaddeus Golas.

"Read this," she smiled. "He has a really clear and simple approach to meditation, to life, actually. He keeps it very simple. Stripped down to the few simple ideas that matter. Like *No Resistance*," she told me, stressing the words. "No resistance is the essence of everything. Yet, traditional teachings never mention it like that. Most teachings make everything too complex, when it's really simple," she laughed. "Read it! It's a great book." So I did. I took it home and I read it. And I kept doing the meditation she showed me.

[Knowing what I know now, I have to warn the reader to develop a healthy respect for the potential to experience powerful states through meditative practices. Yoga meditations at this level, while ordinarily quite safe, should only be formally administered to beginners by a master instructor who monitors the student carefully. Like a climbing instructor would carefully belay a student, high up on a rock wall, the instructor wouldn't take his eyes off of the student, for obvious reasons. I suggest that anyone learning the practice of traditional yoga meditations actively seek professional guidance. Learn yoga meditations only in the physical presence of a qualified master instructor. Based on what you are about to read, it would be irresponsible of me to not admonish the reader with this disclaimer.]

Yoga Abuse

I felt I had made some kind of great discovery about the nature of the human condition. I felt driven by my adrenaline-fueled passions to see how deep I could go into this new state of concentrated attention. I can't describe the powerful surge of energy I was feeling in my body. I was convinced I had pulled back the curtain of our world and found a hidden universe, through the passageway of fixating attention.

This would add the spiritual dimension to my songwriting that I had always heard within the work of so many great artists. Everybody knows universal secrets are woven between the lines of all our favorite songs. Now, I was going to learn how weave them myself. My silent, deepest self took over and I couldn't have stopped what I was about to do for the world. Being young and impressionable, I wanted to make this my really special thing, my *in*. My teenage ego was so empowered and my little inner Jimi screamed out to drive beyond all boundaries of artistic freedom.

I felt the drive of a wild abandon so intense! I needed to make my life happen and I needed to make it happen right now. I needed a kick start. I needed to explode onto the scene and become a rock guitar god. I believed it was my destiny to start singing the hits that were going to bring on the advent of world peace and the end of all war. All the world needed was a song. I believed the right song was going to have the power to change the world. I felt I was opening up into the space where all the great songs come from.

I went home that night and started meditating intensely for hours on end, concentrating all my attention and energy the way my aunt had shown me. As I tampered with these new ideas, I invented my own method to practice this meditation, using a dim LED light on a tape recorder and setting it across the room from me. I would sit in total darkness on a pillow and fixate my attention perfectly on the tiny light. This fixation, the focused concentration, for a sustained duration, became the task at hand. If you could consider this a form of work and this exercise was a job then I worked hard at it, full-time, plus overtime, for days. It didn't seem like work because I loved what I was doing, and the more I loved it, the more intensely absorbed I became in it, and the more this absorption intensified, the more I loved it, until I became actively radiant with a powerful self-awareness of my own energy. No Resistance was the underlying theme.

No matter how much intensity developed, no resistance was always my answer.

> "There is only love and I have no resistance.
> There is only energy and I have no resistance.
> I have no resistance to love.
> Love is non-resistance to power.
> Love is all around me now and I have no resistance."

At first, I felt my attention was a lackadaisical tendril, extending out from between my eyes. It was difficult to hold it still. Its natural tendency was to wander. But over the first day, I worked on it, I practiced. I began straightening my attention and fixating unwaveringly on the light of the tape recorder. Every hour it became stronger and stronger. I went at it with everything I had in me and I never let up. Eventually, the feeling of concentrated energy in my forehead became so powerful; it just felt more natural to let it rise to the point at the top of my head. When I did this, I felt my scalp light up like the fourth of July with tingling sensations similar to intense goose bumps, pricking, dancing all over the top of my head. The warm tingling wrapped around my head from the outside, extending outward like a glow. My entire scalp bristled with sparkling energy and tantalizing sensations of goose bumps danced like ecstatic electricity through my hair.

My whole body lit up. My spine was now overflowing with this same beautiful, warm, tingling goose bumps energy running outward, tantalizing my entire body with sensations of pulsating energy leaping across every nerve ending. The contractions and tingling enveloped me entirely, flowing around my scalp to the tip of the top of my head. Then, the most powerful moment in my life occurred, right then. My entire head began opening up into a jeweled crown of pure energy. The presence of a powerful white light emerged, overwhelming my entire consciousness. I felt myself swooning into a sublime ecstasy. This is the exact point when my visionary experience of the energy I was feeling in my body went off the charts. I let it all go at this point and just surrendered to an inconceivable power that took me over from within. A place where the tip of my head meets top of the sky became a point of inconceivable departure for me. I felt the collective energy, opening into the form of a Catherine window, a mandala of power blossoming over into an inconceivable state of being. I felt everything about who I am transition from the individual into the universal.

My physical brain was glowing in a state without words. The wholeness of my entire mind was vibrating on a singular, pure frequency of one universal tone and that tone was perfectly silent, a state of resonance within a greater universal hum. I was so totally absorbed in this transcendental bliss state. I would have given anything to stay in this state forever. I believe anyone would. The more I loved the experience the more intense it would become. The more I loved the intensity, the more the love became intense. As I opened my heart to a universal love, my identity began melting into a oneness with all the love in the universe.

And the days wore on. I felt as if I were on an extremely intense psychedelic high and, in the end, I began to experience powerful states of consciousness, for lengths of time I was not physically ready for. Without any real training, or experience in how to handle the intensity, once I'd brought it on, I had no understanding of how to return to normal, how to come down. I was kind of like a kitten in a tree. But I didn't care, nor was I aware of any reason on earth why anyone would ever want to inhibit this beautiful experience of giving themselves entirely over to a mysterious universal affection for all that exists. I was entirely successful in finding what I was after, which was something very powerful and new for me. States of singular concentration I had never experienced before became a doorway to the inconceivable. Now I had something to write songs about. I was there! I made it!

I was naturally proceeding into an advanced, esoteric practice without any fundamental understanding of the basic groundwork I needed to have laid down first. Like a kid with a little climbing gear, I was so enraptured by the view alone, I could only see the summit. I was locked firmly in summit fever and rapt in the power and the glory phase of this meditative discovery. So, I kept climbing higher and higher without ever coming back down to acclimatize, or more importantly, to resupply. While I was strong and fresh and focused, I had the stability to keep the experience one-pointed, to stay safe on the mountain. It never occurred to me that once I'd turned on the massive flow of energy, my body was rapidly burning supplies of inner strength. I had no idea how to shut it back off before my supplies ran out. Once I had reached the summit, I burned through my supply of natural strength and now, I had no idea how to bring the energy back down.

After a few days, I became extremely wound up into an intense manic state because I had so much energy I didn't know what to do with it all. I did not yet understand the liability of the verbal mind in this situation and it became a huge problem. I was trying tell everyone I knew about this great thing I'd just discovered. I tried to write songs in an attempt to harness the energy blasting through my body but it was overwhelming me. Trying to use words to make sense of what was happening to me was the only thing I knew. Because I had no formal training in traditional meditation or yoga, I had no working knowledge or terminology to use in comprehending this immensely amplified state I was in. I kept calling my aunt on the phone and explaining to her what I was doing and what I was experiencing. She kept telling me to stop it, knock it off, sit in silence and don't talk, anything to try to get me calmed down to my normal self.

There was a point where she started getting worried for me and began scolding me that I had gone too far. She had warned me, up front, on the day she showed me the initial exercise, not to allow the energy to collect in the top of my skull, in the seventh chakra. She said I wasn't ready for something that powerful and there was a real danger. I could become mentally unhinged if I were to experience something like this before I was truly ready for it. But we were way beyond this point now. I blew through the jeweled crown in the center of the lotus days ago, and had been out soaring with the eagles on my wings of perception for quite a long time now.

One night, on the phone, I had told her about the feelings I had of exploding energy within me. I told her it was like fire raging through my whole spinal column from the base of my spine through the top of my head. I told her I had no idea why it was happening and I had no control over it. I said it was overwhelming, because I kept swooning into a universal ecstasy of tantalizing goose pimply-energy that I'll never be able to find words to describe. She began calling her friends for help. Suddenly, a little psychic first responder's group was being put together on my behalf.

Over the period of about a week, I quit my job and started babbling incoherently to my friends about the meaning of life. I hadn't slept in days and when I did it was only for 10 minutes or so. I began seeing my dreaming states while I was wide awake, mistaking all that I could imagine, as if it were a psychic foretelling of my future, or the future of the world. I entered what, for me, was similar to the book of Revelations in the Bible, but it was a personal event happening within me, for me alone. I reached a state of exhaustion, so intense, that I believed I was dying. I went through the entire experience of dying, where I let go of life, laid down and died. But eventually, I became conscious again. Now, all bets were off. I had just died and come back to life. You know what that means...

I was starting to present a Messianic complex. It would still be many years before I would discover my innate ability to distinguish what is imaginary from what is actually real. If I could have shut down my imagination at this point and just held fast in Square One, stayed in the present moment with no visual or verbal imaginings, I would have sailed through this like a champion. Sadly, I had never heard the words *Be Here Now* put all-together-in-a-row like that before, until I read the little book Marina gave me. I could not have realized how important those three short words could be, or how best to apply them. No resistance came easy, but *be here now* was a real bitch for me. Live and learn.

My aunt called to check on me. She and her colleagues believed I was experiencing an accidental kundalini awakening. The introduction of more big ideas I had never heard of. She briefly explained kundalini yoga to me and what she described matched everything that was happening to me. She lamented the fact that I was now in great danger and probably suffering a mental health crisis. Why no one contacted Howard Britton, I'll never know. I vaguely remember someone saying yoga and kundalini awakening were not Howard's area of expertise; he worked with hypnosis and metaphysics, so they assumed he wouldn't be able to help me in this instance.

I was so far gone. I just shook my head at the mere idea of a mental health crisis. I was the second coming of Christ, that wasn't a mental health crisis, in my mind; it was a gift from God. I was convinced that the *reason* I was experiencing the heights of human consciousness, and entering into a divine realization of the presence of love in all living things, was because it was going to be my job to teach others about it, through my songs.

Nevertheless, I was awfully young. This was all happening during the week of my twentieth birthday, and everything went to my head. All the energy in my whole body was collecting in my head. That's bad. I should have learned how to un-concentrate, diffuse and redistribute all my energy in a balanced way throughout my whole self, before I took up the sport of drilling for cosmic geysers.

Experts on accidental kundalini awakening believe, and there is some statistical data to support this, that the number of people who have these spontaneous experiences, number about one per million in the general population and some have said it can be as high as one in ten million. Worldwide, hundreds of thousands of people have awakened kundalini energy intentionally through yoga practice, so it's not rare for it to awaken; it's rare for it to awaken unintentionally. From what I understand, it is really hard to do. It takes a lot of practice and work on the self. Some schools of thought believe it is gift from the guru, to his students who are ready for it. In all cases, either way, there is an enlightened guru involved, in other words, a master instructor of meditative practices, who oversees and administers the process.

Many unintentional cases wind up committed to psychiatric institutions without ever understanding what happened to them, while a number of others never even bat an eyelash. They just overcome it like a bad flu virus, or pour themselves into their work, running their business, creating their art and they simply move on with their lives when the intense experiences end. The problem for me was, I had this deeply religious upbringing, a wild imagination which I kept constantly active for my artistry and zero experience with the idea of quieting the mind, or staying in the here and now.

If you have this experience and rule out the possibility of quieting the mind and holding onto the present moment, there is no possibility of anything but a total nightmare. This nightmare now became my reality. By the time it was over, my life became a mess and the totality of the nightmare visited every aspect of my physical life. I had lost myself in a cosmic visionary state, brought on by practicing a yoga meditation I had no business attempting on my own. I had given away all my money and my guitar, because I didn't think I was going to need them anymore. In my mind, I was moving on in life to live by a state of grace alone. What I did was a lot like abusing a powerful drug. I had discovered one of the key elements of a very powerful meditative practice; I went at it intravenously and just completely overdosed on it. I took it to the extreme. Plain and simple, I got what I deserved. I got my ass handed to me by the universe itself.

Bringing the Message to the World

Just before Christmas, 1982, I contacted my aunt in an incoherent state and she finally made the call. I was taken to a triage unit. They transferred me to the state hospital in Norwalk. They kept me on observation, with a condition status of 5150, in the psychiatric ward there. I remember seeing my name on the board in the nurse's station with big numbers next to it: Sargenti - 5150. At that point, safely locked away, I began to experience the most severe teeth of real psychosis. Under the circumstances, I think I got there just in time because that previous night in the triage unit, I lost all ability to distinguish one state of consciousness from the next.

I was trying very hard to pull my face out of the deep absorption I had gone into but I couldn't and everything I was trying to do to get back to normal must've looked extremely odd from an onlookers perspective that night. I was making perfect sense to myself, but no one else could see what I was seeing, or feel what I was feeling.

If I had just sat perfectly still. If I could have just remained totally silent. Everything would have been fine. It seemed like an impossible option, suffering from devastating physical exhaustion with so much mental energy still driving though me. If I only knew then, what I know now. The boundary between waking and dreaming no longer existed at that point, and I couldn't return to my normal state. I was trying very hard to do it, but I did not have the skills necessary for the task. Instead, I went deeper in, the other way, succumbing to exhaustion, until I suffered total-incoherence and delusions of grandeur. Once I was fully locked down, that's when the apocalyptic visions hit full-force.

They gave me Thorazine and Haldol, and assigned me to a bed in a ward that looked exactly like the one in the movie, *One Flew Over The Cuckoos Nest*. I only wanted to stay in my bed with the sheet stretched over my head, like I was stuck in between a larva and pupa state. However, late into the morning the orderlies would always come and force us all to get out of bed. There were several other men, just like me, who would have stayed with the sheet pulled over their heads, all day and night, if they were allowed to. We had to take meds three times a day and they let me eat as much as I wanted, but I was rarely hungry. One of the patients told me the staff was putting tranquilizing drugs in the food and not to eat it. So, I was a bit iffy on the food service after that.

Everyday, as I was doing the Thorazine shuffle, down and back, all around the full length of the long, wide hallway, an enormous door would open as I was passing slowly by and a very friendly nurse would reach out and grab me by the arm. She would be inviting me into a giant room off to the side of the ward, welcoming me in. They would have me sit, in my open-back hospital gown, in front of a massive set of three long tables, arranged in a big U-shape. There were always more than a dozen doctors, men and women with pretty white coats surrounding the tables around all three sides. They had binders and folders and books piled high all over it. I had to sit on a hard metal chair with my ass hanging out, in the open area in front of the U. They would fire off questions, interviewing me about my mental state, analyzing my psychiatric condition. Sitting there in my hospital gown with the open back, I felt as if they design that situation to make you feel as self-conscious as possible.

For the first few days, I wasn't self-conscious at all. They seemed like they were all quite happy to meet me. I was truly blasted out of my mind by a devastating psychosis and I barely remember those days at all. What I do remember was being so emotionally distraught by not being able get anyone to understand me, to listen and hear what I had to say about the secret of life: being one with all the love in the universe. I wanted them to know how anyone could do it. I told them I had discovered the purpose of life on earth but no one wanted to believe it.

I tried so desperately to convince the doctors that I knew what I was talking about, I knew the meaning of life! They told me the greatest minds in history could never figure it out. How in the world could I? Who in the world was I, to say I could answer the question the greatest minds in history could not. I held up my hand, pointing my index finger at them and told them, "Love." The doctor threw his pen on the table and shook his head in resignation.

I continued, "It is understanding precisely how to become one with all the love in the universe. And I know how!" I told them confidently. I explained to them that I was here because I just needed *them* to help me share it with the world.

The first few days I met with the doctor's did not go well at all. I remember not being able to use words all that well because of the tranquilizers and I cursed them for using them on me, for forcing me to take them. I remember asking them if I could answer their questions by singing a song to them, which might better explain my situation. I explained that music is a magical vehicle that can lift mankind into understanding.

I remember the first day I did this, the doctors had been getting down on me, admonishing me about how I had behaved incoherently in public and how no one was going to listen to anything I had to say until I calmed down and could speak rationally. That's how I came up with the idea of singing everything I needed to say. I was just crying my eyes out, sobbing because I felt so horrible and raw inside. They told me I was suffering from a deep depression. I told them, "Depression? It's not depression! What I am feeling is perfectly understandable, proportional to the situation, considering the circumstances, doctor! I mean, I just discovered the meaning of life and became one with all the love in the universe. Then they locked me up in a mental institution for it and shot me full of Thorazine. How would you feel?"

They all looked at each other and said, "Why not? Let him sing." So, I pulled myself together and they let me sing for them. I sang James Taylor's *Lonesome Road*, a cappella. I sang it to the back of that big room and into the high ceiling. I filled that space with my whole heart and used whatever bit of reverb that awful room would give me. It was remarkable how emotionally therapeutic this was for me. When I finished though, I broke down again. I just wanted the world to know how much the universe loves them. I could feel all the love in the universe but I had no way to share it with them, no way to help them feel it, too.

The next day, was much the same, I was a little more stable emotionally but I felt my situation was hopeless. I sang them Cat Steven's *On The Road To Find Out*, note-for-note, from memory and just killed it. Everybody loved it and they even gave me a little round of applause at the end. They were all amused but still genuinely moved that I had the heart to deliver the performance of a lifetime to try to help them see our shared connection to all the love in the universe.

The doctor's were friendly enough. They were there to help me. There was one doctor in particular who appeared to be running the whole dog and pony show. He asked most of the questions and appeared to be the one in charge of each meeting. Sitting in his big, high-back, leather chair, he seemed short with big, black-rimmed glasses and greasy black hair with a bald spot on top and a bad comb-over. He had a big, ugly black mustache and clammy-looking, pale-white skin. He asked me to explain to everyone at the table why I believed I had discovered the meaning of life.

I carefully and slowly stood up, then very clearly articulated through the tranquilizers, "We are made of energy, $e=mc^2$. E is energy. Then, there is an equal sign. This equality is very important because to the right of the equal sign, we have the equivalent of energy. M is mass and C^2 is the constant squared. What is the constant?" I asked them.

"The speed of light," the doctor said very matter of factly.

"Ah!" I said, as I pointed my index finger in the air and then toward him, "Speed of love."

He dropped his pen on the table again as his head rolled back. The doctor seemed to enjoy pressing the back of his pen to his chin while asking me questions and then throwing it down on the table in disgust whenever I said something he would rather not hear.

"The constant is love and we have to get our minds around the idea of love being multiplied times itself. Love^2."

I walked over to the opening in the U shaped tables. "Here's the thing, doctor. Imagine this." He picked up his pen and held it to his bottom chin again. "Love times love holds an extremely high value. When we multiply mass by love^2, (who we are)love^2, we become pure energy. Bam! $e=e$, meaning of life. Done."

They all looked at each other like, "What the fuck?"

And I was all like, "Yea, I know, right? Hey, you asked!"

"It all cancels out," I continued, "There is only one thing. Love is the only thing in existence. We are all expressions of it.

"Our life force, our energy, is made of pure love. Men and women make love, they make babies. Love made you and me. What this means is that the universal energy breathing life into everything is made of love," I told them, "This love is not in heaven, it's not out there. Love is all around us. It's present in everything, everywhere. And it's present in you and me. It's present *as* you and me." I told them.

I explained how I'd discovered, through concentrating and fixating attention, we are capable of a radical amplification in our experience of being energized. "The life giving energy that flows through our bodies is the same energy which is present in all things and by practicing focused meditation, mankind can learn how to open up to higher consciousness and there is no limit to how far we can open ourselves, no limit on our ability to give ourselves to love. In giving ourselves over to the point of love^2, who we are passes from an individual into the universal. It is at this point when who we are melts into universal love and becomes one with everything. Only universal love remains, only pure energy. "Like I said, $e=e$. Boom. Done," I reminded them.

I explained that this has to happen in a highly focused way, it takes some training, but it can happen for everyone. I told them that if everyone was made aware of this, as a human possibility, in schools, in universities and meditation centers all over the country, we could end all war, all violence, all crime, forever. The world would be a far better place.

The doctors were amused by my sincerity. As mental health professionals, they had been encouraging me to get whatever it was I needed to say off my chest, because for days it was obvious I had something I needed to tell them but couldn't find the right words. I was starting to enter into a highly energized state again.

The last day they allowed to me sing during these psychiatric interviews, day four, it didn't go over so well. I had been telling them we needed to meet with the President of the United States and ask him to sign an executive order making this kind of meditation a national priority. "He can get Congress to release the funds to build meditation centers all over the country." I told them, "Then everyone in the country can learn how to tune themselves in and resonate with the universal hum, for at least fifteen minutes, two or three times a day. Only five or six days a week. It'll be great!" I pleaded with them. I thought I might finally be getting through to them.

I very carefully explained to them that if everyone did this, we could sway the collective consciousness of the world back over the tipping point toward peace and caring. We could make the world a much safer and better place. At this point in history, we were in the teeth of the Cold War and the fear of nuclear holocaust was ever-present in the minds of everyone. I told them I was convinced that *thought* was the cause of most of the problems in the world. We could solve most of the world's problems, saving millions of lives, by teaching everyone to pause their thoughts and mediate on the presence of all the love in the universe, for a little bit each day.

"It would change the individual and, collectively, with enough people doing it, the change in the mass consciousness would naturally change society." I never understood why this idea has been so hard to put across.

What I wanted them to understand was how the net result would be that violence would naturally go down, the world would slowly grow more calm and sane, (like me). We could stop war permanently and end the nuclear threat. "This is an urgent national security issue!" I appealed to them. "We can stop it all, famine, crime, hatred, killing, by simply teaching everyone how to surrender their hearts to the presence of love[2], through focused meditation. The world will drastically change by people, who are caring and centered, radiating this powerful calm into the world. I can do it! I can show everybody! I just need a little help here."

They still just looked at me, unconvinced. Most of them weren't even listening to me. I asked if I could sing to them again. I said that I had a very special song I was certain would help them understand what I meant. The dog and pony doctor looked at everyone and shrugged his shoulders. "Go ahead," as he tossed his pen down on the table. He seemed frustrated with me.

I slowly stood up and began singing Jimi Hendrix, *Are You Experienced*. I started off very quietly, with my eyes closed, my head turned up toward the ceiling. *"If you can just get your mind together, then come on across to me..."* After the first chorus though, I sang it a lot more freely, with a feeling just like Jimi but they were a little taken aback by the lyrics. They looked at me as if my spiritual realization was threatening to them. Them, they, with their white collars and ties! I would sway in front of my chair and point at them, *"I know. I know. You'll probably scream and cry, that your little world won't let you go..."*

It was perfectly quiet in the room when I finished my song. Gone was the amusement and consideration of our previous meetings.

They had been sympathetic to the fact that I had no history of psychosis and they told me they were trying to determine if my case was a temporary, singular event that would subside, or if I was going to require longer-term care. On the fourth day, as I sat my bare ass down in my little chair after delivering my greatly under-appreciated performance, the head doctor sat back into his big leather chair told me, and I clearly heard him, "You need to consider whether or not you ever want to see the light of day again, Mr. Sargenti." It was like a bell rang in the back of my skull.

He continued, "If you want to know the truth, you have two options. You can be released via *habeas corpus* within nine days, or you will become an admitted patient and held for a period of at least nine months. Once you cross that line, it is going to be next to impossible for any of us to get you released, even after that nine months is up. You'll be kept on Thorazine and Haldol and remain institutionalized. In that situation, the requirements for release are far more rigorous than they are for you right now." That was a very sobering to hear that. "Do you understand what I am telling you?" he leaned forward and looked at me over his black-rimmed glasses. I nodded affirmatively, my eyes wide as saucers. "You have nine days, Mr. Sargenti."

He looked at me accusingly, holding up four fingers. "You have already burned four."

The nurse entered the room and she helped me stand up to usher me out. As I stood, he admonished me one last time. He sat back in his chair again, pointing his plastic finger at me, "I suggest you take your recovery and this brief window of opportunity far more seriously."

Suddenly everything came crashing down on me.

I thought, "These fuckers are all fucking crazy! I'm the sane one here!" My situation had become a huge problem that created terrible trouble for a large number of people. It wasn't just me I was affecting. My family was trying desperately to get me out of there, or at least transferred to a private facility, before the nine-month clause kicked in. Even my mom and dad had contacted each other, which never happens.

It was all immensely unfortunate. I should have gone to a Zen-Buddhist monastery, like I had been begging for, found someone who had kundalini yoga expertise and just spent some time with a bunch of monks and gurus. But nobody I knew had any idea where or how to locate people like that. The internet hadn't been invented yet. They weren't just simply listed in the phonebook. It was much too late for this now. I had gone off the deep end and there was no one there to save me.

Instead, I spent Christmas in the psycho-slammer with a bunch of nut jobs, dangerously crazy people, truly insane and frightening individuals with all manner of serious psychiatric disorders. It was extremely nerve wracking because you never knew when one of these fuckers was going to pop off and start violently attacking someone. Every time it would happen, all of these muscular orderlies would rush in and violently pile on the hysterical, screaming freak and drug the son-of-a-bitch into a coma with a needle in the ass as long as your forearm. Then they'd drag his unconscious ass out by the leg and you see him doing the Thorazine shuffle the next day, like a zombie. It was like being in a prison filled with ghosts, phantoms, lost and wandering through the underworld. It was a real eye opener.

I tried to bring the message to the world and I got crucified. I didn't understand that a lot of people in the world have this same kind of experience I'd had. I would eventually learn that I am not at all unique, in this regard. It took me years to understand that I was only one of countless people who had these same experiences and realizations of a universal love-presence. I actually did make the spiritual discovery that everyone through the ages talks about, in scripture, in literature and in songs. But lots of people do. I finally understood what Pastor Geisler meant when he referred to those religious scholars and monastic visionaries. Now, I understood a little more about what they saw in their visions.

Nevertheless, what I needed to understand, what I miserably failed to really grasp, is that nobody cares. We all have our own lives to live. The people who don't have this experience don't have it because they don't want to. It's their choice. They have other areas of life which are more important to them. Just because being one with all the love in the universe became important to me, doesn't mean it automatically must become important to everyone. Beyond a certain point, I had no business sharing my meditation experiences with anyone. I was just being an annoying pain in the ass. Nobody else needed to understand any of it but me. I didn't realize it was wrong to talk about that. I was being like a little boy running around showing everybody his weeny. I was ignorant of the fact that people keep that stuff personal. Nobody wanted to see my weeny.

The doctors finally did let me get out of the looney bin on New Year's Eve day, when they released me to my brother Bill. Brother Bill to the rescue, once again. He had been working tirelessly behind-the-scenes the whole time, making arrangements with the psychiatric tribunal to get me out of there and I did my part by sobering up and apologizing to the doctors for asking them to contact the President on my behalf. My condition was diagnosed as a rapid-cycling bipolar disorder, manic depression. Either way, it is just as Jimi said it would be, "a frustrating mess." They concluded the psychosis was brought on by an acute manic episode, which could be controlled by taking lithium. I successfully convinced them if they just let me out, I would return to a normal little life and would not talk about the presence of universal love anymore.

I was firmly convinced, now more than ever, the crazy ones were the people running that place. The amount of drugs they force into the patients, in order to control them, seemed excessive and even sinister, to me. It's so sad to live in a world where you have to make that kind of promise or you will lose your freedom and be locked up for becoming one with the universe. I just needed to return to my normal life and everything would be okay.

It was clear to me, it wasn't the becoming one part they wanted to lock me up for, they were actually fine with that, even sympathetic, I found. It was how I was behaving. I had become irrational and grew quite ill. I knew that. I understood. I just enjoyed being difficult. I paid the price of admission to that fucking lunatic asylum, why shouldn't I rattle their little cages a little bit? I paid the price with interest. My little glimpse at the big picture cost me everything.

I was now set loose back into the wild. I was on my own. Even my aunt was afraid to talk to me. The whole thing really freaked her out. She distanced her self from my life after that and I seldom spoke to her in the years that followed.

The fall out from this event was massive. I had quit my job and even though I asked, they didn't want me back after that. I had no money. My guitar was gone. I had no car. Since I had no rent money, myself *and* my roommates all had to move out of our apartment. I had very few people in my life to check up on me and tell me, "No." I could do anything I wanted. Since I was seventeen and out on my own, I had no one to answer to, except employers, landlords and a few good friends who tried to reign me in. I felt I was pushing the boundaries of my own artistic freedom and with role models like Jimi Hendrix, Jerry Garcia and Jesus Christ, well... what are you gonna do, ya know?

The Recovery

I needed to get away from all the weirdoes in Southern California. Before I left Southern Cal, I met with a woman who acted as a counselor for me. I was told she was educated in psychology, understood yoga meditation and understood kundalini psychosis. I was given her number by my aunt Marina, who was put in touch with her by a friend. Her name was Bonnie. She agreed to see me and waived her fee.

When I met her, she was a nice person with an assuring smile, all of about five-foot-two. She radiated a strong sense of calm and inner-strength. Her office was that of any professional therapist but I never did see what her title or specialty might have been, as I was curious what line of professional does this kind of counseling. We just sat down and started talking. She seemed concerned about my situation and told me she was happy to waive her fee because, from what she had heard, I genuinely needed her help.

I told her about the problems I had resulting from the meditation and that I needed to see a spiritual master or someone who knew about what happened to me. She told me spiritual masters are hard to find in the West and many are not as genuine as you might think. She asked me what she could do to help. She assured me she had some experience in helping people in my situation. I asked her if she knew about kundalini and she nodded affirmatively but didn't say anything. I explained how the meditation I practiced yielded a radiant energy, like a psychedelic experience, that I had trouble controlling after a while. I told her the sheer volume of energy going through me was stunning, but over time, when I couldn't turn it off, that's when the trouble began.

She wanted me to know that what I experienced was very rare and that I should consider it a blessing, like a spiritual gift I'd been given. She wanted me to take some time and simply reflect on all I'd experienced and try to quietly digest it and integrate it into my ordinary life.

As I sat with her, describing the events that led to our meeting, I told her, "I'm feeling the intensity well up in my attention again right now."

Bonnie asked me what it felt like.

"It's like a pressure in the center of my forehead, or at the top of my head, which feels a little like vertigo or the spins." I told her I could see lines of energy coming off of everything and when I centered myself within the spin, all the lines of energy would collect and align naturally into a harmonious arrangement around me and the vertigo would spin in balanced way around my whole self. "I feel like I am sitting in the center of a giant lotus blossom made of cosmic energy," I told her. "It's like riding a vortex of flowing electrical current. It's not electricity though. It's like a psychedelic sparkliness." I told her that for about a week it was a heavenly experience. "But after that a week or so, it became much more powerful and prevented me from sleeping. Eventually, as my strength wore down, it became more tedious. I was so tired and I needed a break, but I couldn't shut it off and I didn't know what to do. That's when I went into the psychosis."

Bonnie nodded and gave me a look of genuine concern, "Yes. I hear you had a wild ride. Not all of it was good."

"No," I told her I was afraid of it now. After trying to get myself released from the psych ward, it started to feel like a bit of a curse. Sometimes, I was afraid to go to sleep. That was my problem, why I had come to see her. I wasn't sure what to expect from now on. There was no one, through all of this, who knew anything at all about what was happening to me. A number of people knew a little, but I couldn't find anyone who could sit me down and give me the instruction everyone was telling me I needed.

"I can't find a single, damn person to talk to who knows anything about this," I explained. Beyond a certain point, I became fearful that if I wasn't able to control the flow of the spinning energy around me, I may wind up back in the asylum again. "I don't know what to expect and I can't find anyone who does," I told her.

The Haldol and the doctors helped me shut it off by threatening to lock me up in the mental institution. Now, I could shut it back down by intending to but I was still living in fear of what would happen if I couldn't turn it off again. I was worried I would return to the full manic state and start becoming one with all the love in the universe again, that people wouldn't be able to understand and they would lock me up for being too blissed out, or too excited. Next time, they weren't going to let me out.

She told me my job for the next six months was to keep turning it off. "No meditation at all." She explained that, "Over time, if you feel the power coming on, just turn it off." She said this to me as if were the most casual thing in the world. "Just turn it off." Forget about it. "Your job right now is to exercise the ability to turn it off, at will, and to just remain totally ordinary."

She told me, "Work a regular job, get regular exercise, get plenty of rest and eat right. Don't read any books about meditation. Don't do yoga. Don't do anything like that. In six months, you'll have more control over it and you'll be in a stronger position to begin exploring it again, but not until then."

So, I did what she said, with the exception the books. I had never heard anything about this weird kundalini stuff or read about yoga before and I was curious to learn about what the hell just happened to me. I knew what happened, but I wanted to talk to, or at least read about, other people who had been through it. I needed consensus and human confirmation that I wasn't just another lunatic, that there was something more to it, that it was all served some purpose. Where I was right then, was an extremely lonely place. I needed to be around people who knew what the hell I was talking about. Who wouldn't reject me for it, who wouldn't be afraid of me, or want to lock me up.

So, for the first time in my life I became an absolutely voracious reader. I read for information only. I read everything I could get my hands on about yoga and meditation. I just avoided doing the meditation exercises for the time being. My pursuits were purely intellectual. I read the newspaper, watched TV, went for walks, watched movies and once I found a job again, I worked. I also wrote a lot of songs and a lot of poems.

First stop after leaving Southern Cal, I landed at my mom's sister's place on a three acre hilltop in Ashland, Oregon. I stayed with my hippie aunt Pam and my super fun uncle Riley, for a couple months, trying to get my head together. This is the same sister in Glendale, who took me on the weekend my mom left my dad. They became a sort of Search & Rescue unit for me, it seemed, whenever I was in life-crisis mode, they stepped right in to help me get through it. They confirmed my belief that the world is entirely insane and that eastern mysticism is where it's at. They were big fans of rock music, motorcycles and getting high, so I was in good hands.

I did a lot of reading when I was in Ashland. My uncle Riley and I watched the movie *Road Warrior* religiously, on VHS at least once, everyday for over a month. My aunt Pam had a lot of Zen and Buddhist books. She also had a copy of a book by Ram Dass called *Remember: Be Here Now*. I spent a lot of time with that one. It had elaborate drawings, something of illustrated art book with all manner of hand lettered text, so it was easy to follow. It really helped explain the kind of thing I had just been though. It was exactly the book I needed right then. I was so grateful to find that book.

When I arrived, my aunt was in the process of reading a book called *The Eagle's Gift* by Carlos Castaneda. She said it was really deep. She told me it wasn't the kind of thing I should be reading right now. My job was to turn the fireworks off and just get back to ordinary reality. She gave me the Zen books and the Be Here Now book and told me, "Maybe Castaneda is something you can read someday, but not right now. Right now you just focus on this." She put her finger on the cover design, tapping right in the center of *Remember: Be Here Now*.

"When I meditated, I was practicing concentrating all my attention to a perfect point of stillness, a balanced, focused, perfect, stillness of mind on a singular point in the present moment."

Chapter Seven
KNOWLEDGE

NOT LONG AFTER, in March, I flew to my Mom's house in Crown Point, Indiana for a few months, where I worked for her husband Jack again, just like old times, when he made me work my ass off all summer as a kid, but now I was a grown man, old enough to drive the delivery truck and handle a route all by myself. I knew exactly what to do. I had done it so much when I was young, it was practically automatic. They helped me get back on my feet again. I just focused on work and making enough money to get back to having a regular life.

My daily route was the entire south side of Chicago and, all I will say is, this was an enlightening experience. I worked the streets of south Chicago, selling parts washer services and supplies, out of a big step-side van, to automotive mechanics in every neighborhood of that crazy place. I did it for about 4 months, until summer came. In June, when I had made enough money to restart my crashed-and-burned life, I headed back to Southern California.

I drove home from Indiana in a three-speed Dodge Demon I had bought for $300. It had rusted out floors and the muffler was no good, so the exhaust came into the cab a little. After riding in it for a while, I'd get out with my clothes smelling like exhaust. I was too cheap to get it repaired even though I had plenty of money. I was too excited to get back to So Cal and too impatient to wait for it to get repaired. I hit the freeway and rode the Demon's back all the way across this great country of ours, breathing exhaust fumes and smoking marijuana the whole way. I stopped in Grass Valley, CA to visit my dad on the way home and let him know I was back in the saddle. We had a good visit at what was now, his very successful restaurant.

As a newly-minted 20 year-old, on my own in Southern Cal, I had trouble keeping it together and wound up running out of money again and not being able to pay rent. I might have just been lazy and didn't feel like working much. Either way, it wasn't long before I was homeless and living in the Dodge Demon. I kept getting harassed by the police at night no matter where I tried to park and sleep. I got tired of that in a hurry. So I began living in a condemned office building behind the printshop where I had started out, working after school, at Econo-Print, in Tustin.

The two-sectioned, office building was old and had been sold off to a developer who had plans to tear it down and build new construction there. The print shop was still active on the end section, but the old office side of the building was completely empty, so I moved my stuff in to the back of the old Econo-Print office and kept a very low-profile. I slept on the floor and read a lot of books. I didn't let anyone know I was sleeping there.

I worked in the print shop a couple hours each day. They didn't have a position open which I could have but the owner's son-in-law, who had taught me the printing trade when I was in high school, let me make a few deliveries when they were needed, or he would have me clean up and empty the trash cans. He let me do this until I could a land position somewhere full-time. A big brother-type figure in my life, Terry Harvey not only taught me how to print, he always helped me when I needed money, giving me a job if he could, or just whatever work he could scrape up for me at the time. During this particular summer, he'd just hand me $5 or $10 each day depending on how long I could stay busy. Terry's mom eventually bought the business and if it weren't for her and Terry, giving me work, feeding me and making sure I was OK, I don't know how I could have gotten by. If they didn't have anything for me to do, Terry's mom would always make sure I had lunch.

I did find a position at a big commercial shop across town in Stanton, and they hired me, but set my starting date for September, this was late in June. So, I just lived hand-to-mouth for that summer. I was dirt poor, sleeping on the floor of a burnt out old office building, after my stint in a psych ward. But it was kind of cool, actually. I was young. I didn't have anyone to answer to. No stress. I was on an adventure and it felt like I was heading for some greater awakening.

And as fate would have it, I was in Stanton one day dropping off some paperwork to the new employer, and stopped into a coffee shop along Beach Blvd., miles away from Tustin. I sat down at the coffee shop, ordered a cup of coffee and as I sat there, I looked to my left and sitting at the counter next to me was Howard Britton. I looked at him and he at me and we both broke into laughter. "What a small world," we said in unison.

He and I had lost touch and had not seen each other, even in passing, in a few years. I asked him if he was still teaching Silva Mind Control and he said he was, but it was no longer the same. The program had been sold off to new owners who were making a number of changes and he said they'd tied his hands in regards to the way he was able to teach his classes now. He wasn't happy about the direction it was going. We made light conversation as we ate our breakfast. Howard mentioned he didn't have much time, so before he got up to leave, I began telling him very briefly about the recent experience I'd had with meditation and how I wound up in the State Hospital. He seemed concerned and asked me to explain.

I reminded him of how when I was twelve years old in his classes, I had the experience, during his guided meditations, where I saw a small spot of light in my vision which I felt was some distance in front of me. It was as if I was physically seeing a pinhole of light in the darkness. I reminded him that I had asked him about it. As well, I had asked the question in my mind of what that light might be, it was if the light were at the end of a tunnel and a voice replied, "When you reach this light, you will have arrived where you need to be."

"And. . ." He prompted me.

"And..." I continued, "Last year, before Christmas, I began experimenting for several days with a meditation practice, Marina had given me." I briefly explained the Ajna meditation to him. Oddly enough, he'd never heard of it. I thought for sure he would be well aware of it. But he wasn't. "I kept doing it because the harder I concentrated, the closer I felt that light drawing near to me. I felt so strong and powerful I didn't want to stop. When I meditated, I was practicing concentrating all my attention to a perfect point of stillness, a balanced, focused, perfect, stillness of mind on a singular point in the present moment." Howard was listening very intently. "After several days of this, Howard, the pinhole of light grew so close, as if it were opening up directly above me. Eventually, it become so immediately present that I could walk out into it."

He looked at me with curiosity and bewilderment. I told Howard this pinhole of light grew closer and closer until it came over me, like a beam coming down, it became perfectly, beautifully centered above me and I could bathe in it like pure sunlight. I could open my arms and receive it like the light of day. I told him. "Sublime sensations were emanating from all around the top of my head and I just opened myself up to the universe," I said. "Everything I am was so completely consumed by it, I swooned into it, I became the light," I told him. Howard was staring at me, transfixed. His eyes were welling up and shining with gleaming reflections.

I touched his forearm as I whispered. "And that light, that was peeking into my meditations when I was twelve, Howard… it was the presence of all the love in the universe." I told him. "I became one with all the love in the universe. That's what that light was. The light I asked you about when I was twelve." I stopped and looked at him. He looked at me. "And you want to know what else?" His head tilted quizzically, "The presence of all the love in the universe is all around us right now. It's running through everything, through every blade of grass and it's nourishing every leaf, on every tree. It's the life force running through you and me. It's the shine in those wonderful eyes of yours." I laughed. "I just wanted you to know, I finally made it. I arrived where I've always needed to be."

Howard looked at me and he didn't say anything but I had never seen his eyes shining more resplendently with a caring, compassionate gaze than in this moment. I told him that after a week of continually being in this amplified state, I was trying to tell everyone I knew about the presence of the energy running through the fabric of all living things but no one believed me, and I wasn't making any sense. They all thought I'd gone mad. I became deeply exhausted and manic all at the same time. It unhinged my mind. I told him I handled it very poorly.

"And that's how I wound up in the State Hospital." I told him. "No one could help me. Not even the doctors. It was devastating."

Howard seemed to realize the gravity of that situation. It wasn't simply a lighthearted joy ride. It had actually taken a serious turn for the worse. He didn't seem to have any answers, either. I had hoped he would be able to offer me something more to help me resolve the matter in my mind. But he did tell me with a chuckle, "You know you always want to take your experiences like this with a grain of salt." He assured me, and after a long pause "It's better just to keep them under your hat." He told me, "That experience was a gift for you alone."

With that Howard had an appointment he needed to keep and as he stood up to leave, that beautiful shine returned to his eyes. He spoke with such softness and kindness before he turned to go, "I want to wish you all the love in the world, Vince." He seemed to be on the verge of tears. He took both my hands with both of his. "God bless you and much love to you. Much love." And he paused for an inordinate amount of time and just fixed his enormous shining eyes on me. Both of our hands were joined in a mutual gesture of affection. I thanked him for everything he'd done for me, and with that, he quietly stepped out the front door into the morning sun and went on his way.

❋ ❋ ❋

There was a press operator who used to work a little overtime at the print shop I was living behind, his name was Phil King. When I had my big psychic blowout over Christmas, Phil had heard about it from everyone who was around. Apparently, he had experienced a similar event in his life and he tried to contact me through some friends, who never gave me the message.

I would not have wanted the message, and I wouldn't have called him back. He was kind of a dirty old hippie type who had a reputation as an acidhead. He was a creepy fucker, not the kind of guy a fine young Christian boy like myself would associate with. I didn't like him much. Nevertheless, he had worked for Terry Harvey off and on for years, same as me, so we had a lot in common and a lot of time to chew the fat, now that I was at the shop all the time. He'd been looking forward to having a little chat with me about "my experiences." In Phil's mind at least, as a bonafide hippy tripper, he understood what I had been through, what I had been searching for, what had happened to me and how to best put it all into perspective. Phil saw himself as a spiritual guide, a warrior of cosmic consciousness, someone who knew the secrets of mystical consciousness. Turns out, the guy was a true intellectual and not much different from a much dirtier and grungier version of Howard Britton. He knew the whole cosmic consciousness counter-culture thing like the back of his hand. If he was specialized in any way, one would have to say Phil specialized in the psychedelic aspect of cosmic consciousness, and human spirituality in general. He'd lived through the sixties. I guess that's street-cred, enough for anyone by this time.

So, there I was, living behind a print shop, getting by on about $5 a day and reading a lot of books about esoteric yoga meditations and Tibetan spirituality. Ever since I was released from the State Hospital, I was deeply involved in some abstract form of study, reading ravenously, frequenting new age bookstores, writing songs and looking for some inconceivable answers to these meditation experiences I had discovered. Here comes this straggly hippie-dude, about 11 years older than me, totally bald on top with hair down past his shoulders, a total stoner, and he brings me a book. The same book by Ram Dass, *Remember: Be Here Now*.

I always thought of Phil as kind of a dirtbag but here he was telling me, "The Here And Now! This is the place where you always want to be. This is your center. This is the axis of eternity."

He held up the book, pointing to the words on the cover. "See? It says remember! Four times! So you don't forget. *Remember: Be Here Now*. This is your safety zone."

He leaned in toward me and in a quieter voice said, "No matter how weird and freaky things might get, just take a deep breath and bring yourself back into the here and now, back into your center. This is all about learning how to center yourself, finding your center, staying centered. The more deeply you can do that. . . The better off you're going to be."

"This is all about remembering." He paused, "Be. Here. Now."

Journey To Fictionland

Later that same week, at the picnic table on the patio behind the print shop, Phil King shared something with me that would become yet another life-changing moment. We had been talking about the Ram Dass book he loaned me and the *Tibetan Book Of The Dead*. He mentioned that by now, I had read a lot the eastern religious classics and studied some of ancient scriptures, the Upanishads and some of the Vedas, The Gita and the Koran. I'd read a lot about yoga, learned about Patanjali, tried some of the basic practices and of course, the meditations. He thumbed through the stack of books I had next to me which needed to go back to the library. He seemed amused that I was so into it.

He told me that he thought I was ready to study Carlos Castaneda's *The Teachings Of Don Juan*. He told me that if I wanted to learn about out-of-body experience, Castaneda was the foremost authority on the subject. "But it might not turn out to be what you think," he admonished me. He offered to help guide my study of the material and even show me some of what he knew about Castaneda's version of the practice of "dreaming." He told me that out-of-body experience was another way of talking about what Castaneda called dreaming. He said Castaneda's use of the word dreaming was different from the way it is commonly used.

I listened to what Phil had to say and I found him to be a friendly enough person. I didn't want to hurt his feelings, or seem arrogant by telling him I really didn't like him and I didn't want to hang around with him. But I will tell you something, he really wanted to hang around with me. He was being more than a little bit pushy about wanting to talk about what happened to me last December and how I should read all these books he wanted me to read. He wanted me to believe he had something very worthwhile to show me. He wanted to take me on a little tour of his cosmic view of the universe.

Looking back, I wish this had never happened. I wish I had never met Phil King, or my psychic aunt and I wish I had never heard of Silva Mind Control or ever set foot in a church. I should have stayed in school. I should have eaten my all vegetables. But this was never my fate. Sadly, my fate was to be a more-impressionable-than-average young man with Borderline Personality Disorder, or whatever you want to call it, who was uncannily vulnerable to suggestion. I wish I could find more people and things to blame for all of the bad decisions I've made in life, but I can't. These were the critical flaws in my rapid-cycling manic-depressive personality which have led to more suffering than anyone can imagine, because a tortured mind is one of the most painful afflictions anyone could ever have. Depression is a vicious, vicious killer and I am so glad that I had being a maniac to turn to. It really saved my life many times.

So as fate would have it, I believed what everyone had been suggesting. I believed hook, line and sphincter. As far as I was concerned, all of this was totally real. I went back down to the library and checked out the first three Castaneda books: *The Teachings of don Juan, A Separate Reality* and *Journey To Ixtlan*. Then, I dove right in. I read them all, right straight through.

Phil was quick to point out that Castaneda's work was not found in the typical section of the new age, spiritual, metaphysics or Carl Jung sections of the library. He made it very clear that Castaneda was an anthropologist and what I was reading was his field work. He wanted me to know that *Journey to Ixtlan*, Castaneda's third book was his master's thesis for his degree in anthropology from the University of California, Los Angeles. UCLA. He told me Castaneda went on to earn his PhD. in anthropology based on this work I was now reading.

As I looked through the first book, I noticed the publisher was The Regents of University Press, the publishing arm of UCLA itself. So, this was published by the university as scientific studies in the field of anthropology. Of course, this meant that all of what I was about to read was non-fiction. Phil told me that in most bookstores, Castaneda's books are usually sold in the hardbound non-fiction aisle, sometimes they can be found in the anthropology section. He said, "Sometimes people think he's a spiritual or psychic thing and they "mistakenly" put his books in the new age or metaphysical section." "Oh, dear!" I thought. All pretentious snobbery aside, I was informed, this was scientific work in the field of anthropology, non-fiction, end of story.

So, there you go. The stage is set, the band starts playing. The dealer deals another hand. It was time to roll the dice and make my bet and double down. Everything I was going to read actually happened? The University of California, Los Angeles is publishing *The Teachings of don Juan* so, evidently, this is true. There really is a guy out there named don Juan Matus. Well, I'll be. How could I not respect such academic authority? I certainly dove in headfirst and read the first book in a day. Half of it was just weird field notes anyway. The actual story itself was quite brief... and really weird. I liked it!

The next afternoon, Phil and I discussed the book. He wanted me to understand what happened to Carlos in the bus station. In the book, when Carlos met don Juan, he had been psychically-hooked-on-to by a master shaman's gaze. Phil pointed out how this was a *meant-to-be* situation, where the universe itself was the one calling the shots and the master shaman was a *seer* who saw Carlos was meant-to-be his chosen one, meant to involuntarily become his apprentice. He was careful to establish this unfathomable, written-in-the-stars teacher-apprentice theme that permeates Castaneda's work. I could tell he wanted to play the part of don Juan and have me be his little apprentice. It was pretty creepy. I, more or less, went along with his student / mentor approach. I gave him the benefit of the doubt. I was curious to see where it all led.

As a UCLA undergraduate student in the late 60's, Castaneda had allegedly been looking for an informant for his field studies in anthropology. Specifically, he was looking for anyone knowledgeable in the medicinal uses of power plants such as peyote, datura and psilocybin mushrooms. As the story was told by Castaneda, a friend knew of an old man who, as it turned out was don Juan, and he told Carlos he would try to introduce him.

When Carlos was introduced, at a bus station in Yuma, something in the way don Juan looked at him made him feel very strange, he said it stopped him somehow. It was something in the look in his eye that unnerved him. The rest of the book is about how Castaneda searches for the man and eventually learns where he lives and finds him at home. This is how his story begins.

I was all like, "Wow! I want to be a sorcerer's apprentice! I want to be hooked by a master shaman! That'd be cool!" Everything that was suggested to me, I wanted to experience it. I wanted to know it. I wanted to feel it and live it and just totally go for it. I was excited, I was very passionate about finding the secret of the universe. I was excited that there was somebody out there right now, on planet earth, who knew what it was, and I wanted to find them and talk to them about it, and have them show it to me and then I was going to learn everything I could and take it home and then I was going to wrap it up in a box, and keep it safe, so I could take it out and show it to everyone, any time I wanted!

It seemed like I was on the road to find out. I truly believed this is the best possible thing for me. I believed these experiences were going to help me write really cool songs. Ever since my manic crash and burn, I believed I was put on earth to write a really special song, one that would change the world in a very subtle way. I grew up during the cold war, during a nuclear arms race, in an era when the threat of global annihilation was always immanent. We lived with that fear every day. It was a lot like how the kids of today live with the fear of school shootings. I was going to float ideas out into the public consciousness, sharing the lyrics in my songs, influencing society in a way that would make the threat of global nuclear destruction go away.

I believed I was born to write a song that would cause the button pusher not to do it, to never launch the bombs in the first place, a song which would affect people so deeply they would never even let the situation get that far gone. My songs would guide the hearts of man toward a better, more enlightened world. That was the goal, anyway. So now instead of having my identity tied-in to being only a songwriter, my identity was now morphing into being a humanitarian who uses the mysterious forces of music to communicate the secrets of enlightenment to the world. The nasty Christ-fixation I had was not something which went away politely. It was far more rude and obnoxious, coming back in several forms before I was finally able to realize I am an average ordinary person, and will have to live without teaching the world anything meaningful.

For Castaneda, if this don Juan Matus became his informant, if he were to have in-depth knowledge of power plants and shamanistic practices, in their preparation and use, he would be a veritable goldmine for his anthropology career. It would mean he would have more material than he could ever dream of to successfully write a thesis and get his university degree. Furthermore, he could make a whole career out of carefully documenting the shamanic practices of native people of the Sonoran Desert and publishing about it. Which is exactly what he did in the long run. Any books with information about psychotropic plants could become amazingly popular during this era. There was a huge, drug-hungry audience for information about psychotropic plants and Castaneda's books hit that target market spot-on and sales just exploded.

If becoming a successful Ph.D. candidate is all about publish or perish, then Castaneda's path to success was a cinderella story. Of course, it all seemed a little too good to be true, but Castaneda the undergraduate student, defended the authenticity of his work vehemently, even in the face of criticism and doubt by his contemporaries. He was a masterful raconteur with a kind of charismatic personality very rarely seen. He could convince anyone of nearly anything and he went about doing so in grand fashion because everything contained in his work is completely outrageous.

But Castaneda put it across. He was able to convince a vast majority of people that what he was reporting was the god's honest truth. Since, at that time, he was simply reporting about a culture's beliefs and practices, it was easy to say just about anything and get away with it. This played perfectly into Castaneda's personality because he was just the kind of guy who would say anything, and he could get away with it. So, he did.

Being in Southern California myself, and traveling around to all the new age bookstores and places spiritual seekers might go, I happened to, on more than one occasion, cross paths with people who alleged they had known Castaneda, personally. One such gentleman was on a public transit bus outside of the West Los Angeles area. I had made a pilgrimage to The Bodhi Tree bookstore to look for certain hard-to-find new age titles. This is before the Internet and Amazon. If we wanted hard-to-find new age books, we either had to order them at a bookstore, or call around, then travel 40-miles on public transit to find someone who had it. So, I was riding home on the bus reading a Castaneda book. An older gentleman on the bus noticed the book and commented to me about it. Then he started to talk to me.

"I was at UCLA when Castaneda was an undergrad there." He told me. "My friend was his roommate in the dorms his freshman year, so I knew him somewhat." He said. "You should be aware that Carlos has a reputation for being a fantastic liar." I rolled my eyes.

He said, "No. No. Listen. I just want to tell you he can tell stories like no one I have ever known. Nothing he says is what it seems. You have to take my word on this." He admonished me. "Carlos is like the Coyote in those books you're reading. He is the trickster. Keep that in mind as you read his books. Don't get too wrapped up in them." He told me. "I know you don't know me from anyone, but just remember what I am telling you. I knew the guy. You can never take anything he says at face value. He is always trying to put one over on somebody."

His stop came and he got off the bus, after giving me a final accusatory glance. I thought about what he said. "What does he know?" I thought. "He never had a Kundalini awakening or experienced the cosmic love-energy. What does he know about enlightenment?" And I dismissed his admonishment.

In 1968, the psychedelic counterculture was exploding into the public consciousness and Castaneda's work hit just the right audience at just the right time. *The Teachings Of Don Juan* went viral as soon as it was published. It became a cultural phenomenon. It was ingested whole by the academic community and a psychedelic counterculture thirsty for information about mind-expanding drugs and cosmic consciousness. His book sold all over the world and went into multiple printings, even as he continued his studies at UCLA and his alleged fieldwork in Mexico.

Money, celebrity, professional respect all came immediately to the young Castaneda in the wake of this newly published stunner, subtitled "*A Yaqui Way Of Knowledge.*" He was becoming a Rockstar Anthropologist and, quite against his will, he was publicly considered a contemporary of Timothy Leary, Alan Watts and was even called the Godfather of the New Age Movement. His rise to fame and fortune as a best-selling author was meteoric.

As I started reading the *A Separate Reality* and *Journey to Ixtlan*, Phil was directing my attention onto the practices of dreaming. In the stories, Don Juan had given Carlos the practical task of finding his hands while he was asleep and dreaming. His goal was to wake up in the dream, to realize he was dreaming and to calmly look at his hands before he became lost in the dream again. The idea was to stabilize the dream and to prolong the effect of becoming aware that one is dreaming. Phil was quick to challenge me with the same task. Within a couple of weeks, I had done it for the first time. This furthered my conviction that this was indeed a non-fictional story I was learning from. I was learning the first steps to out-of-body experience.

I continued reading through the first three books and when I got to *Journey to Ixtlan*, I read through the table of contents. This seemed as if I had now come upon a handbook, a set of practices and premises for a complete way of life. Not only was this a series of tasks and practices, said to be part of Castaneda's apprenticeship to two Yaqui Indian Sorcerer's in the Sonoran Desert, this was an entire set of new philosophical challenges, an alien way of thinking about perceiving. It was more than just trying to do something unusual, like going out of body or astral projecting. This was quite literally, a complete lifestyle which is all-inclusive. There was no way to do this part-way.

You had to go whole hog if you wanted to live these unseen experiences yourself. You had to dedicate your life to the practice of this way of life.

Sound familiar? The books put forth the idea that anyone could learn to become a man of knowledge, however, it required nothing less than the complete dedication of one's entire lifetime, up front. Anything less would be a foolish waste of time, because the attempt would be unsuccessful since the goal was to arrive at the totality of the self. How could anyone arrive at the totality of the self without giving their all? Right?

So, for a kid like me, here I come under the influence of Carlos Castaneda and it is being suggested to me that I need to dedicate my life to learning everything I can about the Yaqui way of knowledge, because it is the only way of life worth living. It is romanticized to the point of phantasmagoria that this is a way to successfully become an enlightened man of knowledge. A lot of respected adults and their full-grown organizations, such as UCLA, are telling me this work is true, this is the way to go. I am trying to find my way to real knowledge and define my own success in life because I am still young and I have a lot to learn. These people are all telling me they can teach me what no one else can. They are telling me this is a really special thing and that I am a really special person. I suddenly feel all my answers are this way. So I go.

The initiate is said to be setting foot along a path of knowledge. A lot of people journey along a path of knowledge; it's a common theme for many bodies of work. Many have spoken about yoga as a path of knowledge. I am used to hearing this term by now. So, I continue. Maybe, this is a parallel, a recurring theme in the secret knowledge of universal knowins'?

Then, Castaneda writes that an initiate is someone who is involved in becoming of a man of knowledge. So, I initiate. To briefly paraphrase, the initiate must complete a process of perceptual transformation in which the net result is a specialized ability to *see* with a form of *second sight*. This special kind of *seeing* is an ability to apprehend the world as a living, breathing interwoven fabric of phenomena, events designed by the invisible hand of fate and governed by the supernatural forces which guide men's lives. He writes that we come into the power of knowledge by reaching a state known as *Stopping The World*.

So the idea now, for the initiate, for me, is to learn how to *Stop The World*. If I want to stop the world I need to stop my internal dialogue and learn to master this action of inner-silence, turning off the internal-dialogue. So I am deeply intrigued by these ideas and I am imagining, "How fantastic this must be to live in this way and *see* the world with this enlightened vision." However, the notion is put forth that the initiate is not only going to *see* the world in a new way, but *seeing* the world in this new way is merely a basic prerequisite for acting *intentionally* within a *non-ordinary reality*.

Castaneda is asserting that this new world of pure perception, *The Sorcerer's World*, is a world of *action*. We're not just going there to float around and visit, or trip out. We are going there because we have something vitally important we must do in order to become a man of knowledge. The whole idea is that an initiate is going to learn to *stop the world* as a prerequisite to gaining entry to, and acting with volition in *The Sorcerer's World*. So, everything in *italics* is especially *charged with mystery* because everything in *italics* belongs to a *secret world*, another world that only *men of knowledge* can *see*.

Castaneda's book *Journey To Ixtlan* lists chapter after chapter of subjects the initiate must master before he would be able to rally his knowledge and *Stop The World*. We first have to erase ourselves by erasing our personal history. Personal history is the first part of the self that comes under attack. Everyone who knows you well, everybody, they all gotta go bye-bye from your every day life. Mom, Dad, brothers, sisters, lovers, they're all out. Anyone who could possibly talk you out of it, they all gotta go. After personal history, self-importance is to be eradicated. Warriors are humble, so the ego has no place here. This is a big dent in the personality for just about anyone. To take just that much seriously can be deeply overwhelming and life-altering. Becoming a warrior means checking off on a long list of personal attacks against oneself which include disrupting all your routines so nothing can pin you down in the world of everyday life. Philosophies such as using your death as an advisor and practical premises of the sorcerer's world are intricately described and meant to be consumed whole, without question. Your mileage may vary.

Journey to Ixtlan was a landmark work. However, looking back on it today, I realize the very ideas cults use to isolate their members, break them of their family ties and force them to the cause of doing the master's every bidding is fully present the prerequisites for entry in to the advertised new world of perception. You can't enter into it, or experience *The Sorcerer's World* if you can't let go of the measly little world you are now a part of. You can't have both. The two are totally separate realities, hence the name of the second book, *A Separate Reality*.

If it was truly non-fiction, not only was it groundbreaking, but it was beyond belief how lucky Castaneda was, as an anthropologist, to have dug up such a deep and powerful, intact cultural heritage, which as it turns out, was said to date back hundreds of years, into Meso-American history. What was most mind-blowing, was Castaneda's assertion that not only was this body of shamanistic practices still known, but the guy he met in the bus station was part of a sorcerer/apprentice lineage dating back to the ancient Toltecs. Castaneda asserted the ancient practices were alive and well, with living practitioners in the present day and he had found one... and the guy wanted him to be his apprentice. His career was paved in gold. He was going to document and publish a goldmine of historic information. This was very exciting news for people like me, who were raised to believe in unseen worlds.

The Purpose of Life

As I continued into this way of life, I think you get the idea; one has to learn to shut out the noise and go for internal silence, poo poo the naysayers. My newly forming experience with yogic meditations roughly corroborated the general drift of the spiritual practices side of the story. It's about stopping the world, or entering internal silence, for the purpose of pursuing enlightenment (understanding the way the universe actually is) by expanding perception through entering states of amplified awareness. Not everything was crystal clear yet but I was going to have a go at it. I was going to explore it and see if I could get it all to lay flat, make sense to me, lead me more deeply into understanding the nature of how life actually is.

This sort of thing ran all through the popular culture of the 1970's. Every bookstore carried fifty or more titles on the subjects of mystical knowledge or lucid dreaming practices. The problem of entering into a whole program like Castaneda's is that it becomes a cult of personality with one person idolized as the figurehead of a whole movement. Beside the disempowering feature of becoming a follower of a best-selling author, it's the nature of the business at hand, which comes at a huge cost to the rest of your life. You start to isolate yourself and chase an abstract, idealized goal, one that is said can only be achieved in a highly romanticized solitude, in a program that can only be doled out by the figurehead.

The way it reads is, by virtue of complete commitment to learning the warrior's way, we finally become the masters of the first-attention by *erasing the self* from the world of everyday life. The level of personal discipline required to accomplish this is equal to that required in going to war. Warriors live in *the state of total-war* against their own weaknesses in order to become conscious at night during *dreaming* and act with volition toward specific goals. To accomplish this feat, a warrior needs to master the *second-attention,* by entering into this specialized domain, from both, ordinary reality and from *dreaming,* in order to bring together the *totality of the self.* Without the *totality of the self* as a highly focused, singular unit, driven by *unwavering intent,* there is no hope of harnessing enough *personal power* to accomplish the warrior's purpose. The warrior's purpose is an *act of will* known as achieving *total freedom, total awareness.* It would be like leaving the domain of ordinary words and entering a world where everything is *italicized*.

In Castaneda's work, he elevates the human anatomy to a whole new level by describing, in great detail, how the energy field of human beings appears and how it functions for a *seer* who has attained the ability of *second sight*. To master these *acts of power* is the purpose of a lifetime, strengthening the warrior, so they can obtain the necessary *personal power* to align the first and *second attention* with the energy at-large, energy as it flows through the universe. Entering into the *third attention* is the willful act of achieving *total alignment, total freedom,* becoming *total-awareness* the way the books describe it. The human energy body is described as an energetic cocoon, a luminous egg-shaped sphere of pure cosmically charged life force surrounding the human form. To align the energy within the individual's cocoon with the emanations of the energy at-large, breaks the shell of the cocoon permanently, it is the equivalent of aligning the first and second attention with the third attention in a willful act which ignites the totality of the self with *total-awareness*, the purpose of life on earth, according to Castaneda. After a while the italics become too much to deal with. This is only achieved at the instant the warrior is leaving the world forever, departing on his or her via definitivo, or definitive journey.

It is a beautiful, romantic story that I became totally caught up in. It transformed the way I viewed the purpose of the life. I went from looking at life as a general purpose, one-size-fits-all experience to seeing life as having a highly focused purpose in mastering the self in order to leave the world intentionally, in a flash of radiant light, at the time of one's own choosing. Especially, since everyone around me said it was true. And hell, if it was actually possible, shouldn't that be known? Seems like something you would want to let the President know.

It made perfect sense, if you were a fan of human spirituality and studied as many traditional scriptures and creation narratives as I had by then, this seemed to bring it all together and clarify the mystery of why we're here on this earth. Castaneda's work tackled the big questions of why are we alive and what is the right way to live, then answered them back within a stunning narrative delivering the clear purpose of being alive. The narrative is an intoxicatingly romantic description of warriors, sorcerers, men and women of knowledge, going to war against inconceivable odds to fight for the unimaginable, for total-awareness, the gift of infinite life, to become navigators on a sea of mystery, explorers of eternity. I mean, sign me up!

We have to remember, I grew up in the Lutheran Church where everything in the Christian religion, everything in the Bible was said to be true. Even my parents, grandparents and great-grandparents, hell, all the adults in my life told me I'd better believe everything the Bible said was true. Then I was given a psychic add-on pack to install over my Christian view of the world. It came with Out-Of-Body Experience 1.0, for my mental software needs. This gave me new abilities to reach out into the *unseen world* and take actions which healed others and benefited humanity.

After a time, I suffered so many emotional disappointments and hardships which made me feel needy for something to turn to, something self-empowering and highly-romanticized made sense to me; it made sense to the me-I-had-been-raised-to-be, the person who believes *unseen worlds* are part of life and are our ultimate destination, anyway. I was simply being taught how to load the next-level software iteration, put it all together and live a full, complete life with Absolutely-All-Of-Myself 4.0. I'm just trying to explain how all of this happened. I was born, they told me about all this shit that wasn't real, it took along time because I had to sort through it all and figure out what was actually happening. My whole goal, the whole time was to figure out what is actually happening in regards to how man got here, what are we supposed to be doing while we're alive and where are we going?

When I thought about it, I was taught that Christ ascended into heaven and as he did, those left witnessing his ascension saw only light. I believed maybe Christ was an enlightened man who learned to become a man of knowledge and realized the fullness of our human potential. I was convinced, probably because I was raised to be convinced, that all of mankind possessed a latent ability to become Christlike, to not die but to instead turn into light. He came to earth to show us how it was done but no one really got it.

Yogic traditions also had their transmutation stories where yogis meditated so completely, entering the highest samadhi, so perfectly, for so long, that they physically crossed over from all-of-this, and entered all-of-that, never coming back. At least, that's what I read. These are the stories I heard. The Taoist traditions speak of living a regenerative lifestyle, following a path called *the right way to live*, until their vitality enters the super-regenerative state bringing about physical changes which unite the body, mind and spirit into oneness with universal cosmic consciousness. I'm not making this stuff up. People have been thinking this way for thousands of years. As well, no one knows what happened to the Mayans. We can find their cities, their settlements, but no one can find what happened to them, physically. Nothing remains of them to be discovered. It is believed, as oral tradition relates, they crossed over into heaven on a bridge of light.

Along the way, I came across countless attacks of Castaneda's work in the press and in works written by other authors about his refusal to defend himself against the accusation that his work was fictional, that there was no one named don Juan Matus and that he received his Ph.D. from UCLA through deception. While this controversy raged on, I quietly went about my business of practicing the life of a warrior in order to one day become a man of knowledge. All of the controversy was something I just learned to tune out and disregard.

All Paths Lead To Thee

In Castaneda's absence, I had no one to turn to for guidance but Phil and anyone else I could find who looked like they might know about shamanistic practices and meditation practices. Phil, when it came right down to it, was actually just a big fan of new age authors in general, and loved the subject of human spirituality as much as I did. In this way, we really were birds of a common feather and he simply was like any other buddy who just wanted to share his fandom with me. It could have honestly been about hot rods and race cars, but for us, it was books about the meaning of life.

He became like a big brother who had a nice collection of baseball cards he wanted to share. Only for Phil, it was authors and their books. His favorite authors were Richard Bach, Castaneda, Jane Roberts and Lobsang Rampa. He liked Ram Dass and anything about The Legend of King Arthur. He liked the scriptures and metaphysics, as much as anyone, and he loved great surrealist art. So he had a lot of subject matter to share with me. So after a while, everything with Phil came down to a "Check this out, Isn't that cool!" kind of thing. He just wanted a buddy to share his passion for the world's great arts & literature with. This certainly became the common ground on which a lasting friendship was maintained between us for many years.

I maintained my voracious reading and would even seek out other new age authors to ask questions, go to their workshops or any lectures they offered. I did everything that was out there which I could afford, including The Seth Material and visits with trance channelers. I continued to practice daily meditation, frequented a psychic group that met on Friday nights at a local bookstore and even took up the sport of lucid dreaming. I maintained a general interest in everything people believe and I am still very interested, particularly, in why people believe what they believe.

I had bought a motorcycle, a Suzuki GS550 road bike. It wasn't a fire breathing monster but I used to take off on sunny southern California mornings and head for the hills and canyons beneath Saddleback Mountain. It became an escape for me to hit that throttle hard and carve up the mountainside curves and just let it roar. I loved the feeling of speed, power and freedom that bike gave me. The fantastic Southern California weather combined with the endless territory of hills, mountains, canyons and desert gave a young kid the thrill of a lifetime to just get out on the road and explore with endless freedom.

One morning, I was riding up in Trabuco Canyon, up near O'Neil Park when I came across a sign that said Ramakrishna Monastery. It said open to the public during certain hours. It just happened to be those hours. There was a long winding asphalt road disappearing way up onto the hilltop so, I decided to throttle up and go have a look. I rode up the steep asphalt lane for about a half-mile when I came to the most amazing place. I'd been coming to O'Neil since I was a boy and I never noticed this was here. It had obviously been here the whole time, since the 1930's, I would come to find.

What I found was an old single story Italian architectural style campus with a small bell tower and perhaps half a dozen little red brick and clay shingle cottages and buildings, some with the brick painted white, arranged in various locations along a flat twenty acre, or so, shoulder overlooking the hills and the vast expanse of So. Cal. civilization to the west. It was beautiful and placid with great views, large well-manicured lawns, climbing ivy, just a lovely grounds with ample gardens and plenty of room for the wonderful light splashing all around through the tall, aged trees. It was a fantastically sunny morning, not a cloud in the sky, around 11am, when I pulled up in the gravel parking lot and found a man standing there next to a 1966 Ford Mustang fastback. It was a lot like the mustang my brother used to own when he was in high school. I pulled up to him and shut off my bike.

He greeted me with a wave and I said, "Nice car!"

"You like that!?" He smiled. He was just finishing drying it off after washing it by hand. He began winding up a long, green garden hose and putting back neatly against an ivy covered stone wall.

It took me a second or two to get my gloves off and undo my helmet. As I took off my helmet, piles of long blonde curly hair poured out over my shoulders and down my back. I could see the man's apprehension, until our eyes met and I had a smile on my face the size of Texas. I was grinning ear-to-ear and it seems he found this disarming and he smiled brightly just as well.

I introduced myself as Vini Sargenti and held out my hand. He told me his name was Gurudas and that he was a resident of the monastery. I went on about how I saw the sign at the bottom of the road and I was curious what they were into up here. I asked if they practiced meditation.

"Yes, we do practice meditation here. We are a monastic order of Hindu monks and meditation is our way of life."

I asked if they practiced yoga and meditations of various yoga traditions. Gurudas told me that indeed they did just such a thing. He told me some of the residents were more involved in yoga practice than others, but it was an important part of their way of life. He asked me what I knew about yoga and meditation.

I told him I was raised in a Lutheran school as a Christian and we briefly discussed religion. He said that his monastic order were devotees of Sri Ramakrishna, a famous historic figure who attained the highest state of enlightenment. He lived in India during the mid-nineteenth century. They were practitioners of a specific branch the Hindu religion. I asked if they were like the Hare Krishnas I would see dancing at the airport. He seemed amused by that and said he is asked that question all-too-often. He assured me they were a completely separate lineage of religious history.

He told me about a man from India named Swami Vivekananda, who had come to the West in the latter part of the same century and brought his Hindu religious teaching to the world stage. As a young man, Vivekananda gained a lot of respect in the West and because of him, they were all present in this place, practicing this religion at this wonderful monastery."

We fall under the umbrella of a much larger, worldwide organization called The Vedanta Society. We study ancient scriptures known as the Vedas, the Upanishads and our main text is the Bhagavad Gita. Have you ever read the Gita?" I told him I had. *"For I dwell in the heart of all beings. Chapter 15, verse 15.* One of my favorite verses." I told him. He seemed to like that.

"These are the scriptures of primary importance for us. The Vedas and the Upanishads are ancient Sanskrit writings, which are perhaps three thousand years old. For us, they are Holy Scripture, much like what the Christian Bible is to you. We believe all religions are one religion and that all paths lead to God. Hindu is a religion of peace and our goal is God-Realization, to be one with God."

I told him in a joking tone that, where I come from, many Christians believed people like him would burn in hell for believing such nonsense. He looked at me with a mischievous grin and laughed, "Yes, I would imagine some do. But we would never seek to convert anyone to our religion. If a Christian were to come visit this place and get to know us, we would only hope they would walk away a better Christian."

I told him I would like to learn more about these teachings, the Vedas and Hinduism. I said that I was just entering my twenties, at this point, and I was aware that I was still very young and had a lot to learn. I told him, "There is so much left to know and I'm on the road to find out."

He listened as I prattled on about how I had been practicing meditation since I was young, that my aunt got me started in it when I was twelve and I had no formal training in yoga meditation. I told him I just did a few things I'd been taught and mostly did my own thing, whatever felt right. He thought that was amusing and seemed quite dismissive of me. He laughed and shook his head. I asked him if he knew anything about kundalini yoga.

He said, "I do know a little about it, yes. Why do you ask?" He seemed genuinely bewildered that some longhaired kid on a motorcycle was showing up at his door asking about kundalini yoga.

I told him I was looking for someone who might know something about kundalini awakening. I explained to him how I had an incident, experienced during an extended meditation practice, that culminated over a week or so. I told him I had been trying to find someone I could talk to about it, someone who might be knowledgeable about the practice of it. I tried to carefully explain to him some details about my discoveries, the penetrating power of my attention, the amplification of awareness, the energy that lead to an amazing rush of speed and powerful visions. I told him I felt like I had become one with all the love in the universe and understood the meaning of life, I tried to share the joy I'd found with anyone who would listen but they treated me like I was crazy and the more I tried to explain what was happening the more they laughed.

"I began to become unhinged, because I didn't know what to do. I had so much energy, so many powerful visions, and I didn't know how to shut it off. I am just a typical westerner," I told him, "with no knowledge of yoga meditation. I entered a state of psychosis because I had no practical knowledge of how to handle the rush of energy. I explained how the whole thing got out of hand and landed me in a mental institution.

I told Gurudas I had never heard of it before but I had been told by several people, they believed I had experienced a accidental kundalini awakening and that the psychosis happens to people who encounter the awakening without training. "I admit, it sounded like a ridiculous superstition to me," I tried to explain, "until I read up on it and the kundalini yoga books described my experience to a tee. Ever since then, I've been trying to find someone I could talk to about it, anyone who might know about more it than the folks I knew."

He scoffed at me and it really seemed to piss him off. "There is no chance in hell you ever experienced, or ever will experience, a kundalini awakening, son." He fired back at me, "Chaste and disciplined men live out there entire lives in monasteries such as this one and never experience such things. Only the greatest yogi's and religious geniuses in history experience the kundalini. It is the beginning of God realization! You simply went mad and are obviously on an ego trip that you are such a one who experiences the great awakenings masters work their whole lives to attain!"

"The teacher appears when the student is ready." He reminded me of the age-old spiritual aphorism, "If no teacher appeared, then you weren't ready."

I figured I was facing an uphill battle here, but I was used to it by now.

I told him it was obvious that I wasn't ready. He was being really cocky. I explained carefully, because he already announced he was going to be a dick about this, "In the West, this kind of thing is happening more often and no one knows what to do. Ordinary people are flashing on, speaking of a mysterious fire running up their spines, blasting their brains with energy they can't deal with, winding up in mental institutions, jumping off cliffs or worse. It's not a religious thing. It's simply a feature of human evolution. Kundalini is present in everyone. It's just our life force. In India, you guys have a culture accepting of this kind of thing and ways to recognize and assist people who accidentally awaken this evolutionary energy. I happened to make my way back from dangling off the edge. I had a little guidance from a few kind souls who recognized what was happening and tried to rescue me." He just stood there with his lips puckered up, not at all convinced. I asked him what he believed it was I experienced then.

He shrugged his shoulders, "Could be anything. Meditation is a powerful way, my friend. We have to be prepared for powerful experiences of all kinds. This is why we live such austere lives. So we are ready, should such a blessing come to us."

I slowly and carefully explained, as I asked him once again to hear me out. I told him I had been a religious child and had always wanted to unravel the mystery of God. I explained my long-standing curiosity of the supernatural growing up, asking my aunt about astral travel, the whole deal about discovering the chakras, which I had never heard of. I explained the meditation Marina told me to try, which, at that point, I had never known there was a name for it, he immediately recognized what I was referring to and expressed horror.

"Who on earth would give a beginner the Ajna meditation?! Oh, my dear God!" He was shocked and completely indignant. Now he seemed to be shifting slightly toward concern about my predicament.

"What did you call it? The aja...?" I asked.

"Ajna," he said slowly. "Ajna is the name of the sixth chakra. It is the seat of the third eye. The meditation you just described is called the Ajna meditation. It should never to be shown to anyone but serious devotees and only as part of formal meditation instruction by one's master." He told me. Then he had a nice chuckle at my expense. "Boy, *that* would be something, wouldn't it? For the third-eye to open without any knowledge? That would be shocking, wouldn't it?"

"Yes." I squinted, "Very."

I continued on, about the tape recorder light, the way I *willed* the straightening of my attention and became completely silent and still and fixated on the light for hour, after hour, after hour, for day, after day, after day. How my concentration grew stronger and stronger and stronger, until my energy and awareness became amplified in a great rush when all manner of visions and phenomena began to arise for me. I told him about the light and the universal love energy from which all things emerge. I told him I spent the next week or more in a long series of progressively intensifying visionary states and I am just trying to makes sense of it.

He looked like the whole story just seemed ridiculous to him. I could see him struggling to get his mind around everything I just told him.

"Why would anyone choose to do something like that, Gurudas?" I asked, "Why would I be so interested in discovering what was happening and so daring that I would meditate that intently, on the present moment, for that long, until my own energy opened up like a thousand-petalled lotus blossom? I mean, how does this happen to ordinary kids like me? I mean what did I do to deserve this?"

"Well, obviously," he retorted, "You did the Ajna meditation, right? What did you expect?"

"I didn't know what to expect. There were times when it was like a nuclear bomb was going off at the base of my spine and I could not have controlled it for the world. I was completely consumed by it, as if I were enveloped in invisible flames shooting out of my ass." That got him laughing.

"Seriously though, Sir." I continued, "My body felt like a flamethrower and my whole spine was like the barrel of the gun, throwing fire out the top of my skull like the fourth of July. Would it occur to you that this sort of thing is possible? I had no idea! Do you think if you discovered it was possible, how it was possible, that you would have the balls sit down and just do it? That your ability to concentrate would be powerful enough? That you could love intensity without fear and feel no resistance even in your most powerful moment of universal presence?" My eyes glowed with the wild power again.

I felt all the juice I had during the weeks after the experience coming on in me. I was turning it on, in the moment, trying to get him to understand I sincerely meant business.

"I am looking for help." I said softly.

"If you had a kundalini awakening you'd be answering the questions, not asking them."

I laughed, "I like that!" I said, "You know it's funny. You're a funny guy. I think I just told you that I was trying to get anyone I could to listen to me and no one would. It seems to be the ongoing theme of my life here. I did not neglect to mention how I tried to tell everyone about this powerful experience of oneness with a living energy that is made of love, which can be found through meditation. I tried to tell them, I tried to tell everyone the meaning of life, that the secrets of the universe are revealed by training the attention in meditation, and through practice, they would come to understand God is living in the here and now, he's all around us as the life-force of all things, he's the power of love which is everywhere, and we are all made of love because we're all made of energy! It's impossible to explain in a way anyone will understand. I can't make anyone understand! They can only do that for themselves!"

"I tried, Gurudas!" I laughed, crying at the same time. This guy was driving me mad. "I stood in front of a team of twelve doctors, all gathered around a table and tried to convince them that I knew the meaning of life. I tried to answer the meaning of life for everyone but they all thought I was crazy and they put me in a mental institution." I shook my head, "Fuck, man! I just wanted someone to help me find a real spiritual master, so I could plant myself at his feet and learn the right way to continue pursuing this meditation I had discovered. But now even you won't fucking listen. Jesus Christ has the entire world gone fucking mad!?" I was pissed, frustrated, sad and drowning in self-pity all at the same time.

He just looked at me with a face that did not betray his complete bewilderment. "What a waste." He scowled, and now he was practically in tears. "What a total waste of a great opportunity. Just think of what you could have done if you had been properly guided!" He looked like he just wanted to kick the dirt and have a go at all the gravel in the parking lot.

"Well, it's too late now." He shook his head and looked at the ground. "You'll never know what you could have done. It's just a waste of a once-in-a-million-lifetimes opportunity." As if I had won the lottery and just set the cash on fire. As if reincarnation is actually a thing.

So, I just looked at him and shook my head. "You're really just hellbent on putting me in a box, putting some label on it, [waste of opportunity] and burying the whole thing like the bricks in this wall, aren't you. Wouldn't that be convenient for you? To just act like this conversation never happened? Just stay in your comfortable monastery and go about your business, sit in meditation three times a day whenever the bell rings?" I told him. I had to admit, though, that kind of life sounded a lot better than mine.

"You want an answer?" I asked him, leaning in toward him, challenging him directly, man-to-man, now. "There are no labels. And all your thoughts are simply an empty hand full of nothing. If this war is over then why is my spine still lit up like a torch? Why do I suffer this raging column of fire that is burning my brains out? It's not over. The here and now is never over, my friend. Sitting in place, with dazzling energy spinning all around me, exploding at light speed into a conscious awareness of everything around me oozing radiant energy is not something we just get over."

"Okay! Okay, okay" he said holding up his hand. "Just try to relax. Relax already."

My blood was boiling and he could feel it. My brains were unstable and he was beginning to realize it. I honestly needed his help or someone's help, anyone's. My attention was piercing his eyes out and it was freaking him out a little bit.

"Look," I said, "I just need some guidance from someone who actually knows what I am talking about. Do you have anyone like that here or not?" I said in frustration.

"I'll tell you what." He said as if conceding somewhat, "If you think you had some degree of kundalini awakening, then who am I to say otherwise? But I don't think you did. I think you're just some crazy kid." He laughed and patted me on the back lightly in a kindly way. "But here's what I want you to do." He motioned for me to walk with him and I quickly followed along. He put his hand on my shoulder and smiled. "Let's take a walk up to the bookstore. They have a leaflet with the public hours and events we have here at the monastery. Why don't you start there."

We walked in silence toward the door leading into the main area of the monastery. There was statue of Vivekananda sitting in meditation over a reflecting pond and behind all that, what an amazing view of Southern California! We walked along the covered patio area up the steps into the bookstore and he introduced me to Swami Viprananda, who happened to be there at the moment. They both explained some of the upcoming events, which would be taking place, mostly lectures and readings. They invited me to keep coming back to the monastery and learn more about how everything works. They had a Sunday morning event they thought I might enjoy and encouraged me to start attending it every week, if I could.

Viprananda told me I could come back during the week, in the morning after they had breakfast, that all the monks gather and go for a walk together, either on the shrine trail or down the driveway to the bottom of the hill to the mailbox. He said that would be a good way to get to know everyone and he had found instruction sometimes has a way of unfolding more naturally during long casual walks.

"Come back at any of these times and we'll help you learn any way we can." Swami Vip told me. I really liked this guy.

Gurudas looked at me with a big grin on his face, "There you go! You're on your way now. You good?"

I shrugged my shoulders, "I'll find out." I smiled. I thanked him for taking the time to talk with me. He gave me one of those electric smiles only someone who sits in meditation six or more hours every day can give.

As it turns out, Viprananda was a professional Jazz musician at one time, who toured all over the country playing his saxophone. He got tired of sleeping in vans and airports so he joined the monastic life. We hit it off pretty good, he and I. He would become a fine mentor for me, though we were not many years apart in age. He didn't know much about kundalini awakening but, in the years that lie ahead, he helped me calm myself down pretty good and just go with the flow.

Looking Outside Oneself For Confirmation

In the months and years to come, I spent a lot of time with those guys up at the monastery. They became like a surrogate family to me, these meditation men. From time to time, the big wigs, important swamis would pass through for a big event and I was encouraged to question senior people like Swami Swahananda, when they came around. I would drive up to the Hollywood temple and get to know the guys up there as well. Everyone was very friendly and welcoming. They all tried to be as helpful as they could. I went to several of the locations for special events and I met a lot of lifers, men and women who were totally committed to meditation as a religious way of life. They were full-timers on the road to find out, professional meditation practitioners who did this for living. I fell right in line with them and we spent a lot of quality time together, though I had a regular day job and a life in the real world.

None of them seemed to know much about kundalini, but they had no problem sitting peacefully in meditation for hours at a time. My life-event was like a phantom phenomenon nobody had any real answers about. And I'll be damned if I could find a single soul who could sit down with me and talk shop about it. I began to wonder if it were all somehow just make-believe and if was I simply imagining all of it. Could imagination really be so powerful? Part of me felt certain that it was the labels that were make-believe, my verbal and visual thoughts were make-believe, anything we have to describe it with is useless, empty, but the underlying experience had an undeniable power and validity that simply could not be spoken. That was really hard to deal with. I think all the monks knew there was no way to talk about it so, they were reluctant to even bother. Part of me wanted something concrete but it just wasn't there.

Eventually, since I was still young, the question arose of whether or not I would like to lead a monastic way of life and I thought I might, but I wasn't sure. So they allowed me to come and go as I pleased in order to consider the possibility, if the call to monastic life would be true in my case. They said I could become a lay brother at first, if I wanted to explore the possibility more deeply, without making formal vows. They showed me to a guest room I could stay in and they let me be. I would show up for meals, for work periods on the grounds and help with the massive amount of yard keeping duties on the huge forty-acre property. The rest of time I was to seriously contemplate if I wanted to take formal vows and dedicate my life to meditation and God-realization. The schedule of the monastery was set up around three meditation periods lasting two to three hours each with a short break in the midst of each. But I found meditation time was rather open ended. They came and went from the hall as they pleased but they all put in their time. Morning, mid-day and evening, these cats were logging anywhere from six to nine hours of nose-to-the-grindstone meditation every single day.

Swami Tadatmananda was one of the longest-standing residents of the monastery. I think he told me he was age fifty-seven when I knew him. We often worked together on the grounds and became fast friends. I just called him Ted. We would cut up big piles of branches and throw them down in the ravine together. It was kind of a strange practice, seemed like a real fire hazard. But I really grew to love that old guy. He was as sweet as could be. He never taught any classes or gave any talks publicly. He never blew his own horn. He just sat in meditation and quietly lived out his days working on the monastery grounds, doing whatever needed to be done. He was practically invisible around there.

One day, after spending the morning in the meditation hall, I felt the urge to leave the monastery and never return. I couldn't identify with hinduism and needed to pursue the Castaneda teachings further. This wasn't my battleground. Mine would be in living a normal daily life in the workaday world. I did not see myself living away from the world, I felt I needed to go out into the world and be part of it, get a real job and take my lumps. I knew I didn't belong there. I had someday hoped to marry and settle down. I wanted children of my own. I didn't think I wanted to live a life of celibacy. I knew I had too many issues for that. The rigid formality of monastic life, the ritual, the pomp and circumstance of it all, to me, seemed unnecessary. Just sit down and focus. Badda Bing, badda boom. Why you gotta do all that? I loved the monastery though. It was a surreal place to live.

I went to the mediation hall after lunch to explore these feelings. I sat in there for about two full hours in total silence, just watching the incense and the candles slowly burning down. Then, one of the brothers would show up and refill all the incense and candles, water all the flowers and the room would remain the same. Swamis and brothers would come and sit for a while, then leave for a bit and return to the silent stillness of the meditation chamber. I really like that meditation hall at Ramakrishna Monastery. That is a wonderful space to sit and simply be. It was perfectly set up for peaceful repose and seemed to be completely sound proof. It was deeply quiet with nothing distracting in there. Even when people came and went, in the low-light setting, their movements were barely noticeable. The whole site, no matter where you went, seemed to have this deep silence emanating from every corner.

Those boys had a real nice place to live and do their thing up there. As I sat there, I simply wanted to feel what I was feeling and expand my awareness into my own subtle sensations. I would evoke a query regarding how I felt about living out my years within the experience of regimented days quiet religious practice, a religion I was not born into. I tried to get in touch with how I really felt about becoming a member of a monastic order, living the life of a renunciate, making formal vows of poverty and devotion. Eventually, I stood up, went back to my room and gathered up my stuff. I only had a small backpack. I made one last walk around the shrine trail, saying not a word to anyone, then walked out through O'Neil park. I hitchhiked back to the city of Orange, to the dingy apartment where I paid one-hundred dollars a month to sleep on the couch. It was a real rat hole, next to the railroad tracks, I had been sharing with some friends. I never looked back, until now.

Gurudas, in regards to me, came down on the side of imagination and make-believe in our discussion. He denied any validity and decided I simply imagined any powerful experiences I'd had, even while he himself practiced a religion and believed in reincarnation. Over the years, he never did cut me any slack. He always called me "the crazy kid." I argued that, while there was a great deal of make-believe occurring in my experience, in all the chatter and outward expressions of finding words to make sense of it, there had to be some underlying physical validity to this experience of universal love and life-energy. I was looking outside of myself for confirmation of a deeply personal observation. He wasn't going to confirm anything for me, nor would anyone else ever confirm anything. I was totally on my own in life. I eventually came to realize nobody cares about me or what I did or didn't experience in my life. We're all totally self-absorbed.

I know now that this is a deeply personal adventure in absorption and it is nearly impossible to talk about one's own encounters with meditative states. If you have a similar experience and find yourself in the company of a master of meditation and a welcoming crowd of knowledgeable people to discuss your experiences with, consider yourself very fortunate, extremely blessed. My own experience was a long slow grind, on a very rough road out of the wilderness toward a deeply silent understanding that is nearly impossible to share. More often than not, when I try to describe what I think and feel I just wind up sounding like an idiot.

I knew Phil King for many years after those early times of going through the Castaneda material. Sadly, all my friends and he fell prey to the cocaine epidemic in Southern California in the late 1980's. The unsavory element, the kind of people that drug magnetized into my friend's lives and the catastrophic negative events that followed, gave me a bad opinion of everyone involved in the whole scene and I wanted out.

Castaneda's books spoke of allies, spirit entities contained in power plants and even Phil The Acid King had his affinity for his LSD molecule, the love of his life. She seduced him and he became devoted to her. For me, cocaine was very close to being an evil life-form all-its-own. I believed cocaine contained the vicious monkey of addiction, which once ingested would climb on one's back and take over a person's entire life. Being a musician, I saw this happen too many times, to people I cared very deeply about, people I depended on. It was very sad, very sobering for me, a kin to losing all your best friends at once. It was just more tragic events in what was already sizing-up to be a very bewildering life for me. It was very much like watching Fred Gomez die in the street and there was nothing I could do. I could take them to rehab, push them in the door to AA and CA meetings, but they would pop right back out and go straight for their sweet addictions.

In the 1980's there was AIDS and there was the cocaine epidemic. At that time, with AIDS, the people you cared about simply withered and died, as if they were victims of a horrible, incurable cancer. With cocaine, the people I loved slowly became unrecognizable to me. It was so hard to tell what was happening, to see the accident coming, to recognize the disease progressing because they could hide the severity of it. As they changed, smoking the cocaine was turning a wonderful person into someone I didn't want to know anymore. And that was heartbreaking because I needed them to be there for me, but they could no longer be. They would betray anyone for another kiss from their crack-pipe lover.

The cocaine people would always be trying to drag you into their world, like emaciated zombies, checking your pockets for anything you had which they could take from you. It changed them and rewired their brains permanently. My dear friends now, could do nothing more than try to use me to get what they wanted. None of them were ever the same after that and our life-long bonds in close daily friendships were completely destroyed. Fortunately for me, I was not a cocaine person, or an acid person. The idea of hoarking piles of detergent up your nose just seemed ludicrous to me. The idea of taking LSD, and suffering the chemical burn-out and hangover, to reach the same state a little disciplined meditation could deliver, was absurd. I cut my losses and got the hell out of there.

On the last day of 1986, a friend of mine, Tom Hess, who had turned me on to a novel by Dan Millman, *The Way Of The Peaceful Warrior*, picked me up where I was renting a room in Costa Mesa, CA. He got me the hell out of there and I went to stay at his place in San Francisco, so I could start a new life. I cut my hair on New Year's Eve day, and from then on, slept on the floor in his tiny studio apartment until I could find a job and make enough money to get my own place. Tom and I shared similar interests in esoteric spirituality and in many ways we were kind of kindred spirits. Looking back, it was quite a selfless gift from my friend to help me get out of that degenerating world taking over Southern California. I couldn't have done it without him. He changed my life forever. I stayed on his floor for nearly two months until I was able to rent a converted garage bedroom, near Golden Gate Park, in San Francisco's Inner Sunset district. As it turns out, the inner sunset is what occurs just before the long, dark night of the soul.

Once I was all set up and living in my little converted room in a garage, I focused my daily life in the clean, tight living of traditional spiritual paths. My friend Tom had a budding interest in formal yoga practices and eventually settled into the teachings of Iyengar. I went to studying with Dan Millman, who happened to be teaching in, of all places, Mill Valley. I had taken some of Dan's training workshops while I was still living in so cal.

Eventually, I had taken all the workshops he offered until there were no more to do, and one day, out of the blue, he called me and asked me to assist him, along with some other students, in his trainings. He mentored me the best he could but I eventually started falling back into my old ways. I was a party animal, a lazy musician at heart and couldn't elevate permanently or morph into a vital, athletic personality, the way Dan was naturally. I was never the athletic type, nor did I have that natural pizazz of a new age spiritual teacher. I am a sedentary beast. I think this is why meditation suits me. Evidently, I had a lot more in common with Tadatmananda than I realized.

I would go between hard austerities of regular fasting, strict raw vegetarian dieting, daily meditation and regular exercise to bar hopping nights of binge drinking, smoking cigarettes and weed, going to rock concerts with my ordinary friends. It made no sense but this is how everyday people live. We just live normal lives. I wanted to live the divinely inspired life of the spiritual warrior but that was a very solitary world and I would get lonely and need the warmth of friendships and good company, so the next thing you know, all my friends are stoners, so I am off drinking beer and getting stoned silly with them. (And having a great time, I might add.)

By the time I showed up to help Dan with his workshop, I was a mess again. I was totally ordinary, in terms of my energetic state. The light in my eyes, the benefits of fasting and all the austerities were totally zapped out of me in one fell swoop by a few long nights of hard partying at Grateful Dead concerts. I did the workshop, but of course, he never asked me to help again. I was still a kid with a lot of issues I needed to work out with myself. Maturity was still quite a ways off for me yet. You can imagine how rewarding it might be for a teacher like Dan to see his students grow to successfully embody everything in his teachings, or not. That special spark of a spiritual warrior's personal excellence he had seen in me was once again diffused by my bad habits. It had gone dark, possibly the difference between my manic and depressive personality traits.

I had already moved on to Dan's original teacher, the community surrounding the alleged spiritual master Da Free John. Dan started there, so I figured I would go there. This community vacillated between times of hard partying and times of rigid austerity. So it kind of suited me. They would maintain critical self-examination through both hard partying and rigid discipline to fixate on what is constant throughout, the self that remains prior to the mind.

I liked all the people I met there and they were quick to accept me. I made friends quickly there as we were all birds of a feather. They all had known Dan for over 10 years, so that kind of gave me an in with them. So, I joined that group and was quickly ushered right in to the level I and level II practices. I spent a few years heavily involved in the teachings and meditation practice and the tithing; let's not forget tithing, of Da Free John's spiritual community. This was all happening in Marin County, California, a place I absolutely loved living. I rented shared a house in Novato, with a few other devotees who were all musicians.

I eventually met my first wife, through mutual friends, at a community theater presentation, in which some friends and I performed a song I had written for the show. From our dressing room window, before the show, we watched the crowd below gathering out front, as we anxiously endured the jitters before our performance. I saw a beautiful girl down there, with long flowing brown hair and just knew I had to meet her. My co-performer told me her name was Denise.

Eventually, I would meet her and we would begin an intense relationship and end up moving into an apartment together. I wrangled-in the girl who would become my first wife. Poor girl. For being such a "super spiritual guy," I was anything but an emotionally balanced person. At the age of twenty-four, the two of us set up housekeeping together but I was a real mess when it came to being content and trusting her. The scars of my upbringing left me with deep abandonment issues, not to mention, Jack had left his mark on my temperament and it wasn't good.

Denise and I argued all the time and she was the nicest lady in the whole world. You would never think she would be involved in such conflict but it got to the point where we needed relationship counseling, so we went. We found a wonderful therapist named Sally, yet another friend of the Millman's, coming to the rescue. It seemed everyone in Marin knew Dan and Joy, and we happily spent all our extra money on couples counseling, tithing, workshops and Grateful Dead tickets. As a couple, we went into heavy credit debt just living a normal hippy lifestyle in Marin. You know, the American Dream.

The medicine man is a high priest, he protects sacred traditions and runs all the traditional spiritual ceremonies. He is the keeper and teacher of the traditional medicine ways.

Chapter Eight
THE MEDICINE PEOPLE

AFTER THREE YEARS together in Marin, Denise and I eventually moved up to Windsor, CA in the wine country of Sonoma County, north of Santa Rosa. Rent was more affordable up there. We had finally had enough of the high-rents-for-tiny-spaces lifestyle in Marin. I had lost track of Dan long before and had taken up the game of golf by then, a horrible addiction to suffer from. We rented a nice three-bedroom house and for the next five years, except for my constantly changing printing jobs every three months or so, our lives were relatively stable, thru the end of 1995, when we broke up. During that five years, I began exploring the mountains of the Mendocino National Forest. I spent a lot of time in a wilderness area on the Pacific Ridge near Snow Mountain.

One year, it was getting toward the end of summer and I had been out in the wilderness by myself for a several days. I was making my way back home out of the mountains. I had just passed the sign that says, "You are now entering the Mendocino National Forest" as I was exiting the forest. I had come down to the bottom of Elk Mountain and was rounding the last turn near the Middle Creek Campground. That is a point of great relief for a driver because you've finally made it off the steep mountain switchbacks and reached the flat straight road.

I was just heaving a big sigh and jumping on the gas when a large buck came bounding out of nowhere right onto the road. This huge set of antlers and fur suddenly jumped out of the manzanita brush, right in front of my truck as I was accelerating out of that last turn. I only saw him for long enough to scream and brace for impact. I hardly got my foot on the brake before I hit him at full speed, maybe 40 mph. There was no way I could have missed him. It was as if he had waited for me, then jumped right in front of my speeding pick up truck. I nailed him hard. He actually bounced off the front bumper and fell over like a tin soldier. He stayed down, motionless, where I couldn't see him.

I had time to put it in park, undo my seatbelt and open the driver's door. I was stepping out of the vehicle when this beautiful, enormous animal sprung back to life, righted himself onto all fours and literally bounded off, disappearing into the manzanita in the direction he came from. I could not see him or hear him at all after that. He was just gone. I thought for sure I had killed him, I had hit him so fucking hard, it jarred my teeth.

Examining the front of my car, I could see it was wiped out. I could see the impression of his head and antlers running off one side of the hood and the curvature of his shoulders torso were impressed into the grill and bumper toward the passenger side. My headlights on the driver's side were dangling by one tiny screw and the plastic grill was all smashed and cracked. I grabbed a piece of the grill that was laying in the road and threw it in the back of the truck. It really messed up my truck in the front. I couldn't get the hood open and I was worried the radiator was punctured. The latch was buckled under and bent against the underside of the hood. I just hoped like hell the radiator hadn't hit the fan and I could still make it home. No fluids were underneath, so I went for it.

I figured that amazing animal, as tough as he was, to take a hit like that and walk away, was most likely staggering off to die on his own terms somewhere in the brush along the mountainside. I felt upset that I had hurt such a majestic animal, what looked like a mature trophy buck. They are so nervous at that time of year, only coming down off the mountain near dusk, to drink in the river valleys, as hunting season is getting underway in the area.

That week, as I worked my normal printing job, in a shop in Santa Rosa, CA, I contacted my insurance company about the damage the deer caused to my vehicle. They set up a claim for me to go ahead and have it all repaired. However, even though I had gotten a couple of estimates from local shops, I kept driving the truck. I returned to the mountains that Thursday night.

My Holy Jumping Off Place

It was supposed to be a quick road trip to drop off some gear and secure a specific campsite for that weekend, which would be Labor Day. Denise and I had been planning this camping trip since the beginning of summer and we were excited the time was finally drawing near. We wanted to get as far away from the world of everyday life as we could and just enjoy the solitude for a few days. I knew of a rustic campsite way up on the ridge in the wilderness. It was near the end of the Pacific Ridge road. There was tiny little spring, which came up out of the earth there and trickled down, across a grassy oak meadow, as it made its way down into the forest and then off the side of the mountain. The views from six thousand feet were spectacular. There was a soft, flat gravel area for pitching tents and setting out chairs and tables around the stone fire ring. I had my heart set on securing this site, which is usually no problem, but with it being Labor Day Weekend and hunting season starting soon after, the possibility loomed that I could drive all the way there after work on Friday night only to find someone had beat me to it.

I decided to make an extra three hour drive, each way, on Thursday after work, drop off some gear, set up a cheap tent and some chairs, then make the three hour drive back home, sleep, go to work, then enjoy the weekend. This way, since we weren't going to be able to get to the camp 'till nightfall, I might pull a fast one and keep someone else from taking it earlier in the day.

Hitting the deer had screwed up my headlamps and I hadn't given them much thought since the only time I drove at night was usually under the city lights in town. One was kind of dangling and not at all steady. I never thought about needing them outside of town at night. As I made my way up the dusty red clay roads of the forest in the twilight of that summer night, I reached an exposed, narrow stretch of road way up toward the top of the ridge. It was a good three hour trip from my house and I was getting close to the rustic campsite where I was going to drop my gear and head back home.

I could swear the road went straight. It was hard to tell in the deep twilight with my headlights all fucked up. I remember the moment of indecision as I put my foot on the brake, realizing my headlights had forsaken me. I had the strangest moment of perception, as if I were hallucinating a road that went straight. Somewhere between the reflection caused by ambient glare, the accumulated dust across my windshield, my wobbly headlights and the cloud of fine red clay dust I had been kicking up in the air around my vehicle in the afterglow of twilight, there was a manifestation of ephemeral appearances.

I was having one of those, "what the fuck?" moments where I couldn't tell if I could believe what my eyes were seeing. By the time I realized I wasn't sure of what I was seeing, I decided to stop. But by the time I actually stopped, I felt like I stopped, and yet one wheel slid, ever so slowly, off the edge of the road and went just barely off the side of the steep terrain. I very nearly came to a full stop, I thought, and I almost made a sigh of relief, before I plunged off the side of the mountain.

I was at a elevation of six-thousand feet when it happened. The pitch of the slope was not totally vertical but it was a good seventy degrees and it pulled my truck around dead perpendicular to the road before I left it and squared my vehicle to the slope, so I didn't roll over. I was heading directly straight down the steep vertical drop as if I were still driving the vehicle but I was no longer in control, gravity was.

In the moment, I was convinced this how my life was going to end. I even remember telling myself out loud, "This is it!" In one instant, I was a driver, and in the next, a passenger of gravity plummeting straight down the side of the mountain toward my death. As I left the road, as I went from nearly stopped, to tipping over the side ever so slowly, to the sudden rush of acceleration down the side of the mountain, I went from disbelief to a sudden, complete shock and horror. My adrenaline shot through the roof in a single instant and I was screaming as loud as I had ever screamed.

It was growing very dark but I could still see through the dirty windshield that I was really, really high up on the mountain. I caught a flash of the dark valley thousands of feet below in the distance, but in front of me, in my immediate vision, I could only see little trees, about the size of small Christmas trees. My pickup plowed straight through them. They had no effect whatsoever on the gravity accelerating my speed down the slippery mountain. My truck simply ran them right down.

As I came through the first patch of those little trees which had grown clinging to the mountainside, they went over like matchsticks under the truck to reveal a group of three large Douglas fir trees coming into my view. I tried to steer straight for one in particular but I don't think it made any difference at all. I piled straight into the center tree. I watched the front end of my truck push up toward me, buckling under my accumulating velocity and the weight of the vehicle, and it caught me. My unbridled glissade off the side of the steep mountainside came abruptly to a complete and total halt. The loud rush of hurricane force sounds were instantly hushed. The big fir tree had caught me and I remember saying to myself, "Oh! Thank God." It all held, my free fall firmly arrested by the steadfast, firmly-planted fir tree. Everything fell suddenly and completely silent... and I lived.

Then I realized I had just totaled my truck, 40 miles from the nearest paved road, at the edge of night, six thousand feet above the valley floor. Then I just started yelling the word fuck over and over again, because I was truly fucked right then. I had just totally fucked myself. By the time I got out of the vehicle and scrambled my way 100 feet up the steep, bare-dirt slope to the road, I was really freaked out. I had to really fight and scratch my way up, sliding partly back down, and wanting so badly to get off that slippery steep hillside where gravity was still the master of the game. It was very, hard dry clay, which I had just made smooth with my passing and I just remember having to exert a great effort to get enough traction with my street shoes and hands to claw my way back up the steep slope without sliding back down. I just had to get myself up out of there and that ignited my sense of primal desperation, of fight or flight.

By the time I reached the nice flat, stable stretch of road where gravity no longer had me directly in its grip, I was in a state of high anxiety and excitation. I remember having to make a concerted effort to calm myself down and gather my wits. I walked away uninjured. Well, I climbed away from what was literally a horrible accident, but that was going to wind up being the easy part. I knew this was going to take everything I had to make it out of the mountains alive because no one was going to come along and rescue me. In that day, there were no such thing as cell phones and I was deep out in the wilderness. It was going to be a long night's trek out of there to find help. It was 9pm. The last light was totally gone now.

I was one mountain ridge over from the nearest paved road. So I had to go down several thousand vertical feet then, back up to the top of the next ridge over, before I could even begin to hope to find a ride out of the mountains. It was possible I might see a ranger or some other folks in the morning somewhere. But now, I needed to get out of the mountains and let my wife know I was okay. The nearest phone was at least fifty miles away from where I was standing. She would be expecting me in a few hours and when I did not arrive, she'd be worried, not to mention I needed to call my boss in the morning to let him know I couldn't make it to work and why. The way I saw it, I just completely and totally fucked up my life. My only means of transportation was totaled and if I couldn't get to a phone I might lose my job for a no-call, no-show.

Walking The Red Road To Forever

In this part of the California wilderness, during the summer months, the soil is a fine red powdery clay. When it is dry and you drive on it, it turns into a huge choking plume of fine red dust. The dust gets into everything. There is no way to keep it out of your vehicle, your mouth, your lungs. You become part of the earth when you go out there and the earth becomes part of you.

I was way out onto the rutty forest roads and through the rocky creek crossings of the Mendocino National Forest. I had traveled way out into the Snow Mountain Wilderness Area, then up to the top of a god-forsaken peak called Goat Mountain and south along the Pacific Ridge. This is where I met with the Hand of Fate, or my own stupidity, one or the other.

Suddenly, I found myself way up on top of the Pacific Ridge with no wheels. Not only that but all my gear was a hundred feet below me in the truck. Now, my only options were the extremely harsh ones. I had to climb back down to the truck one more time to grab my backpack and to make sure I had enough water, warm clothes and food with me to survive for a while. I grabbed my flash light and some extra batteries which I would need to get myself out of there. Once I was back up on the road, and I was sure I had everything I needed, I started off into the night, on foot.

I headed back the way I came, walking on the ridge road toward the main forest road. About an hour later, when I came to the five-corner intersection on top of the crest line of the ridge, near the Snow Mountain cut off, I had a critical decision to make. Was I going to set off east toward the Lett's Lake Campground? This probably would have been the wise choice, because it was relatively close, by comparison to the town of Upper Lake. But if I went there, toward the direction of the forest service office and ranger station in Stonyford, I would undoubtedly wind up introducing myself to a lot of people I would rather not know. My other option was to anonymously head off the ridge to the west, where I might eventually catch a ride, with no one in particular, back to Upper Lake, maybe in the morning?

At that point, I thought it might be best just to try to sneak out of the wilderness without making myself known to the rangers or the County Sheriff. I thought it might be a bad idea to come walking out of the night into Lett's Lake Campground and consult the campground host, who could probably radio for help. I didn't want to have to explain what I was doing so far out in the wilderness without a vehicle.

I looked out toward the west and the vast deep blackness of the Snow Mountain Wilderness at night, toward Bear Creek thousands of feet down in the valley below, and I set off toward the side of the starlit sky with the setting moon. I headed down the mountain into a deeply black dark area of the Mendocino National Forest. Looking across the landscape at night from the top of the ridge, there was not a single point of light to be seen anywhere in the vast expanse of territory before me. It was, in the truest sense, a perfect wilderness. I had enough moonlight at this hour to see pretty well, but the moon was making a slow arc for the horizon and it already was most of the way there. It would only be a few hours before I would be under a moonless sky. The sky was as clear as a bell and the stars were spread out across the sky as far as the eye could see. Though I had one of the most amazing sky views on earth spread out before me, with zero light pollution, I wasn't interested in marveling at the wonder of the Milky Way galaxy, at all. I had a whole lot of earth to contend with right then.

I knew the road like the back of my hand, I was just a little worried about bears, herds of elk and mountain lions, all of which I hoped would be sleeping. I would have been totally unprepared for an attack at that instant. I had nothing with me but a backpack with a little food and about a gallon of water. I decided to leave the sleeping bag in the truck because it was summer, still rather warm and I didn't want to carry it all that way. The bag I had brought was kind of heavy, more for camping, not for a trekking expedition.

Over a period of about six hours, I made my way down off of Snow Mountain and the pacific ridge into Bear Creek Campground area. The campsites in this area at the time were classified as rustic campsites. There was nothing there but fire rings made out of stone and a few picnic tables. There was no one in the campground when I arrived about 3am. Even the moonlight was gone. I thought I might sleep on one of the tables and make my way out in the morning when it would be more likely to cross paths with someone. Besides, the downhill section of my journey was now over. It was all uphill from this point on.

I lay down across a tabletop to try and get some sleep but I started to get the shivers. Down in the valley, next to the rushing waters of Bear Creek, it was suddenly awfully damn cold. I was wearing only a light jacket, which I thought would be fine for that time of year. I was exhausted, I had been awake since before I left for work at 5am Thursday morning and here it was Friday morning and bedtime appeared to be a long way off.

I decided it was best not to temp fate, to fall asleep and invite hypothermia to feast on my exhausted body. I pulled myself up by my bootstraps and looked across the deep, dark valley toward the river crossing, where I was going to have to get my feet wet, then start my climb several thousand vertical feet up out of Bear Creek toward Elk Mountain Pass. Off I went, dreading the thought, not having any idea how hard it was going to be to climb that mountain on foot. It had always been a bitch, even in a truck. It was a long, steep, winding dusty road that just never seemed to end. It was difficult to imagine what it was going to be like to walk up thousands of vertical feet in about fifteen miles. I had no choice. I was going to have to do it. So off I went, with waves of dread as my only companions.

By Grace Alone

When I finally came to the river crossing, it was after 3:30 am and I was truly exhausted. I walked over as many stones as I could find but eventually had to wade through the water to get to the other side. My shoes and my socks and my feet inside were now soaked through. Immediately as I walked out onto the dry road on the other side, I thought I saw a flash of light. I wondered if I might be seeing things. I stuck my neck up and tilted my ear to the night air, listening. As I waited for any sign of human life approaching, I didn't hear anything. I thought I might be hallucinating. I decided I hadn't seen anything and I would just keep walking. All of a sudden, there it was again, a flash of light across the hillsides of the valley surrounding me. Then there was nothing. No sound. No light. Nothing.

I was hoping beyond all hope that someone was making their way down through the switchbacks on the mountainside toward me. I stood there next to the river crossing transfixed; listening and looking for any sign that rescue might be approaching. It was totally silent and dark. I dreaded to think no one was coming. Sure enough, within a minute, I could see headlights streaming through the trees and light pouring across the valley as the sounds of a vehicle made their way down the main forestry road toward the crossing. I breathed a sigh of relief hoping the people coming would be interested in helping me and not just be some straggly hillbillies or methamphetamine-fueled gun freaks, or even worse, cops.

As the lights of the vehicle came swinging around the last switchback and bumped over the ruts on the slope toward the crossing where I stood, I could see it was a large Chevy Suburban, with huge off road tires, certainly a more than capable rig for handling these roads. I waved as they approached and the vehicle rolled up next to me and stopped. The driver rolled down his window.

It was dark in the cab except for the lights of the dashboard. There was man behind the wheel with long black hair. He was wearing some form of ceremonial regalia under his light jacket. Across his chest, I could make out, what in actuality was, an intricate Dakota Sioux Native American bone breastplate, though I didn't know it by name at the time. Other than this, he appeared to be dressed ordinary clothes. Next to him in the passenger seat was a woman holding the most adorable little girl with big dark eyes, and a ton of messy long black hair tumbling down all around her face, looking very curiously at me. Before the man spoke to me, it was as if he was finishing a conversation with a voice coming from behind him in the vehicle.

He said, "All right, all right. No problem. Okay, I got it." Then he looked at me. "What's up, bro? Are you okay?"

"Thanks for stopping. Actually, I'm not. I lost my truck off the side of the mountain up on top of the ridge and I have been hiking for about six hours." It was more than a little awkward as I wasn't sure what to ask him for. We were heading opposite directions. He was heading into the wilderness and I was trying to get out.

"Are you guys going to the campground to camp?" I asked, "I need to get to Upper Lake to let my wife know I am okay, she's going to be worried about me. I know it's a long way. Will you be going back that way tomorrow?" I asked, meaning later that day. "Do you have a blanket I could use tonight and maybe I can catch a ride into town whenever you, or someone is going that way?"

He kept turning around to his right as if gesturing to someone behind him who was telling him something. Then he said to me, "I'll tell you what, bro. You seem like a good guy. We don't normally help people out here because there are a lot of Yahoos out here. Ya know, Rednecks and gun-toting crazies." He explained. "I own Bear Creek Ranch and you are standing on it. So, my house is right there." He pointed to a small hill across the river. "Why don't you get in. I'll give you a place to sleep tonight in one of my little cabin units and we can work the rest of this out in the morning."

As the driver said that, the woman opened the front passenger door, the dome light popped on, as she and the little girl scurried over the front seat into the back. I went around the passenger side and climbed into the seat, collapsing my weight into the soft, warm, leather upholstery of that sweet Suburban. I felt a sense of infinite relief wash over my entire body as I sat back into the comfortable seat, knowing I didn't have to walk up the side of that mountain that night. I remember thinking, "Damn, I need to get me one of these Suburbans. This is nice!"

Still parked, the driver turned to me and smiled. He said, "Hey, bro! My name is Gino. This is Leticia and this is my daughter, Jade. Fermín is in the back." I only registered the little girl and the woman. I could not see anyone else. "It looks like you have had better nights!" he laughed as he let the truck idle. "I own all this property around here. 640 acres. We are kind of in the same boat as you right now." He explained. "We are just now returning from a long journey. We had to eclipse our travels because we received some very bad news and we are coming home to check it out and see what the damage is."

He told me, "We have been at the bottom of the Grand Canyon. We were involved in ceremonies with the Havasupi, along the Colorado river there, when we received a message that someone has broken into our home here and vandalized it. They said who ever it was stole a lot of our equipment. I am pretty sure I know who it was."

With that, he put the big Suburban into gear and blasted out across the water. "Hang on!" he yelled as the front of the truck splashed into the river. Crossing the river got his adrenaline pumping as he roared across the water he began shouting out loud. "Those damn Yahoo motherfuckers breaking into my ranch and stealing my family's private property! Nothing but bunch of redneck yahoo motherfuckers!" Gino yelled. The truck rocked back and forth wildly as we accelerated out across the water and the stones of the riverbed, until we popped out the other side of the river onto the road.

"We'll see what the damage is right now. We've been on the road for over fifteen hours!" he told me, "I hope its not as bad as they said."

I could see the house now. I remembered it from my many passages across the river. I didn't think anyone lived there. I always assumed it was an old abandoned place. It had an old tin roof with a big stone chimney. When I would drive by, I used to tell myself that sorcerers lived there, like it was don Juan's house. The view of it was mostly obstructed by fir, pine and tall dense manzanita which covered most of the hillside. He drove past the house to the top of the hill, then pulled into a dirt driveway. The driveway passed back down the hill through the manzanita and over a ways to a six-foot high chain link fence surrounding the main compound. The fence had three rows of barbed-wire extending along the top, all around the compound, to keep wayward creatures from breeching the perimeter. Gino jumped out, very excited and angry yelling the same kind of statements he had been making as we crossed the river.

Leticia and Jade climbed out of the back of the vehicle. Then, as I stood outside the passenger door, suddenly an agile figure appeared from the very back of the vehicle. A man with long, brown, thin hair came sliding over the back seat, reaching out through the open window of the back door, his hand latched onto the luggage rack on the roof. He pulled himself by his arms, sliding through the damn window in one fluid motion, landing feet-first on the ground. He moved like an acrobat. He looked at me with his wild eyes blazing, his long, brown hair framed his chiseled face making him look quite striking. He gestured by jutting his chin. He seemed to regard me very seriously. I said hello to him but he did not speak a word. He then smiled broadly and seemed to regard me with amusement.

Gino was fumbling with the keys to the lock on the heavily chained gate as Fermín held the barbed wire down with one hand, pulling himself up and over the fence with the agility of a gymnast. "That's Fermín, brother. It's okay, he doesn't speak English." He explained to me. "He is a medicine warrior. You need to thank him. He's the reason we picked you up. Like I said, we rarely help people out here." The lock finally came open as Gino rolled aside the big section of chain link gate. As he was rolling it he began yelling in anger again.

"Because when you do, this is what happens. These Motherfuckers! These damn Yahoos always stab you in the back! You try to help people and all they do it steal from you. They take your shit and they break in and they ruin everything. This is so fuckin' violating!" He screamed as he entered his compound surveying the damage. "They violated our sacred site! Our sanctuary!"

Leticia gestured for me to stand at a spot next to the house and said I should wait here. She was a very soft-spoken woman with long, straight black hair. She spoke English, well-enough. She appeared to be very gentle and naturally friendly. I think she was tired after the long trip and it was after 3 a.m. Then she quickly entered a small sleeping cabin, just off the main house, with the little girl. Gino and Fermín had gone around the front of the main house. I could hear Gino rattling things around and swearing loudly as he made discovery after discovery of things that were damaged or stolen. Every time he found something not as he left it, I could hear him banging stuff, exclaiming loudly and letting out long strings of swear words as he cussed his way around the compound.

About five minutes later, as I waited, tired and cold, he eventually made his way back toward his truck, where I was standing nervously. I did not want to enter the area until he invited me in. "Oh, sorry. It's okay, bro. I'm not always like this. Forgive me." He said. "Why don't you come this way and I'll show you where you can make yourself at home." It was such a relief. Gene's voice was so calming on what was such a monumentally horrible night for me, and for him too, evidently. Whatever he was angry about was understood. I had clear feelings that, underneath it all, he was trustworthy person. He was someone I could have confidence in. I was just struck dumb at my luck in meeting him right then, of all people. I liked him. I could tell he was a good man, a high-quality person, a decent man of moral character, even though he was pissed off and swearing like a sailor. Under the circumstances, it wasn't out of proportion to the situation.

He took me around to the front of the house under a ramada, where there was an antique cast iron wood cook stove in a outdoor kitchen and dining area. We entered a screened-in porch and he showed me the damage to the front door where they had broken in. They had kicked it in, tore the lock right off and busted the door frame clean through. The inside of the main house was very spacious and although it seemed old, originally built in the 1920's maybe, it was clean and had a lot of character. It was unexpectedly comfortable. Aside from being a rustic hunting cabin on the outside, it was obvious it was under the care of a woman's touch. Many items were there purely for decorative aesthetics. Arrangements of dried flowers and native plants were placed in all the right places around the main living space. A stunning collection of Navajo style blankets were draped, just so, across furniture and chairs and the walls were hung with Native American art and artifacts in just the right locations, so as to lend balance to what would be otherwise empty walls. It was not at all overly-cluttered. Though the place had been tossed rather thoroughly, none of what made this house a home was touched by the burglars. They were after something specific, in my opinion, items of immediate resale value.

The rectangular shape of the main house was divided in two by a bedroom off to the right. The main room, contained the full kitchen, dining table and an ample living space in front of the large stone fireplace. This was about two thirds of the rectangle, the bedroom off to the side was about one third. There was a small walk-in closet-sized room off the back wall of the house, just big enough to sleep in, where Gino told me they kept all their sacred medicine. He told me this area was left completely undisturbed.

"They knew better than to mess with sacred medicine objects." He chuckled. "I would hate to think they would be that stupid." I could see a buffalo skull and feathers and Native American style blankets and beadwork, all manner of skins and drums, bags of sage and other ceremonial objects. He took off his chest plate regalia and laid it across the pile of materials in that room then he came out and quietly clicked the door closed behind him.

He and Fermín looked at each other and spoke in Spanish. They both agreed that it was pretty bad, a couple of generators were taken. One of the outbuildings had been broken into and some ranch equipment was stolen, but what were they going to do? They agreed to call it a night and deal with the rest in daylight. Fermín quietly left and I could hear him make his way around the back of the house and join Leticia and the little girl in the tiny cabin. I could hear their muffled conversation going on for quite a while after. Gino had already started a fire in the fireplace as soon as we'd come in. I had been helping it along, getting it going while he was settling in. There was a couch, a coffee table and a soft, fur rug on the floor in front of the fire place. I was just sitting on the rug with my back against the table, tending the fire.

Gino finally sat down. He took a big sigh and shook his head, "I don't know, bro. People these days. They just don't respect what is sacred anymore. You know?"

"Yes, I know, my friend. The whole world appears to be going insane." I replied. I was anxious to ask him what his plans were for the next day. I really needed to get to town where there would be a payphone and I could call my wife.

Gino anticipated my urgency. "I know you've been through quite an ordeal and everything tonight. I just want you to know, that in spite of all of this," he gestured to everything around him, which was ransacked and in disarray, "We're going to help you out."

"Like I said, we normally don't help people out here. They are not like us, the people who come out here. They come out here with .50 caliber machine guns on the back of trucks shooting all the trees and killing every creature that moves. For this reason, we prefer to keep to ourselves and do our own thing and prefer to just be left alone. We don't socialize with the folks out here." He laughed. His smile was soft and kind. He was as tired as I was. I told him I spent a lot of time in this wilderness and I was well aware of all the creepy people and scary behavior that went on out here. I made sure to mention that once you get away from these more central places around the rivers and campgrounds, there is a lot of deeper wilderness where no one ever goes. I told him, "There are places out here I could show you, beautiful places, in the more remote areas, way up on the ridges, where you could sit for days and never see or hear another soul."

He was listening very carefully to what I was saying. Then he said to me, "We are medicine people. We practice the Lakota way of Native American spirituality and we do our ceremonies here, next to the river. This property is our sacred sanctuary. We come here to pray and be with one the natural world."

He began to tell me why they decided to help me. "The guy you met here, his name is Fermín. He is a medicine warrior." He recognized the confusion on my face. "A medicine warrior is a different from what you hear about when people speak of a traditional medicine man. A medicine man is like an advisor to the tribal chief, but he is more of a priest, with a direct tribal affiliation. A medicine man is solely responsible for the spiritual life of his tribe, like a Father, or a Rabbi. The chief is the tribal leader, he's a politician in many ways, both within the tribe and to the outside world. The medicine man is a high priest, he protects sacred traditions and runs all the traditional spiritual ceremonies. He is the keeper and teacher of the traditional medicine ways.

"Fermín and I are still young men. We are medicine *warriors*." He stressed the word warriors to distinguish it from the status of a medicine man. "We have no singular tribal affiliation but we most closely identify with the Lakota. We are very involved in their medicine way and spiritual life. Their way is our way." He laughed. "So you can think of us as Lakota Sioux, if that helps you. We just travel around the country and attend ceremonies wherever we are invited and we live in a sacred way. We know many tribes. It's best to think of us as Lakota Sundancers," he told me, "but we go all over. We are medicine warriors and all that means is, we just practice a ceremonial way of life. That's all that means." He waved his hand in a dismissive way, as if to say it's no big deal. He didn't want me to make too much of it. It was as if he wanted me to associate his faith as no different from being a Presbyterian, or Catholic, only they were Lakota Sioux medicine warriors.

"We recently returned from the Great Sioux Reservation," he continued, "where we are involved in the Sundance every year." He explained. "Have you ever seen the movie, *A Man Called Horse*? Yeah? It's kinda like that. That's a movie," he laughed, "but out there, those guys are really doing it."

He told me that according to the white man's laws the Sundance is technically illegal. Sundancers pierce themselves, through the skin of their chest and attach themselves to the sun pole with tethers. They can also pierce their backs and drag buffalo skulls while dancing around the sun pole. After dancing four days of ceremony in the hot sun, they tear themselves loose from the pole in an act of self-transcendence. I kind of understood. I had seen the movie, so I knew what the Sundance was. I knew enough to realize these guys were into some awfully heavy shit.

Apparently, Fermín had been a Sundancer for many years. He would travel every year from his home in Guatemala to join the Sioux in ceremony. Gino explained that Fermín was in his seventh year. He danced the traditional four years, in the ceremony and re-upped again for another four year commitment to dance in the ceremony.

He explained to me that when they came to the river crossing and saw me standing there, Fermín had told Gino that I was a warrior on a spiritual quest. By tradition, if medicine people are involved in an endeavor directly related to their spiritual practice, (as they were in returning to their sanctuary) and they encounter a warrior on a quest, no matter where it is, they are bound by the spirit to do whatever the warrior asks of them. They are not under any obligation to help ordinary civilians, only warriors, and only those who are actively in the midst of a spiritual quest, actively engaged tasks of spiritual self-empowerment. When a warrior is actively engaged in the act of seeking his own self-empowerment, he is said to be on a quest, such as a vision quest, for example. If anyone, in the midst of their quest, crosses their path under conditions of distress, they feel it is their heartfelt duty to assist them in any way the warrior asks. He explained that Fermín saw me as a warrior on a quest and I was definitely in distress.

"You asked for a blanket and a ride into town." He said, "A very humble request in your situation, bro. So, I have no problem helping you out."

"Normally, you don't want to let the people around here get close to you.

They're just not like us." He said, "But Fermín said you are okay. So, I trust his judgment." He pointed in the direction of the cabin unit behind the house where they went to sleep. "That guy is a really heavy dude in the medicine world." He whispered. "You'd be surprised the people he knows and how respected he is in the medicine circles we go to. His knowledge of medicinal plants is extremely impressive. He knows about plants of all kinds and their healing properties. He finds them growing all over the U.S. and Mexico and he gathers them, shares them, because he knows how to use them."

Gino explained how he drives down to Mexico every year to pick up Fermín and they travel around together visiting different reservations and trading for art objects with the Native American tribes. Gino told me he made his living as an art dealer. In his travels, he would purchase Native American art and artifacts and sell what he could in his art galleries in the city, to keep himself going. "I am a medicine warrior and a Sundancer myself." He confided in me. "I am just not as far along as he is. Like you, I come from the ordinary world. But he lives out here full-time. He lives by Grace alone." Gesturing toward Fermín's direction. "It's just very humbling to be allowed to see the things I've seen and go to pray with the traditional medicine people we know."

We finished talking and he called it a night. He told me I could sleep in front of the fire, or on the couch if I wanted, and he would take me to town in the morning. Then he disappeared into the bedroom and I was alone in front of a nice warm fire on a very comfortable fur rug. I couldn't believe my luck that night. What a night. I counted my blessings as I fell quickly into a much-needed sleep.

A Warrior's Quest

It seemed like I blinked and it was full daylight already. I was anxious, knowing I needed to get to town and let my people know I was all right. Gino was still sleeping but I felt compelled to let him know I was awake and would need to get to town whenever he could manage it. He was very gracious and let me know he would start getting ready soon.

I went outside and tried to fathom my situation. I had just dumped my car off a cliff on the mountain, then I walked about 25 miles in the middle of the night, where I crossed a river and was rescued by some Native American medicine people. I remember wondering if Fermín would know anyone like don Juan Matus or Carlos Castaneda. As I sat near the river and listened to the sounds of the natural world out there, I started hearing the sounds of

Gino and the others stirring in the compound.

I walked back up the hill to find Gino making some coffee and getting some breakfast for his little girl. Leticia was Fermín's wife and she was helping to care for Jade, the little girl. Gino's wife was visiting family in Hawaii and she would not be back for a couple of weeks, he told me. Gino said they were going to stay at the ranch until she returned from Hawaii at which time they would return to the city and fetch her at the airport.

Fermín came out of the cabin at that time and sat under the ramada with us. He talked to Gino in Spanish and they conversed for a bit.

"He wants you to come back, if you are able to." Gino told me, "Once you get home and everything gets worked out with your truck." Fermín' looked at me and smiled. His eyes were extremely clear and bright. He was very intense looking. Fermín was rather small, maybe 5' 7", 120 lbs. He was very slight of build, very compact. He was relaxed yet, intense.

"We have an Inipi, a sweat lodge set up down below there where Bear Creek runs off into the Eel River. There is a soft flat area there and that's were we do our ceremonies. Fermín is going to run the sweat lodge for the next four days so we can clear out this dark spirit that has descended on this place since we were gone. We left here a couple of months ago and went to South Dakota for the Sundance. After that we were in New Mexico and then down in the Grand Canyon. The season is basically over for this year but Fermín will be back next year and he has some other places he would like to go which are closer to home, around California. If you have time, he would like to know if you would like to go with him."

I looked at him in dismay, kind of puzzled. He jutted his chin and kind of smiled at me. It was a knowing smile, a very friendly and mischievous smile. He was looking at me like, "Hey, dude. I know what you're into... You need to see some of what I got to show you." I smiled back at him. It was a feeling of mutual kinship. Suddenly, I saw him in a different light. I felt differently, as if he were somehow a close friend I was meeting for the first time. I was excited to know these guys. We were going to become good friends. These guys were all right. They were just about two of the most down-to-earth people I'd ever met.

Just then Gino said we could go now and he'd take me to town. We put the coffee cups away, then he, Jade and I loaded in the big Suburban and we roared off across the river again. As the big V8 engine powered up the switchbacks toward civilization, Gino mentioned a few more things to me about Fermín. He said, "Bro! You should really take him up on that, if you have a chance." He shouted over the roar of the motor as we banged our way over the rutty, dusty road up the mountain. "I have never seen him do that before, ask someone to go to ceremony with him like that. He said he knows something about you, about your quest. He wants to help you. That's a very rare thing, bro. You need to think about that." He told me.

"He is a specialist in medicinal plants and he's just really well-connected to a lot of people in the medicine world. He was showing me all these different plants on the ranch. What they were called and what can be done with them. He knows more about plants than some botanists would." He laughed. He smiled at me and said, "Yeah, we'll get you to town here in another hour and you can call home and let everyone know you're good. But try to come back before we leave and join us in the sweat lodge. You need it after the kind of night you just had." And this time he laughed even louder.

As we had rounded the corner out of the forest, at Middle Creek Campground, I thought of that damned deer, how I would probably have never met these guys had it not intervened in my life that evening and damaged my headlights. When we finally pulled up in the small town of Upper Lake, not long after noon, he dropped me off right at the pay phone at the gas station. I thanked him and tried to give him gas money but he refused it. "Nah, bro! This one is on me. You let everyone know your okay and we'll see you soon." And with that he disappeared into the market across the street, with little Jade in-tow, to gather some supplies. He called her mommy. "Come on, mommy! Let's go to the store and get something to eat."

I called Denise at work to let her in on the whole horrible story. I told her that I was okay and was going to need a rescue because I was stranded in Upper Lake. Within a few hours, Denise pulled up in her little white Nissan Sentra and rescued me. I had called my boss and told him I had been involved in an accident the night before, that I'd totaled my truck and was unable to reach a phone until now. He was wondering what the hell happened to me. I let him know I still needed the job, now more than ever, and that I would be back to work the day after Labor Day. So, all was okay there.

Denise told me how once, she had known a Native American Medicine Man through her friend, Gay Luce, who founded the *Nine Gates Mystery School*. Gay had invited her to peyote ceremonies before I knew her. The ceremonies she attended were actually held for paying attendees of the very pricey, new-age Mystery School in Marin County. She had done office work for Gay and would housesit for her when she was away. Gay would invite

Denise, from time to time, to attended events held by the Mystery School. Although these weren't traditional ceremonies, it offered her some experience with a traditional Native American Medicine Man, so she held a healthy respect of what the people I met that night were into. She thought my wreck was horrible but she also believed it was kind of magical how that event lead to my meeting those folks and the invitation I received.

It was now Friday afternoon of Labor Day Weekend and all my problems had resolved themselves just fine. While we weren't going to be able to go camping now, I still had three days off, a sunny holiday weekend to enjoy and plenty of time before I had to re-enter the world of everyday life. We made our way back down south to our happy little lives in Sonoma County.

On the way home, I began realizing how close I came to my death. If the physics of how my truck left the road had been only slightly different, had the angle been such that I had rolled, in that little pickup, with no roll bar, I might not have walked away from it. I might still be up there, either trapped or dead. Shivers went through my spine and I felt sick to my stomach, thinking of what that would have put my family and friends through. For being a warrior on a spiritual quest, I sure did a lot of stupid shit. Not repairing my headlights before going back up into the mountains at night is one of the stupidest things I've ever done. It threw a glaring light on my bad habits of neglecting significant concerns. It was one of those unforgivable sins, which I came very close to paying for with my life.

Chapter Nine
CEREMONY

It would be a few weeks before we could get back up to visit the medicine people and thank them for helping me that night. We made a bunch of fruit-filled cakes and bought a few Navajo blankets, as a gesture. My wife told me it would be a sign of respect to bring a gift of tobacco. The same as when I happened upon yoga meditations, I didn't know anything about Native American traditions until after I was suddenly immersed in them, so I took her word for it and we put together a nice leather pouch full of fresh rolling tobacco.

We were ordinary working people, so we had to wait for our next day off to make the trip up to the ranch. On Saturday morning, we left our house around 9am, traveling in Denise's little white car. It was another beautiful California late-summer day, nearly Fall. The bright blue sky was perfectly cloudless as we left town and headed out into the countryside on the northern end of the Sonoma Valley. We drove for a couple of hours to the town of Upper Lake, then headed north through a valley mostly filled with orchards and small farms. Once we reached the Middle Creek Campground, at the upper end, where I'd hit the deer, this is where the world ends and of any sign civilization ceases to be.

As Denise and I reached the river crossing where I'd first made contact with Gino and Fermín, it was mid-September, the driest point of the year and we just splashed through the river like a song in the breeze. No problem for her little tiny roller skate of a car. The path through the river was well established, this late in the season. From there, it was a stone's throw up the riverbank to where the Bear Creek Ranch cabin was perched. As we pulled up to the gate of the compound there were a lot of people there. Children were playing and an older gentleman with some younger men was working around a large diesel engine in a open shed out back, their new replacement generator for the one stolen. I asked if they knew where we might find Gino and Fermín. He pointed toward the house. We went around to the front, beneath the tin roof awning there were several ladies sitting at a big table and cooking on an old cast iron wood stove. Leticia was there with a woman possibly in her seventies and a younger lady with some toddlers. One was the little girl I'd met that night, little three year-old, Jade. She recognized me, "Hey! I know youuuu."

"Ah! I see you know each other!" The younger woman laughed. She introduced herself. This was the lovely Bernadette I had heard so much about the last time I had been here, Gino's wife. She was of diminutive stature and of Filipino and Polynesian decent. I thought she might be Hawaiian since Gino had said she was visiting relatives in Hawaii. She was a beautiful charming woman, standing all of 4'11" with long black hair, big, bright, round eyes and a kind welcoming smile. She and Denise seemed pleased to meet each other, even thankful to have more female company around. Hanging out with a bunch of guys isn't always as fun for them. We offered Bernadette all the gifts we had brought and she helped us set everything down. I told her who we were and that we had wanted to come back and thank them for their kindness in helping me get home that night.

"So you're the guy they told me about!" she marveled as if witnessing a living legend, "Gene told me the whole story about finding you out here on the road." She explained. "Well, I'm glad you're okay and that you made it back all right. I'm sorry to hear about your truck but, wow, what a story!" she laughed.

"Gene and Fermín are down by the river getting ready for ceremony. You should go down there. They are preparing the lodge right now. Just go that way and you'll find them." She pointed out into the forest, upriver, toward the south side of the compound. The compound was perched on a small hill above the river. We walked out a narrow gate in the chain link fence, down the hill about a twenty to thirty foot decent, and out into the forest following the only path away from the compound.

Eventually, we could see smoke and made out a couple of figures in the clearing. Then, we could see we were entering an area of a traditional Native American ceremonial site. The sweat lodge was merely a primitive dome structure covered with green canvas surplus tarps and we could see everything opened up into a clear flat area. The soft sandy clearing contained a large circular arena, defined by a long continuous line of piled river stones, about 100 feet around. There were openings in the line of the circle at each of the cardinal points of the four directions. There were flags of different colors on long sticks at each opening defining the cardinal points. The sweat lodge sat in the eastern portion of the circle with its door opening toward the center, facing west and to the altar which was set up in the center. In the western portion of the circle was a mammoth fire pit, defined by a circle of large river stones. They were just lighting the fire as we approached and it was only just starting to kindle and crack a bit.

We cautiously approached the sacred circle, calling out to Gino and Fermín who now made eye contact with us as we entered the clearing. They lit up when they saw us and called back to us.

"Ah, Vincent! You made it!" Gino shouted as he walked toward us. "He came out of the circle to greet us as we stopped. Something about the way everything was set up suggested we did not want to enter the sacred circle without being invited in. "Bro!" He said in a laughing gesture toward my wife, "You look so much better than the last time we saw you!" He was obviously teasing me.

He turned over his shoulder and spoke to Fermín in Spanish and they both laughed like Gene had said the funniest thing ever. He turned back to us and he told Denise, "This guy looked like he had been out walking on the moon, last time we saw him." We all laughed at the hilarious gesture Gene made, opening his eyes as wide as he could, as if he had been spooked and holding out his hands as if trying to balance in low-gravity.

I introduced him to my wife and we talked about that night we met along the road. He explained a bit more about the break-in they had experienced and what was stolen, who he believed was behind it. I told him about my truck, that the insurance company sent a flatbed rig up onto the mountain and they actually fished it out from off the cliffside. It was in the repair shop as we spoke. He seemed genuinely amused. I really liked this guy and I could tell he seemed to take a liking to me, in return. It seemed we were just ordinary twenty-somethings meeting for the first time, it could have been anywhere. He explained to my wife about the circle and walked her around the outside of the ring telling her about who he and Fermín were and what they were doing here. He asked her if she had ever had any experience with the inipi, referring to the Lakota word for the sweat lodge. She told him how she had experience with the sweat lodge ceremony, through a specific medicine man and she had been to a non-traditional peyote ceremony.

"See?" Gino laughed to Fermín and I. "I knew these two had something in common with us." He smiled broadly and his eyes seemed to gleam beautifully in a way I had really never seen before. Gino was a very striking young man with an engaging charisma. He was a dead ringer for a young Carlos Santana. He looked just like him only much healthier and more vibrant. Fermín was a very mysterious, but friendly and approachable guy. Fermín had the same kind of shine in his eyes, only his seemed more diffuse, more distant and at-peace. The only problem with Fermín was that he spoke only a word or two of English and, approaching the age of thirty, really had no desire to trouble himself to learn it. So, communicating with him had to be done through a translator or by means of my broken Spanish. There were no apps in those days. Someone had to sit between us and tell us what the other had just said. It could be laborious for the person translating, and out there in the mountains, Fermín and I could only talk to each other in short spurts because no one was interested in having to work too hard. I spoke a little Spanish, just enough to hablo the ol' español. I knew the swear words but Fermín was a religious man, so those words were of little use as conversation starters here.

When Gino asked me if I had gone with Denise to the ceremonies she had been to, I told him I had not ever been to any ceremony or Native American gathering. I told him my 3x-great-grandmother on my dad's side was full-blooded Cherokee. I never tried to act like I knew anything about the actual ceremonies themselves because I really knew absolutely nothing other than what I'd read about in books. At this point, I had become more about formlessness than structure in my ideas about human spirituality but I realized that here, I was approaching a new framework for talking about man's place in the universe. I was coming into contact with a distinct spiritual taxonomy, with it's own glossary of terms and forms of expression. I had respect for this fact and was honestly completely open to experiencing anything they wanted to throw at me.

My only experiences in shamanic spirituality came from adapting the warrior's way to my daily life and reading books like *Black Elk Speaks* and others. I said that I had only read about the sweat lodge. I asserted that I was a voracious reader, and I openly admitted this was no substitute for life-experience. However, I had only read books about medicine men and traditional ceremonies. I had always wanted to experience it all first hand, but I'd never had the opportunity.

Gino broke into laughter. "Well, we're going to change this, bro." He smiled, "I am not laughing at you at all, brother. Forgive me. It's just that you reminded me of a story from my past." He shook his head as if he were speaking of something utterly absurd.

"It is just the idea of these guys who write books about our way of life. As if it's some sort of yuppie, new-age, fashion show." He chuckled, "I know you know this but, our personal experience of our ceremonial way of life is a very here and now type of thing. To talk about it and take photographs of it, and for white guys to stand before university auditoriums giving lectures and writing books about it. . . professing to know what we are all about, why we do what we do..." He seemed to struggle for words. "It's just not what we do. It's not our way." He shrugged his shoulders. "I have read their books and they don't truly understand us. The descriptions they give and the conclusions they come to are often wrong or condescending and misleading." He told me. "Our way is a way of silent knowledge. There is no way to talk about it. It can only be experienced, firsthand. You'll see." He assured me.

"It is possible to learn general information about the medicine way from books, about the philosophy and the way we think about life. But our way is not about thinking. Our way is about knowing, about experiencing. And this knowledge only comes from our deeply personal connection to our ancestors, the Great Spirit and our Mother Earth. She teaches us everything in silence. She teaches us about peace, and respect for life. She teaches us about balance and gratitude.

If people were to read the words of tribal leaders, teaching what their way of life means to them and their people, I can see how this would help. It could act as a good primer, for those who are becoming interested in it. But to think you could understand what our rituals do for us, that you could understand who we are and what this all means to us, without experiencing the ceremonial life for yourself. . . " He paused, as if looking for words, "Well, it's just wrong. It's not going to happen." He laughed.

"You tell me you have never been in the Inipi, or been in ceremony, with medicine people, and yet Fermín recognizes you as a spiritual warrior on the path. I mentioned to you how you're not like the other people we see around these parts, bro." He chuckled, "...all straggly with rotten teeth and gaunt. You look strong and your eyes are clear and bright. Your smile is so infectious, it gives you away, bro." He laughed. "This guy smiles like a warrior." He and Fermín spoke to each other in Spanish, laughing. "It's just something about you we recognize. Fermín told me you are on a quest. We don't know what your quest is but we feel obligated to help you along your way. And you've never been in the purification lodge? Well, let's start here. We are going to change this much today. All I can say is, this is your time, brother. You're overdue." He smiled, "This is where you belong. The Mother Earth is welcoming you. You are one of us now."

The Sacred Circle

Because I was with Denise, who they were only now first meeting, Gino explained to her several things he had already told me, that he and Fermín were Lakota Sundancers and medicine warriors. He explained that they were not Lakota Indians, by birth, but that they were ceremonial brethren with the

Lakota. He explained to me how the Lakota had taken them in, as their own, and given them what they feel as their spiritual identity. They took part in the Sundance and other ceremonies on the Great Sioux Reservation in South Dakota.

A Lakota medicine chief had come to visit them at Bear Creek Ranch and blessed their new site, when they first acquired the ranch. He helped them select and dedicate the site for the circle and had bestowed them with the right to hold traditional ceremonies. He gave Gino the soapstone with which he would fashion his first Chanupa, his sacred peace pipe, which made him a respected pipe carrier, giving him the right to conduct legitimate Native American ceremonies, pow wows and celebrations on his site.

"So, we're not just some punks off the street." He laughed.

"Fermín is highly-regarded by several Indian tribes around the country for his knowledge of plants and curing." He went on about how they had been friends for many years that they had met in ceremony with the Havasupai and then travelled together for quite a while. He said they just stayed in touch after that. "When he reaches the states, each year, I drive down and get him and we go all over. He knows a lot of really heavy weight people in the Native American world, Medicine Chiefs and tribal elders." He seemed to be thinking for a moment. "These ceremonies and events we go to" he paused, "You can't just read about them in the paper and go." He laughed, "There's no way to know when or where they are. You have to be invited and know the families who host them. This is the result of friendly relationships, tribal trading and ceremonial brotherhood with other medicine warriors. A lot of times we'll be at one event and get invited to three more throughout the year."

Gino was a young entrepreneur, a property owner and an all-around businessman of sorts. He had acquired the Bear Creek property, 640 acres, surrounded on all sides by miles and miles of national forest lands, because of its location and its history as an early settler's cabin at the confluence of the two small waterways.

"Come with me." He said, and he guided us around the outside of the circle toward the west. "Where we are standing is a place of power." He led us along the bank of the river and suddenly we noticed we were at the confluence of Bear Creek and the Rice Fork of the Eel River. Bear Creek was the main watershed for everything coming down out of the Snow Mountain Wilderness area. By the time the creek reaches this far down into the valley it has built up a pretty good head of steam and the water is rushing past as it joins the river. As it enters, there is a large pooling area surrounded by soft sand, red clay dirt and the large stone outcroppings which are basically the foot of the great Elk Mountain," he said, as he looked upward toward the summit. "Heya! Heya!" He yelled in a gesture to the spirit of the great mountain and chuckled a bit. You could see they had done a lot of work piling stones to make a swimming area a few dozen yards down from where the two waterways converge.

"All the life-giving waters of the vast Snow Mountain Wilderness flow down to here, feeding Bear Creek. All the watershed from the mountains south of here are feeding the Rice Fork and everything from all of these vast areas flow together and meet right here. It is quiet now. The water is peaceful at the end of the summer." He told me.

Then he shared more about the shaman's system of thought, "For us, water is the blood of the mother earth, a sacred, life-giving nourishment to all the living things out here. There is so much of it right here. This spot is very special, very sacred to us. This is why we placed our ceremonial circle here. This is where we come to pray. Fermín and I go all over and enjoy ceremony with tribes all over the country and in Mexico. We pray with them, we sweat with them and dance in their ceremonies. But this..." he said motioning with his hand, palm down as if patting the earth, "this is our home, right here. This is our private church. This is where we come home to pray. This is our sacred sanctuary."

To All My Relations

Gino asked us to wait a moment at the entrance to the circle. He lit a bundle of white sage and retrieved a large eagle feather from the primitive altar he had built outside the door of the Inipi, in the center of the circle. All of his medicine objects were neatly collected onto a table made with the round end of a cut log, covered with blankets and furs. A buffalo skull, feathers, shells, blankets and all manner of dried plants. He lit the sage bundle with a stick match and fanned it with the eagle feather until it was smoking on its own quite nicely. He fanned Denise down using the feather to move the smoke of the white sage around her. The sage smelled sweet and somehow faintly familiar though I had never seen this being done before. It felt very medicinal and relaxing. He smoked her down from head-to-toe to purify her with the cleansing spirit of the sage smoke, so she could enter the circle clean and clear. Then he did the same for me.

Once he had invited us to enter the circle, we silently entered into the traditional ceremonial life of Native Americans, in my case, for the first time. Fermín quietly tended the now raging fire. These guys were nothing, if they weren't well equipped. They had numerous buckets of water, a ton of firewood, which they had gathered from the land around the site. Gino had all manner of feathers and medicine objects. From the buffalo skull to dried bundles of white sage, fresh bay leaves, incense cedar and chunks of copal resin the size of baseballs, his abalone shell, he had so many objects, too numerous to name them all here. He was so generous with information about everything in his ceremonial life. He shared everything with us and explained in great detail every aspect of what they were doing, when and why they did it, as if he were training me for a day when I would carry on this way on my own. He also shared with us the thought which went into each piece. He gave us the backstory and taught us both about his Native American beliefs and the system of thought they came from.

He explained how they believed in the living presence of a Grandmother Earth and a Grandfather Sky. They believed all of life was related, through these two great beings, the way a family is related, that overriding everything was the Great Spirit, the combined, collective presence of all living things, the web of life. This is their creator. He explained how the Sun and the Earth had a relationship that started long ago, like grandparents, they gave birth to life and from this beginning, came forth nations, including our own lives. He believed the plants and the animals, all the wildlife everywhere throughout the ranch, and beyond are our brothers and sisters."

They spoke a ceremonial language using terminology which was all new to me but deeply meaningful to them. He began to teach me about everything in his ceremonial world. He would say, "Aho! Mityake hoisan," which in the Lakota native tongue meant, "To all my relations." He said he was making a gesture from his heart to everything, the Grandmother Earth, to his ancestors, to the plants and the trees, to the fire, air, earth and water which were all coming together here. For him, they were all his relations. He told us about his trips to the Pyramid Of The Sun, to Oaxaca and ancient ceremonial sites all over Mexico. He had a great love and knowledge of the rich spiritual history of ancient Mexico. He named his son, Quetza and his daughter Jade, (pronounced Hah-day) he had given the name of the sacred stone people. His entire being was wholly committed to this way of ceremonial life.

Gino, once again assured us, "If you feel awkward or unsure about anything, if there is something you don't know about, it's no problem, bro. Just ask me anything and I will try to share why we do things the way we do." He pointed toward the altar, "This is our way of life. It's not the only way. Mankind has many ways, but these are our beliefs, our faith and this is how we have been taught by our ancestors how to worship the creator. Now, it is time for us to share this all with you. We respect the Christian ways, as we respect the Hindu ways. We also hope they respect ours."

It was only a matter of time before the fire they built became a truly powerful thing. This was no ordinary campfire. This was a scary huge-ass fire. Fermín was on top of it, keeping it under control, but you could tell he had his hands full. He had gone from blowing on it to get it started to where now he was throwing water all around to keep the grass outside the circle from catching on fire. He was swinging a 5 gallon bucket full of water across his body like a baseball player would swing a bat, in order to allow a thin wave of water to pass from the bucket out onto the ground with each pass. He slowly made his way around swinging a little water across the ground within the circle as well, until the general area was nicely wet with fresh water. It was oddly refreshing to everything around, especially inside the circle.

"It helps keep the dust down a bit, too. " Gino quietly mentioned as I watched Fermín put down his bucket and walk over to sit with us. I noticed a healthy-size, gas-powered water pump half-covered in the ground outside the circle, with a pipe running down into Bear Creek. He smiled and said it was for emergencies only.

The heat coming off of this fire was intense. It had to be sending up tongues of fire thirty feet in the air. It would singe your face off if you got too close.

"Heyah!!!" Gino would yell, when the fire cracked loudly from time to time, as his way of acknowledging the power of it.

"It will calm down in a bit." He said quietly. He had seen this a thousand times and whatever fear we had about the fire's intensity starting a forest fire was gently put to rest by his soft assurance. "We'll head back up to the house in a little bit and let this burn down for a few hours. Fermín will keep an eye on it, then I'll come back down and give him a break. We will enter the Inipi just before dark. "

Though Gino was explaining to me what being a medicine warrior meant for him, he was introducing me to the entire spectrum of Native American spiritual practices, as if it were his sworn duty. He was treating me as his equal the entire time. It was as if he had already somehow come to know me as his friend and a kindred spirit. He never talked down to me for my unfamiliarity with his ways. It was always straight across. He was training me from day one, so I would be prepared for the customs and rules of the culture when it came time to follow Fermín into his medicine world. He was wasting no time bringing me up to speed.

I did not realize it then, but if I was going to follow them into the traditional and respectful world of the medicine people, as a white man, there was a lot I needed to know and respect about their customs and culture, so I wouldn't unintentionally embarrass myself or them. This was my opportunity learn what I needed to know about how to operate within the medicine circles, so I would do everything the right way, but most importantly, not do or say things which the more traditional elders regarded as offensive. I would soon learn there was a fine line there, especially when traveling between tribal affiliations. As in traveling between any culture, I found the moral dilemma in the inversion of right and wrong would flip suddenly, depending on who we were with.

He already knew I was like him and Fermín in my own way, because I honestly was. Their ceremonies were active meditations. For them, prayer meant communion with the living energy in the world all around them, the same as it meant for me when I was in meditative states, what I have described as being one with all the love in the universe. We were involved in identical pursuits. I wanted nothing more than to understand what the mystery of life actually is. They were content with the Native American labels they used to describe the world around them. They knew damn well when they were using words as placeholders to represent experiences which are impossible to describe with mere utterances. Their spiritual experience began at the edge of silence and extended outward in every direction to all their relations. They had an entire matrix of practices and lexicon of terms to provide a context within their culture for ceremonial experience to become a launching pad into the great mystery of existence. I had just come from somewhere different yet, we were very much the same.

Unbroken Circles

The afternoon passed. We returned to the house for a while and visited with the family. We had chance to get to know Bernadette a little better and even met Gene's mom and dad, as well as one of his brothers, Alvin. We changed into clothes more suitable for the purification ceremony. Eventually, we returned to the circle to tend the fire for another hour or two, giving Fermín a chance to take a break and spend some time with Leticia. Bernadette and Jade came down to the circle for a while but did not stay. Her and Gene had an infant son, Quetzal, who was sleeping up at the cabin. They went back to the house to get dinner ready and to keep an eye on the baby.

I wasn't aware of it, but the entire family were playing important supporting roles in the ceremony, by making sure everything that needed to happen for the rounds to proceed smoothly, was taken care of. While they did not participate directly, the ceremony was for everyone. It was a blessing. It was an honor to be a part of supporting the experience for the participants. In this sacred event, they all had a beautiful and ancient course of action to follow and through their duty to each other, there was a very deep bonding experience occurring for everyone, a renewal of their mutual affection for each other, for their sacred sanctuary and for the traditional the ways which brought them together. Everyone was equally involved, equally appreciated for everything they they were doing to hold the ancient traditions intact for one another.

The course of action was laid down centuries ago by the Ancestors and provided the road map for maintaining close-knit family and community ties. Everything Al Jackson told me to never forget, I found here entirely whole. All of the same elements of honor and moral decency, hard work, love and respect were all here and held in very high esteem by every medicine person. I would go on to witness, many times over, how their way of respect for each other and for life produced deeply caring and lasting bonds of affection, not only within their family units, but in their sense of brotherhood among warriors and in their extended community as medicine people. The medicine people are faithful. They are tenderly living their lives inside self-regenerative circles of energy and they know it. They know the power and strength unbroken circles provide and they are well aware of how difficult it can be to maintain them. They know if they are faithful to the medicine ways, acting with honor and respecting the living and all their relations, unbroken circles can be protected, kept unspoiled, and what is contained within in them is a warmth and closeness, a rewarding quality of life like no other.

They are well-aware of how rare and valuable this experience is, how fragile it can be, how few people in the world can even conceive of it. What they know and hold sacred is invisible to 99% of the world. They've witnessed the rest of the world trample it underfoot without ever knowing what they've destroyed. These are the survivors of genocide, a culture defeated by the white man's rise to power in America, a subjugated and conquered people. They know all-too-well how easily precious things, sacred circles can come apart, so they continue to walk in a sacred way. They have learned respect means to touch the world lightly. They want nothing more than to enjoy this exceptional tenderness in their experience of being together with the people who mean the most to them in this life. Being together is the most important thing in the world to them, to spend quality time together and enjoy life's bounty. The ceremonial life of the medicine people, in the natural presence of Grandmother Earth and Grandfather Sky, keeps them cleansed within and the hard work it all requires provides the solid foundation they need for this vitality in healthy relationships to blossom within their lives.

Gino, talked about what the lodge means to the medicine people. "This is the womb of the mother earth." He told us. He spoke about how it is a dome and vaguely resembled the shape of the womb of a mother. We were entering the womb of Mother Earth for a time, to be purified," he explained. "The fire, air, earth and water all come together in the womb of the mother, to give birth to a new life, our spiritual life. We are challenged by the heat to grow and be strong in spirit, but humble and down to earth. Because it's hot in there, when we pour water on the super-heated stones, the heat rises, so we humble ourselves by lowering our heads, becoming closer to the earth. Our prayers will rise up to the heavens with the steam." he told us.

"We will all speak our prayers, or sing our songs, or simply enjoy the silence and all of this will be purified by the fire, air, earth and water. At the end of each round, I'll open the flap and everything we did, everything we said, everything we felt inside the womb, all of our tears, all of our pain, all of our prayers will rise up with the heat and the steam, sending our prayers up to be heard by our grandfather sky. We will experience a spiritual cleansing together. We'll help each other be strong. As it should be. Together we are many times stronger than we are alone."

"Sometimes the heat feels like a challenge for us and we feel like we have gone through a tremendous ordeal just to make it to the end of the round. This is the toxicity of the world burning away, the purification of the body, mind and spirit. After four rounds are complete, we will conclude the ceremony, open the flap for the fourth time and quietly come out into the fresh air. Like a child being born, we experience a spiritual rebirth as we re-enter the world, as if for the first time. Usually, we come out of the Inipi and dive right into the river. It's up to you. Sometimes the water is too cold but today, we went swimming. It's good," he grinned.

In time, the fire burned down and the end of the afternoon approached, Gino invited us to enter the lodge. Once we were settled he calmly entered and called out to Fermín to begin bringing the stones out of the fire to him. Once there were sufficient stones within the inipi for prayer. Fermín joined us and as he entered, he brought the flap of the dome down behind him and everything went pitch dark.

* * *

Out of respect for the traditional ways, I won't describe the experience of ceremonial life inside the inipi. What is intended to be only a firsthand experience of the here and now, should forever remain precisely that. The place of the purification ritual in the life of the medicine people is sacred to them and I wouldn't want to diminish the intention of their ceremony. We were honored to be invited to share in the experience with them and to learn more about how they felt regarding the mystery of being alive. As the years went forward, I was honored to travel with them and enjoy the ceremony of the sweat lodge countless times, with so many wonderful people, under so many different contexts. Many, many rounds of prayers were sent up into the sky.

After we came out of the inipi and took a splash in the river, we spent the rest of the evening in the circle quietly watching the fire burn down the rest of the way, before quenching it and going to bed. The next morning, very early, we kicked it over again for another round of sweats before leaving the ranch for the season. We had shown up in time to enjoy the last two days of their final four-day ceremony. It was a good weekend. We got to know Gino, Fermín and all our new friends quite a bit better by then, but they were leaving so it was time to say good bye for now.

Before we left, Gino asked me to sit down with he and Fermín. He asked me to give him my contact information so we could stay in touch. He said when they returned to the ranch, maybe in the early spring, he would call me and I could make the trip with them again. He began translating for Fermín. "I know you want to fly into the spirit world and learn as much as you can about the mystery of life. I know people who can help you in your pursuit of understanding, if you want." Gino translated for him, "Next year, I am going to a special event in the Sierras. It's called *The Gathering Of The Elders*. I would like to take you there with me. There will be a lot of warriors there and some Medicine Men, Chiefs and tribal leaders. We'll be doing ceremony for four days. I would like for you to meet them.

Gino continued explaining the event in his own words. "The Elders from all the tribes in the region will come together to hold meetings, to talk, and to pray together. It's on the Tule River Indian Reservation next year, kind of near Tehachapi, not really, but kinda near there. He's going to need a ride. If you can drive, he says you could all go together." Fermín was referring to his wife, himself and I. This would be an honor for me, I told him but I would need a bit of a heads up beforehand, so I could schedule time off work to go. He agreed and it was all-good. Gino explained to me how he would not be able to take Fermín to this particular event next year because of other business, which was required of him that week. He said Fermín was looking for a way to get there, since he didn't drive. He told me it was a good opportunity to help him out and perhaps the Great Spirit would reward me with something special for my efforts." He smiled. His eyes shining, "You never know!"

When we drove off, I told Denise, Fermín had invited me to go with him to The Gathering of the Elders, next spring. She was already in complete dismay how I could wreck my car off the side of a mountain in the middle of the night and come away from it with an invitation to a Native American sweat lodge ceremony. Now, she just shook her head. "You really amaze me, you know?" She couldn't believe my fortune. She completely understood what a rare opportunity and an honor it was.

The Gathering Of The Elders

I figured Fermín just needed a ride and there's probably not a lot more to it than just that. How many people he could ask who would take him up on that? As it was, it would be a solid nine hour drive to get there from the Santa Rosa area, since I had to go to San Mateo first to pick them up and this is how it played out when the time finally arrived. Over the years that followed, I would travel with, either, Gino, Fermín, or both, all over the West to native American ceremonies. Gino would invite me to the ranch nearly every time he went. I had an open invitation to stay at the ranch whether they were there or not and I took advantage of that opportunity.

My home, north of Santa Rosa, was several hours closer to the ranch than they were and I would make the three hour drive once or twice a month, even in the off season, if the roads were dry enough. They would call me and I would give them updates on the conditions up there. I became a kind of caretaker of the ranch when they couldn't be there and helped keep an eye on things up there. Having that base gave me greater access to explore the Snow Mountain Wilderness Area and the Mendocino National Forest, which I had grown to love so much.

I would often go up on my own and just spend time alone on the ranch, sleeping in their little cabin units very early in the spring when there was still snow on the ground. I would make myself at home in the patio area, cooking on their wood stove and eating on the tables set up outside the main cabin. I would build myself a fire at night and simply enjoy the sacred sanctuary of my medicine friends. It was six hundred and forty acres, precisely a square mile of deep quiet, surrounded on every side by endless miles of protected National Forest. Late in the night, the silence was deafening.

Eventually, the day came when Fermín returned and asked me to drive him to The Gathering of the Elders. I had to drive several hours to pick up Fermín and Leticia at Gino's place. He and Bernadette were there when I arrived, as was little Jade. After we loaded up the car and went to leave, little Jade broke out of her dad's arms and wanted to get in the vehicle go with us. She ran up and tried to climb in the back of the camper with Leticia, who was more than happy to care for her. I found it quite funny and so did Gene.

"No, Mommy, you can't go. They are going to ceremony, you have to stay here," he laughed as he pulled her back into his arms.

She struggled against him. "No! No! I wanna go! I wanna go!" She said.

"You want to go to ceremony?" Gino asked her. She puckered up her bottom lip and nodded her head at him. She looked sad to be left out of the great event. Gino tickled her and played with her and she kept laughing and saying over and over, "I wanna go. I wanna go. I want to go pray with the Elders." That comment stopped us all. We all looked at each other, like, "What the hell did she just say?"

I remember Gino looking at Bernadette and saying, "Mommy? What do you think? She wants to go pray. Can she go to ceremony?" Bernadette looked at Leticia and Leticia had no problem with taking her. " I said, "What fun! She can represent the whole Mendoza Tribe there." We all had a good laugh. I was actually surprised when Gino and Bernadette let little 4 year-old Jade come with us.

Gino and Bernadette's reason was clear, "Who could deny a child the right to pray with her ancestors?" She was a little bitty medicine girl. She was so cute. She was so happy to be going to ceremony with us.

As we drove off, Gino was kissing her good bye, with tears in his eyes. He was waving good bye. "My little girl… She's going off to ceremony! She's going off to pray with the Elders. Be good, Mommy! Come back safe!"

And with that the four of us began our adventure other, just like the night we'd met. Only now, Gino was taking a break and I was driving the gang in his place. The whole thing was kind of surreal.

We arrived late in the night after an incredibly long drive to this extremely remote location at the foot of the Sierras, north of Tehachapi, southwest of Yosemite. We had to first cross the reservation and then proceed out into the foothills, until we found a river. We started seeing campsites and Fermín signaled me where to park. We set out our tents with flashlights, as we needed to be quiet. Others were sleeping all around the area, though I could not see more than a few cars parked around. We set up camp in an empty site next to the river. Fermín removed all the food out of the truck and loaded it into the bear box next to the campsite's fire circle. He locked the box up tight and climbed into his tent with Leticia. I was so tired from the drive. It had to be 3 a.m. I fell fast asleep in my tent.

I have no idea how long I was asleep but it was still pitch black out. I was awakened by the sound of rushing air, wind, as if in a hurricane. My face was against the wall of my tent, which was made out of only the thinnest fabric. I awakened and without moving, I realized the sound of rushing air was that of the air moving through a large black bear's nostrils. The bear's nose was pushing against the wall of the tent to sniff my ears and face. The sound of wind and rushing air was the bear's nose against my ear! I could feel his massive body weight moving across the ground next to me.

As I lay motionless in the tent, I felt as if I were I were staring down two barrels of a loaded shot gun. The sheer volume of air moving in and out of his nostrils, was a powerful indicator of his superior strength, as he searched me for any signs of food I might possess. I tried hard not to panic. I was completely unarmed and had no way of defending myself had the bear wanted to eat me. I was actually in a pretty bad spot all of a sudden, I realized. I was terrified, instantly in fear for my life and decided playing dead was my only option. I experienced a short reprieve when the bear slowly lumbered away from me. I could hear him rattling around the campsite, looking for food. He came back to me and sniffed at the wall of my tent again before disappearing back into the dark night of the forest.

I was still very tired and decided he wouldn't be back. Though I was freaked out, I could hear others rustling around shouting at the bear to leave so, it had been a long drive and I had no trouble going to back to sleep. When I woke up again it was bright daylight and I heard a lot of commotion outside. When I climbed out of my tent a lot of people were all around and I noticed they were pointing at the bear across the river. He had returned for the breakfast hour. I noticed he was an adolescent male, probably only three or four years old and hadn't learned to have better manners yet.

A number of the warrior men and one of the elders came by admonishing us to keep our food safe and not to feed the bear anything, or he would not leave. I wasn't too worried. This kind of thing is an everyday part of life in the Sierras around Yosemite National Park, although I had never been nose-to-nose, or ear-to-nose with such a powerful creature in the deep of night. I felt he was personally welcoming me to The Gathering of the Elders. One of the local Tribal women mentioned he was the cub of a mother who had been killed by hunters a year or two before, when the bear was still quite young. They all thought he would perish but they kept seeing him around. She said he had a brother who also survived.

"People have given him food and that is why he keeps coming back. He thinks humans are a food source. Adolescent male bears are very dangerous and unpredictable. Stay away from him and don't feed him," she scolded us. Then she made her way down the line of campsites admonishing all the campers in the same way.

We made a nice breakfast and coffee, taking a long, slow time to wake up. It was not yet 8 a.m. So it wasn't like I was able to a good night's sleep. As I did slowly come to my senses, I noticed we were in a large flat space along the river and it looked like there was a big, colorful pow wow going on. The place was full of life. Families of all shapes and sizes were camped out everywhere. I'd say there was probably three to four hundred people there. There was a large arbor made out of cedar logs which appeared to be the focal point of the site, the main gathering area. I noticed the sweat lodge steaming away up the road, along the river.

Leticia would help me understand what Fermín was planning and when he wanted me to do things. Fermín told me that after breakfast he would take me to the sweat lodge and introduce me to some of the people responsible for holding this event. I soon learned when one is arriving, it's appropriate to seek out the senior elder, at any event, and respectfully acknowledge them, asking for their permission to join in the event. In our case, Fermín was an old friend but it was necessary for me to introduce myself and respectfully ask if it was okay for me to stay. Of course, they welcomed me with open arms. I mean, who wouldn't. Right?

The gathering was a coming-together meeting for a number of tribes around this part of the country. Among several Tribal Chiefs which were present, there were also many medicine warriors, like Fermín and the large extended families of all the Tribal Council members from perhaps five, or more, different regional tribes. Families upon families upon families, kind of like St. John's but for native American medicine people.

The sweat lodge ran all day and night at events like these. I soon realized the sweat lodge was a purification ritual, which was merely a component of these larger rituals, not the focus itself. At the ranch, sweat lodge was kind of a focal point, but at these larger events sweat lodge became the entry point to each stage of the larger event. Participants went there to cleanse themselves before entering the arbor and taking part in the dances and larger meetings. I was invited to go to the lodge as often as I wished, so I went three times a day while I was there. Morning, afternoon and then later at night with the medicine warriors. The later sweats with the medicine warriors came with a warning that they are able to tolerate intense sweats, so women and children were forbidden from these late night rounds. I went. I liked it. It was hot as fuck and they sang really fucking loud. It would get super, super intense in there. It was awesome! The Warrior Sweats were killer!

One of the people I was introduced to, as I waited inside the Inipi for the flap to come down, was a familiar face to Fermín. He spoke to the man at length outside the lodge and they were having some laughs together in

Spanish. Once they climbed in, Fermín noticed I was already there and he pointed me out to the man and told him my name. That's how I met Chief Crowbear. He was a Medicine Man and Peyote Chief who ran all the ceremonies of the Native American Church near Atascadero, California. He had a winning smile and seemed genuinely pleased to make my acquaintance. He didn't feel pretentious at all toward me. He spoke to me in English and we made light conversation before the sweat began.

Toward the end of the gathering, we had entered the arbor to hear the Tule Chief, the host of the event, give a moving talk and speak his heart to the Tribal Chiefs and everyone who was there. The Chief carried a strong and powerful presence as he strode over and sat down on a round of wood, on one side of the arbor. He respectfully addressed the Elders first, calling them each by name and speaking of their long friendships. Then he welcomed the crowd and thanked everyone for coming to support this event. He spoke over the gentle sound of a roaring fire, late in the evening at the close of the event. He was soft-spoken and though very tough looking, he had a gentle heart and it was obvious, he was a deeply loved and respected man. Everyone I met spoke very highly of him, with great admiration of his ability to lead and inspire his people. It was honestly a very beautiful and moving moment in the gathering. The Chief spoke with great tenderness about the plight of the Native American people and the fate of the Indian nations in today's world. He said their time in the world was short, that progress had closed-in on them and their days on Earth as a Tribal people were waning. It was an all-too-common theme at gatherings like these, I noticed in the years I spent with these folks.

He spoke of their young people migrating out into civilization and their inevitable assimilation into the common culture. He wanted to implore those in attendance, those who were able, to keep the beautiful medicine ways alive in the world as long as possible. He spoke of the teachings of morality and family trust, which are imparted by example at medicine gatherings such as these. He spoke of the special and unspeakable qualities, the heartfelt warmth experienced by those who live inside the natural power of sacred circles, respecting the medicine ways. He begged the Elders and everyone in attendance to keep their sacred traditions intact until the day when the last Inipi would finally be extinguished for the last time. There wasn't a dry eye in the house when he finished addressing the crowd. There was a great reverence for their sacred medicine ways and a tremendous finality in what the white man's world had spelled out for them. They knew they were the last holdouts, the last remaining flame of an unbelievably rare, beautiful and fragile way of life.

Then, everyone began picking up their things and leaving the arbor for the night. As if inviting us to play cards one night, chief Crowbear walked by, noticing Fermín and I sitting there, he casually invited us to visit him and "sit up the night" with his family of warriors, whenever we might have the chance to find ourselves in his neighborhood. He spoke to Fermín first in Spanish and then, very respectfully, turned to me and repeated everything he'd said in English. That was all he said. We acknowledged him with respect and thanked him.

It's never broadcast on the evening news when these things happen, or where they are. You can't pick up a paper and find an announcement of their ceremony times. Many of these traditional events are very private, almost secret, so you have to ask around and form relationships with others to learn about them. Just by their very nature, the white man is freaked out by the powerful experiences contained in many of these ceremonies. When governments conquer a people, they do not want them connecting to their own self-empowering rituals and religious beliefs. They would rather the conquered people be assimilated into the dominant culture. For this reason, the authorities have made some of their ceremonies illegal.

Gino had explained to me once how the Sundance is illegal according to the U.S. Government. That only meant they had to hold this traditional ceremony more privately on the reservation and keep it more secretive. The same was the case, in almost every state, for the Native American Church. It was almost entirely banned by the U.S. Government. It has found some lenience in a few western states. Mostly, it is held on a reservation and kept on the down low. The use of power plants is a subject of mixed emotions among Native American Tribes. Some tribes are very conservative and disagree with it. They don't acknowledge it and don't want the world to perceive it as a part of their sacred culture, while others embrace it completely and hold it as sacred sacrament. I don't need to tell you which side my friends came down on.

The Gathering Of The Elders

I figured Fermín just needed a ride and there's probably not a lot more to it than just that. How many people he could ask who would take him up on that? As it was, it would be a solid nine hour drive to get there from the Santa Rosa area, since I had to go to San Mateo first to pick them up and this is how it played out when the time finally arrived. Over the years that followed, I would travel with, either, Gino, Fermín, or both, all over the West to native American ceremonies. Gino would invite me to the ranch nearly every time he went. I had an open invitation to stay at the ranch whether they were there or not and I took advantage of that opportunity.

My home, north of Santa Rosa, was several hours closer to the ranch than they were and I would make the three hour drive once or twice a month, even in the off season, if the roads were dry enough. They would call me and I would give them updates on the conditions up there. I became a kind of caretaker of the ranch when they couldn't be there and helped keep an eye on things up there. Having that base gave me greater access to explore the Snow Mountain Wilderness Area and the Mendocino National Forest, which I had grown to love so much.

I would often go up on my own and just spend time alone on the ranch, sleeping in their little cabin units very early in the spring when there was still snow on the ground. I would make myself at home in the patio area, cooking on their wood stove and eating on the tables set up outside the main cabin. I would build myself a fire at night and simply enjoy the sacred sanctuary of my medicine friends. It was six hundred and forty acres, precisely a square mile of deep quiet, surrounded on every side by endless miles of protected National Forest. Late in the night, the silence was deafening.

Eventually, the day came when Fermín returned and asked me to drive him to The Gathering of the Elders. I had to drive several hours to pick up Fermín and Leticia at Gino's place. He and Bernadette were there when I arrived, as was little Jade. After we loaded up the car and went to leave, little Jade broke out of her dad's arms and wanted to get in the vehicle go with us. She ran up and tried to climb in the back of the camper with Leticia, who was more than happy to care for her. I found it quite funny and so did Gene.

"No, Mommy, you can't go. They are going to ceremony, you have to stay here," he laughed as he pulled her back into his arms.

She struggled against him. "No! No! I wanna go! I wanna go!" She said.

"You want to go to ceremony?" Gino asked her. She puckered up her bottom lip and nodded her head at him. She looked sad to be left out of the great event. Gino tickled her and played with her and she kept laughing and saying over and over, "I wanna go. I wanna go. I want to go pray with the Elders." That comment stopped us all. We all looked at each other, like, "What the hell did she just say?"

I remember Gino looking at Bernadette and saying, "Mommy? What do you think? She wants to go pray. Can she go to ceremony?" Bernadette looked at Leticia and Leticia had no problem with taking her. " I said, "What fun! She can represent the whole Mendoza Tribe there." We all had a good laugh. I was actually surprised when Gino and Bernadette let little 4 year-old

Jade come with us.

Gino and Bernadette's reason was clear, "Who could deny a child the right to pray with her ancestors?" She was a little bitty medicine girl. She was so cute. She was so happy to be going to ceremony with us.

As we drove off, Gino was kissing her good bye, with tears in his eyes. He was waving good bye. "My little girl... She's going off to ceremony! She's going off to pray with the Elders. Be good, Mommy! Come back safe!"

And with that the four of us began our adventure other, just like the night we'd met. Only now, Gino was taking a break and I was driving the gang in his place. The whole thing was kind of surreal.

We arrived late in the night after an incredibly long drive to this extremely remote location at the foot of the Sierras, north of Tehachapi, southwest of Yosemite. We had to first cross the reservation and then proceed out into the foothills, until we found a river. We started seeing campsites and Fermín signaled me where to park. We set out our tents with flashlights, as we needed to be quiet. Others were sleeping all around the area, though I could not see more than a few cars parked around. We set up camp in an empty site next to the river. Fermín removed all the food out of the truck and loaded it into the bear box next to the campsite's fire circle. He locked the box up tight and climbed into his tent with Leticia. I was so tired from the drive. It had to be 3 a.m. I fell fast asleep in my tent.

I have no idea how long I was asleep but it was still pitch black out. I was awakened by the sound of rushing air, wind, as if in a hurricane. My face was against the wall of my tent, which was made out of only the thinnest fabric. I awakened and without moving, I realized the sound of rushing air was that of the air moving through a large black bear's nostrils. The bear's nose was pushing against the wall of the tent to sniff my ears and face. The sound of wind and rushing air was the bear's nose against my ear! I could feel his massive body weight moving across the ground next to me.

As I lay motionless in the tent, I felt as if I were I were staring down two barrels of a loaded shot gun. The sheer volume of air moving in and out of his nostrils, was a powerful indicator of his superior strength, as he searched me for any signs of food I might possess. I tried hard not to panic. I was completely unarmed and had no way of defending myself had the bear wanted to eat me. I was actually in a pretty bad spot all of a sudden, I realized. I was terrified, instantly in fear for my life and decided playing dead was my only option. I experienced a short reprieve when the bear slowly lumbered away from me. I could hear him rattling around the campsite, looking for food. He came back to me and sniffed at the wall of my tent again before disappearing back into the dark night of the forest.

I was still very tired and decided he wouldn't be back. Though I was freaked out, I could hear others rustling around shouting at the bear to leave so, it had been a long drive and I had no trouble going to back to sleep. When I woke up again it was bright daylight and I heard a lot of commotion outside. When I climbed out of my tent a lot of people were all around and I noticed they were pointing at the bear across the river. He had returned for the breakfast hour. I noticed he was an adolescent male, probably only three or four years old and hadn't learned to have better manners yet.

A number of the warrior men and one of the elders came by admonishing us to keep our food safe and not to feed the bear anything, or he would not leave. I wasn't too worried. This kind of thing is an everyday part of life in the Sierras around Yosemite National Park, although I had never been nose-to-nose, or ear-to-nose with such a powerful creature in the deep of night. I felt he was personally welcoming me to The Gathering of the Elders. One of the local Tribal women mentioned he was the cub of a mother who had been killed by hunters a year or two before, when the bear was still quite young. They all thought he would perish but they kept seeing him around. She said he had a brother who also survived.

"People have given him food and that is why he keeps coming back. He thinks humans are a food source. Adolescent male bears are very dangerous and unpredictable. Stay away from him and don't feed him," she scolded us. Then she made her way down the line of campsites admonishing all the campers in the same way.

We made a nice breakfast and coffee, taking a long, slow time to wake up. It was not yet 8 a.m. So it wasn't like I was able to a good night's sleep. As I did slowly come to my senses, I noticed we were in a large flat space along the river and it looked like there was a big, colorful pow wow going on. The place was full of life. Families of all shapes and sizes were camped out everywhere. I'd say there was probably three to four hundred people there. There was a large arbor made out of cedar logs which appeared to be the focal point of the site, the main gathering area. I noticed the sweat lodge steaming away up the road, along the river.

Leticia would help me understand what Fermín was planning and when he wanted me to do things. Fermín told me that after breakfast he would take me to the sweat lodge and introduce me to some of the people responsible for holding this event. I soon learned when one is arriving, it's appropriate to seek out the senior elder, at any event, and respectfully acknowledge them, asking for their permission to join in the event. In our case, Fermín was an old friend but it was necessary for me to introduce myself and respectfully ask if it was okay for me to stay. Of course, they welcomed me with open arms. I mean, who wouldn't. Right?

The gathering was a coming-together meeting for a number of tribes around this part of the country. Among several Tribal Chiefs which were present, there were also many medicine warriors, like Fermín and the large extended families of all the Tribal Council members from perhaps five, or more, different regional tribes. Families upon families upon families, kind of like St. John's but for native American medicine people.

The sweat lodge ran all day and night at events like these. I soon realized the sweat lodge was a purification ritual, which was merely a component of these larger rituals, not the focus itself. At the ranch, sweat lodge was kind of a focal point, but at these larger events sweat lodge became the entry point to each stage of the larger event. Participants went there to cleanse themselves before entering the arbor and taking part in the dances and larger meetings. I was invited to go to the lodge as often as I wished, so I went three times a day while I was there. Morning, afternoon and then later at night with the medicine warriors. The later sweats with the medicine warriors came with a warning that they are able to tolerate intense sweats, so women and children were forbidden from these late night rounds. I went. I liked it. It was hot as fuck and they sang really fucking loud. It would get super, super intense in there. It was awesome! The Warrior Sweats were killer!

One of the people I was introduced to, as I waited inside the Inipi for the flap to come down, was a familiar face to Fermín. He spoke to the man at length outside the lodge and they were having some laughs together in Spanish. Once they climbed in, Fermín noticed I was already there and he pointed me out to the man and told him my name. That's how I met Chief Crowbear. He was a Medicine Man and Peyote Chief who ran all the ceremonies of the Native American Church near Atascadero, California. He had a winning smile and seemed genuinely pleased to make my acquaintance. He didn't feel pretentious at all toward me. He spoke to me in English and we made light conversation before the sweat began.

Toward the end of the gathering, we had entered the arbor to hear the Tule Chief, the host of the event, give a moving talk and speak his heart to the Tribal Chiefs and everyone who was there. The Chief carried a strong and powerful presence as he strode over and sat down on a round of wood, on one side of the arbor. He respectfully addressed the Elders first, calling them each by name and speaking of their long friendships. Then he welcomed the crowd and thanked everyone for coming to support this event. He spoke over the gentle sound of a roaring fire, late in the evening at the close of the event. He was soft-spoken and though very tough looking, he had a gentle heart and it was obvious, he was a deeply loved and respected man. Everyone I met spoke very highly of him, with great admiration of his ability to lead and inspire his people. It was honestly a very beautiful and moving moment in the gathering. The Chief spoke with great tenderness about the plight of the Native American people and the fate of the Indian nations in today's world. He said their time in the world was short, that progress had closed-in on them and their days on Earth as a Tribal people were waning. It was an all-too-common theme at gatherings like these, I noticed in the years I spent with these folks.

He spoke of their young people migrating out into civilization and their inevitable assimilation into the common culture. He wanted to implore those in attendance, those who were able, to keep the beautiful medicine ways alive in the world as long as possible. He spoke of the teachings of morality and family trust, which are imparted by example at medicine gatherings such as these. He spoke of the special and unspeakable qualities, the heartfelt warmth experienced by those who live inside the natural power of sacred circles, respecting the medicine ways. He begged the Elders and everyone in attendance to keep their sacred traditions intact until the day when the last Inipi would finally be extinguished for the last time. There wasn't a dry eye in the house when he finished addressing the crowd. There was a great reverence for their sacred medicine ways and a tremendous finality in what the white man's world had spelled out for them. They knew they were the last holdouts, the last remaining flame of an unbelievably rare, beautiful and fragile way of life.

Then, everyone began picking up their things and leaving the arbor for the night. As if inviting us to play cards one night, chief Crowbear walked by, noticing Fermín and I sitting there, he casually invited us to visit him and "sit up the night" with his family of warriors, whenever we might have the chance to find ourselves in his neighborhood. He spoke to Fermín first in Spanish and then, very respectfully, turned to me and repeated everything he'd said in English. That was all he said. We acknowledged him with respect and thanked him.

It's never broadcast on the evening news when these things happen, or where they are. You can't pick up a paper and find an announcement of their ceremony times. Many of these traditional events are very private, almost secret, so you have to ask around and form relationships with others to learn about them. Just by their very nature, the white man is freaked out by the powerful experiences contained in many of these ceremonies. When governments conquer a people, they do not want them connecting to their own self-empowering rituals and religious beliefs. They would rather the conquered people be assimilated into the dominant culture. For this reason, the authorities have made some of their ceremonies illegal.

Gino had explained to me once how the Sundance is illegal according to the U.S. Government. That only meant they had to hold this traditional ceremony more privately on the reservation and keep it more secretive. The same was the case, in almost every state, for the Native American Church. It was almost entirely banned by the U.S. Government. It has found some lenience in a few western states. Mostly, it is held on a reservation and kept on the down low. The use of power plants is a subject of mixed emotions among Native American Tribes. Some tribes are very conservative and disagree with it. They don't acknowledge it and don't want the world to perceive it as a part of their sacred culture, while others embrace it completely and hold it as sacred sacrament. I don't need to tell you which side my friends came down on.

The Native American Church

Chief Crowbear had invited us to a sacred ritual dating back hundreds of years, possibly thousands. No one knows. As the Medicine Chief of his Tribe, he was solely responsible for being the present day keeper of this tribe's traditional spiritual ways and practices. He was the tribal authority in charge of keeping this tradition intact for future generations. We located his site in a panic when we arrived late in the afternoon and were unable to find the address. We were a late arrival and everything felt rushed through so we could get inside the Inipi for purification. We could not enter the big tipi until we had been purified by the sweat lodge and the last round was about to begin. They held the flap of the sweat lodge open, waiting for us to get smoked down and properly enter.

Once we came out of the lodge, the world felt completely different. The sun was setting fully and we were invited to enter the big tipi, now glowing with the golden flames of a smokeless fire. I had no idea what to expect. This was my first formal Native American Church ceremony and I did not know the structure of the event yet or a single thing about how it worked. Once again, I did not know jack squat about an advanced practice until after I was fully immersed in it. Seems to be the theme of my life, to fly by the seat of my pants and learn as I go. I have always worked on my feet. Since Gino was with us this time, I had the benefit of his experience, his ability to speak English and his constant willingness to explain everything to me as we went along.

He told Crowbear this would be my maiden voyage and I may need some explaining to keep up with the pace. Chief Crowbear acknowledged my deficit and told me I could come sit next to him after the ceremony got going. Chief crowbar was a friendly enough guy, standing about 5'10" and of very slight build. He was a clean-shaven man, with shoulder length black hair and several grey strands setting in here and there, especially in his sideburns. He wore, what I can only describe as, a headscarf, which appeared to be a traditional medicine man type of do-rag. It was a solid color, made of unbleached canvas or some similar shade of cloth. While he appeared benign and friendly, we were now on his turf and his eyes blazed with a calm authority.

He was no different than a general, with vice-captains, lieutenants and many soldiers under his command. Nothing would happen unless he approved of it and gave the order. Most of all he was, at the same time, like any other teacher you would find at any ordinary school across the country. He was both. He was a strict and fierce leader of warriors, the senior authority in command, and yet, he was a loving friend and steward of a specialized knowledge, which needed to remain intact on this earth long after he had passed. So his presence came with an air of awe and reverence for the sacred, for a stewardship which has existed for thousands of years.

There was always an unspoken acknowledgment of our grave responsibility in handling such a fragile treasure. The tradition was practiced as much for the present moment as much as it was practiced for the sake of it being maintained and passed down to future generations. Crowbear was always actively involved in answering questions and pointing out how to do things correctly and not do things incorrectly, as everyone scurried around preparing the area for ceremony.

Since this is a quieter and smaller ceremony with about forty to sixty participants inside the big tipi at any one time, much is known of it and has been written of it already, so I do not feel any breech of confidence in describing a bit of the details here. On the first day, I had no idea what I was in for, my experience of the event is something worth sharing. I feel an assurance Crowbear would not have any problem with anything I am writing here. As with my Native American friends with whom I travelled, I would want for them to find this book represented them well, that their ways of life have been respected and honored.

There was so much going on, so much activity, gentlemen and ladies of all ages, children running everywhere playing. With forty to sixty people participating in the actual ceremony, there was an equal to greater number of folks acting as staff in supporting roles of the ceremony itself. As with most Native American ceremonies, they are traditionally held over a period of four days, with one full ceremonial cycle each day being considered one round. Also, it is true that each daily ceremony consists of four rounds. Some aspects of the ceremony, the sweat lodge, for instance, may occur within this larger format but happen in threes; morning, noon and night sweats, for instance. Once the fire was burning in the big tipi right nicely, he got the big ball rolling and the ceremony began to unfold in cycles. There was a water drum that went around the circle with a hand basket of dried peyote pieces, along with another jar full of peyote powder. Also circulating was a giant pickle jar of liquid I was informed was a tea made of peyote. Take your pick, play your song, here's everything you need to get your thing on with.

Crowbear gestured for me to come sit next to him. I was just miserable. I had woken up at 6 am and just driven ten hours to get there. When he explained to me that the Native American Church was about "sitting up the night," I nearly died. It was an all-night ceremony from dusk-to-dawn and the sun had just gone down. I could only shake my head. I was in for a long night. He explained the ceremony is a process of four very precise rounds, which occur over the course of the night, and in each of the rounds the warriors sing their peyote song and pass the drum to the next participant. I would guess we had about fifty to sixty people in the big tipi that night. So, I figured we were in for about two hundred and forty full-length peyote songs, plus time in between to pass everything around, not to mention the prayers which began and ended each round. Sleep was going to be a long way off and I was not accustomed to sitting in the dirt cross-legged. My legs kept falling asleep and I was miserable. Even with the big pillow I brought to sit on, my Peyote Pillow, I was still in for a night of great suffering.

Chief Crowbear explained to me that the suffering was part of the whole experience. "Your body is not going to want to sit up the night but you will focus on the ritual and you will overcome your little self. With the help of Mescalito," a traditional name for the sacred spirit contained within the life of the plant, "your big self will take over and that is the whole point," his guidance gave me reassurance that I could do it. "Your song is the vehicle which will allow you to pierce the spirit world with Mescalito. Do you know a traditional peyote song?" he asked me. I sang him part of a song I had learned from a collection of recordings I had of Native American Peyote songs. He told me that one would not be appropriate for his church. At that time, Gino had the drum and was going *off* singing his own original peyote song. He was proud of it because he wrote it himself. Crowbear just looked at him like, "Really, Dude? Are you kidding me?" Gino was over there with his eyes closed, just going for it. Singing his little heart out. Crowbear could only shake his head and laugh quietly to himself. "It's my job to keep these ceremonies on track. Then, I got guys like this, doing their own thing," he smiled.

He went over and took the water drum from Gino, after he politely let him finish his all-new peyote jam. He brought it back and sat next to me again showing me how the strange object worked and how to play it. Then, in front of everyone, he taught me a traditional song I could sing, in order to "participate *correctly*," he said scowling at Gino, "in the ceremony." He glared playfully at him. Everyone laughed. Gino shrugged his shoulders impishly. I learned the song and Crowbear took the drum and gave it to Fermín so it could continue on its way, uninterrupted, around the circle, in order.

This is a very strict ritual with not a single movement out of place. Everything is done as it has been done for hundreds of years, according to Crowbear. He leaned over and told me he was only fifty seven years-old and already a great-grandfather. He was a very friendly and casual guy, always relaxed and at ease. As we sat up the night together, he pointed out his son and his son's seventeen year-old daughter who was holding her newborn infant child. They were all in the circle together, inside the big tipi with us. This is what struck me most about the medicine circles I was invited into, they were family-based events, like any barbecue you might attend at a friend's house in Anywhere, U.S.A.

However, the medicine circles each contained the additional element of being centered in the ceremonial, which becomes a doorway to another world. Each world was so incredibly beautiful it would leave me breathless every time. These were family people and the nature of their ancestry placed a very high value on ceremony, specifically because, through participating in these events, respecting the ritual of togetherness, they were receiving a gift of ever-deepening affection for each other and for all their relations. These events enriched their lives in ways impossible to describe.

Their sense of powerful family unity comes to them through their ancestral ways. Ceremony brings the family together and keeps them close. It brings friends and community together and binds them in tribal alliance. It opens the individual to the universal and cleanses body, mind and spirit. At the most esoteric and universal level, every living thing within the natural world is a beloved family member to them. When deeply respected for their natural power, life inside these sacred circles takes on qualities so rich with warmth, outsiders could never imagine it. The only way to know happens by participating in it. The gifts of the heart one receives inside the sacred circles are of a measure impossible to describe. To say they have become one with all the love in the universe seems like a great understatement, since respect and gratitude are all equally inherent within their shared experience.

As the night wore on, the more peyote I could hoark down without throwing up, the better I felt and the less distracted I became by how much my legs hurt. I took very little at one time and I ingested it very, very slowly. I had a fear of vomiting. I did not want to vomit in the tipi. What I found difficult to process was how, for the medicine warriors, both male and female, vomiting was an accepted part of the peyote ceremony. It appeared as if it were the price of admission. It was the deeply humbling price to pay for the experience of journeying into the spirit world with Mescalito. They believed the humility evoked, by vomiting in front of sixty people, was a requirement.

They would all lean forward, periodically throughout the night and vomit into the dirt in front of them, usually very little, if anything, would come out. It was more like retching than any profuse vomiting, a side-effect from the naturally occurring strychnine in the peyote plant. Crowbear explained to me that he went to great lengths to get as much of the bad stuff out of the peyote material as possible. This was why they offered it as dry powder and also tea, along with dried cut-up pieces, it helped lessen the involuntary need of vomiting. As soon as someone would vomit, sitting cross-legged on the floor of the tipi, the ceremony assistants, ushers, if you will, raced forward to scrape the dirt into a container and another usher would quickly replace the spot with clean, fresh dirt. They would cover the bucket and empty it outside after each round.

After a while, I became deeply absorbed in the rhythmic flow of the ceremony. I began to experience a dreamlike ease with which my perception shifted back and forth between being in the tipi and the invisible events occurring, for me alone, within other total worlds of my own perception. The shift between states was effortless and completely unnoticeable. One moment, I would be in the tipi, and in the next instant, I would be involved in dream activity in a completely separate time and place, with different people, no less real. After a while, both seemed to be occurring simultaneously, like being present in two worlds at once.

Then, at once, it became obvious I was capable of two separate channels of perception simultaneously. One contained the physical world inside the big tipi and the other was equal, yet made of dream. Occasionally, the dream would overtake the world and occasionally the world would overtake the dream. While I was most grounded in my presence within the tipi, this was when I also experienced the greatest clarity. This is when I became most capable of reaching all the more deeply into the dream, with an ability, not to actually control, but to guide my activity along through the places I was traveling through. While I was playing the drum and singing my song, I was penetrating the void and experiencing personal empowerment and clarity of purpose in a way I had never known before.

It wasn't until I was actually sitting in ceremony with them, when I realized what the Native American Church was all about. It is a very formal, very ritualized and extremely structured peyote ceremony. The peyote is not mandatory. It's only there for those who want to make use of it as a sacrament. Nobody cares if you take it or leave it.

Even before I knew Gino and Fermín, I knew The Native American Church was a peyote church, but until I went, I really didn't understand it. I didn't understand giant tipis and how to erect them and take them down pole-by-pole. I didn't understand how to build a smokeless fire and maintain it throughout the night, as Crowbear soon taught me. I didn't understand peyote, how to take it, why they take it, how everything in the ceremony feels. I didn't understand the songs or what a water drum was, or how to play it correctly, but soon they taught me and then I knew all about it. From then on, I did everything exactly right and I became a part of their medicine family. I participated in the traditional ceremony precisely the way I was taught. By the end of the four day ceremony, I had experienced it all for myself, firsthand, many times.

For me, formless warrior that I perceived myself to be, I didn't know why every movement had to be so exact, why everything happened in fours. I mean no disrespect, it just seemed as if their ancestors were a little obsessive compulsive to me, superstitious, step on a crack and break your mother's back type stuff. However it may have seemed to me, this was their traditional way and I was honored to join them for the moment we were in. I was blessed to join them in this sacred experience of connection with Mescalito, to finally meet the spirit guide contained in the plant, to learn the lessons only Mescalito could teach. Crowbear was my doorway into that world, Fermín and Gino, my ushers.

I was entering a world where dreaming and waking were simultaneous, not that I hadn't been there before, because I had. I had made it to this region of consciousness before on my own, without any grease on the ol' ball bearings. However, this time I wasn't going to need a psychiatric ward, or tribunal of twelve doctors to bring me back out of it. Crowbear's authoritative presence served well enough to ring the bell in the back of my skull, letting me know it was time to stick to my guns and bring myself out of the state of deep meditative absorption. The medicine people's code of honor and respect provided the path back to solid ground in the ordinary world.

We sat up the night, in the Native American church, because we were bringing waking into our dreaming and dreaming into our waking. We were steadfast and upright all night, rather than horizontal. We were strong. We did not sleep, we flew on the wings of perception with Mescalito and kept in the right mind by having to painstakingly perform the songs correctly, in time, as part of a larger event, where our strict behavior mattered. We did not lay back and trip out. We would not have been allowed to, even if we wanted to. Our perceptions were powerful, but not intoxicating.

The ceremony was designed so no one could lose themselves and wander off into bad places of the mind. The reason it had to be so hard is because, if it weren't, you would never get to where you needed to be, in order to benefit. You had to be pushed, until you learned how to jump on your own and fly on your wings of perception. Each participant had the full support of the Medicine Chief and Tribe around them, giving them confidence and bravery to enter spiritual dimensions and take flight. The ceremony required lock-step activity, so there was no way to become lazy and drift off. One had to be aware and tuned-in to the present moment and function with the group, so when Mescalito took you away, you could not go so far as to be lost, or have any reason to succumb to terrifying visions. Your feet had to remain firmly planted on Earth. It was a safe environment for spiritual awareness with love and support surrounding everything. The sure hand and trained eye of chief Crowbear, his mordant sense of humor, made absolutely certain every step of the ceremony was performed perfectly to the traditional ways.

Over the course of the four-day ceremony, we were repeatedly invited to comeback whenever we were able and participate in any ceremony they might be having. We were welcomed as members of their ceremonial family. As long as our behavior was respectful and in line with their traditional ways, we would always be welcome guests, friends, and fellow travelers along the medicine road. It struck me that if I'd had this same kind of support and structure when I experienced my kundalini crisis, at age twenty, I wouldn't have wound up in the loony bin and there would never have been a crisis, it would have been a singular blessing. I may have come away from it with a lot less wear and tear and a great strength of certainty, rather than so many problems.

Now, here I was ten years on, and there was no crisis here. I was being shown how warriors behave in the face of immense challenges of a spiritual nature. I was safe in the presence of a master teacher acting within his area of specialization. Chief Crowbear welcomed me beneath the umbrella of his guidance, then demonstrated the natural power of the sacred circle.

Life within an unbroken circle was indeed filled with very rare and beautiful things, far more rare and far more beautiful than most people can possibly imagine. The masses fail to respect and hold sacred the immense value of unbroken circles, family circles, community circles, natural and universal circles, the give and take in marriage. My own ancestors had no such knowledge of how to carefully nurture healthy, deeply bonded relationships such as those I witnessed in the medicine world. There is no context, no path, no mention of the possibility anywhere in modern culture other then in our churches, and the white man's religion seemed cold and distant, to me, lifeless by comparison. This practice of familial and tribal empowerment is more of a lost art today, than ever.

What a sacred unbroken circle actually is, what it means, how truly precious and valuable the invisible qualities are in every aspect of their lives, this is the gift of the medicine people, which today is all but lost to anyone but them. This is the reason why there is so much sadness and harm in the world. The sacred circles through modern society have all been trampled and broken through ignorance of the fact they were ever even there. Only traces remain, both within modern society and within each of our individual lives. Most remain ignorant of the sacred knowledge of the unbroken circle and its natural value to mankind.

Those who come into contact with this magical power of universal affection for all of life are transformed to the point where they would give anything, sacrifice whatever they had to, to live the right way, giving whatever is required of them to maintain these deeply sincere bonds of caring and affection with the people who mean everything to them in life. These are the lessons of the Native American Medicine people. These are the kind of intensely personal lessons participants walk away with from the Native American Church, or any of the ceremonies and rituals of the medicine people. Most can't comprehend, don't have the capacity or just plain could care less, how rare and wonderful, how fragile and rapidly disappearing these medicine circles are in today's world.

Sundance and Ghostdance

Both the events, *The Gathering of the Elders* and *The Native American Church,* came with the expectation we would return year after year from then on. As well, there would be additional invitations from tribal leaders and medicine people befriending us at each, to come and attend ceremony with them, if we were ever in their area. We were building relationships and forming lasting friendships, sewing and nurturing new possibilities for personal growth into the future. This kept extending my access far deeper into the Native American medicine world than I ever believed I might go. I would also be invited to drive Fermín to the *Ghostdance*, traditionally held late in the spring, down in the desert east of Temecula.

The Ghostdance was another ceremony, which required, not just sitting up the night, but traditionally dancing within the circle of the arbor until dawn. You're looking at a solid eight to ten hours, at that time of year, on your feet, involved in vigorous movement, an active meditation, entering trance states while in motion. After dark, a large bonfire is lit in the center of the arbor, and once the ceremony commences, the participants dance counterclockwise in a circle around the ring with only the firelight to illuminate the time. It's a long time. It's a challenge. It's an honor to be challenged in such a way.

The Ghostdance is such an unspeakable, hauntingly beautiful event, which I did not expect, nor will I ever be able to strike it from my memories. It will live with me and haunt my memories for the rest of my life, as a part of me was changed through the experience of simply being there. It was so deeply moving. The songs on the air, the struggle of the dancers to keep pace with the marathon night. It's a fight in a war against weakness, against pain and fear, to rise up and endure to the very end, to dance the dance of the spiritual warrior, showing the ancestors, once and for all, what you are made of. The darkness, the countless stars, the fire light, the cool night air, the colorful costumery of the many, many dancers all shaking and vibrating in halting, arresting rhythm and sound. The breathing, the dust rising off the feet, flowing movements of a circular group of human souls animating both skeletons and flesh, clearly underscored the ephemeral nature of the living.

There are traditional songs which we would sing in unison, mesmerizing, haunting melodies, all the participants gathering in a harmonization of movement and vibration, the steady rhythm of deep and powerful drums filled the night, as if to represent the heartbeat of the ancestors long gone silent. We were entering a higher realm. There would be times of song and rhythm, times of wonder as if returning from a trance into a world of soothing silence in between each round of what seemed like an endless dance. Through the course of four rounds, over the course of four nights, we made the commitment to return for four straight years and dance with the spirits, to honor the ghosts of our ancestors and learn what they had to teach us. The pain in our bodies, the suffering in our minds and the weakness of our spirits are all sent through our prayers, which are taken up into the sky through the flames, through the songs, riding up within the smoke, transformed through being touched within a moment by forever.

Now, I understood what Gino had told me from the outset. There is no way to understand from the outside looking in. We have to participate and live the experience, first hand, to know how deeply it runs through us, how heartfelt, how intensely human their spirituality is. We need a vehicle to propel us into oneness with all of life. We can't do it alone. We need each other to be one with everything.

I could write a book about everywhere I went traveling with these two gentlemen, Gino and Fermín, and all of the wonderful people we met and the incredibly deep and rich experiences we would enjoy. The experiences, which would come from opening myself up to these opportunities, would bring me a daily sense of self-renewal and empower a peaceful connection to the earth, to all living things, for a lifetime to come.

Within a period of about four years, I had attended a fairly large number of very powerful ceremonies with them and had developed many new friendships along the way. At one point, they were preparing to go to Sundance and they told me they wanted me to come with them, they wanted me to become a Sundancer.

It was as if they were going out on the town for drinks and dancing. "Yeah, you can go with us! Tether yourself to the sun pole for four days. Rip yourself loose. It'll be great! We'll only be gone for a month or two." Sadly, for me, the month-long journey thing was the deal breaker. I am certain I would have gone, too, had it been possible. I had no fear of the sun pole, only of my inability to live outside of the white man's world I had been born into. I would have been honored and proud to wear the scars of the Sundancer's piercings for lifetime.

It's just that I could never financially afford to live outside the white man's world the way they were able to. I was born in it and I was stuck in it, a creature of the energy grid and monthly rent, a slave to the capitalist society, which had conquered the Native people. I had bills to pay. Steep rent and car payments to make each month and no safety net. I had a printing job in a small shop and I lived paycheck-to-paycheck. I couldn't afford to take a month or two off of work to go tether up to the sun pole in some far-off reservation in South Dakota. The thought of not being able to go and the reasons why angered me. Such anger is not part of the medicine way of life. Only reverence is, awe and humility. It was an honor to be asked, but for the first time, I had to decline an invitation to just pick up and go to ceremony with these guys. My circle broke.

These were unmistakably beautiful ceremonies, which are beyond the scope of this work to describe. There are just too many and too much is going on here to describe everything, to do them any justice. The experiences I had and the people I met could have continued indefinitely, but at a certain point, I could go no deeper into their world, due to time and money. I wasn't truly a member of their world. I was a guest. I was a warrior on a quest and they there to help me when I most needed them. From Gino and Fermín to Crowbear and all the rest. They just cared about my path and wanted to help in any way they could. They were all good and decent people who honestly cared about me as a person who wanted to learn about their ways. They lived to nurture anyone who held any potential at all to be a kind, decent and caring, as well. They would befriend anyone who was honestly sincere and help them learn whatever they wanted to know about the medicine way of life.

But I would never be able to make the break into living by grace alone full-time, as much as I would have absolutely loved to. It just wasn't my calling. I had to work to live. My fate would lie elsewhere and at a certain point, we all knew it. The break was instantaneous. I couldn't go. They left for the Sundance. I never saw either of them again. It's not that we couldn't see each other and it's not that I couldn't go down and visit with Crowbear, or the others on my own. We just didn't. Gene and I spoke on the phone a few times after that but never seemed to actually reconnect. I talked to Alvin a couple times, here and there but, out of respect for each other, and for our separate paths, we simply parted ways and travelled separate roads. Our time together had come and gone. Like dancers at the end of a song, we simply parted for the time being. These were beautiful years, with wonderful people all of whom remain among my fondest memories.

> *"Fred Rogers and Arnold Palmer, two men who would never come up dirty no matter how deeply we investigated their lives. Why are men of character such as these two the exception, not the rule?"*

Chapter Ten
OF GOOD
AND DECENT MEN

THE PURPOSE OF religion and spirituality is to make us better people. We practice spiritual traditions because we believe they offer a path toward the very best in us. Often, they provide a challenge, which helps to give our lives meaning. They challenge us to be the very best we can be, to overcome our selfish, petty concerns. We believe rising to meet these challenges will lead us to the highest quality, most rewarding life here on earth. I have long looked around, throughout today's world, for examples of what a good and decent man might be, once he has realized the fullness of his spiritual practice. I would assume spiritual maturity would extend into every area of a man's character, making him steadfastly honest, an example of common decency with not one skeleton having ever hung within his closet.

If a person were to practice a spiritual path for an entire lifetime, as many say they do, and reach the full maturity of the wisdom of their years, shouldn't there be examples of this exceptional personal excellence we could find? Wouldn't these people standout from the crowd, either in public life or as people we know in our private lives, as men of impeccable character? How would we recognize such a person? Why do so many of our cultural hero's, political leaders and religious figures come up dirty in the media and, to our dismay, fall from grace for alleged sexual misconduct or other horrifying failures of character when we once held them in such high-esteem?

Shouldn't we be able to find numerous examples of good and decent men who are completely honest, fair, morally incorruptible and extremely generous with their time and attention? And in fact, yes, they appear in the most ordinary of places, and they appear to be especially prevalent among athletic coaches, master craftsmen, teachers and all-time greats in sport. For example, Fred Rogers and Arnold Palmer, two men of excellent character, good and decent men, I always aspire to become more like. They both grew up in Latrobe, PA and even knew each other as kids. For the sake of conversation, here are two examples of the kind of human kindness, personal decency and moral character I am speaking about. Two men who would never come up dirty no matter how deeply we investigated their lives. Why are men of character such as these two the exception, not the rule?

I would have thought men of this caliber existed in droves considering how popular religion and spiritual traditions are in the world today. I expected to find a few good men who had absolutely no skeletons in their closets whatsoever, beyond any trace of corruption, men with hearts of gold. And while they do exist, men such as these are far more rare than I ever imagined, only a few in every thousand, maybe. I am certain there are a several in each of our lives, who slip by us barely recognizable. Looking back in my own life, I learned to recognize them and began find them where I least expected it, sometimes only after their passing would I come to realize they had lived a life beyond reproach, only to reassess how I thought and felt about them. Only then did their fine example, of what it meant to live well, to live the right way, reach me.

When I contemplated spiritual paths as a young man, I did so hoping I would come to know role models who were living examples of everything a given way teaches. I had hoped to find enlightened men and women who were kind, generous, truly forgiving, wise, knowing, radiant and joyous all the time. The sure mark of darkness which betrays a man's true character is contempt for his fellow man, he will rat himself out, demeaning others with a sharp tongue mostly due to his own ego. Listen for what a man makes jokes about for there lie clues to his weaknesses. When you find his weaknesses you can go after his faults. Do a little looking around and most likely, the skeletons will start turning up in his closet.

Men are weak and we are easily morally corrupted along the lines of our weaknesses, whether it be money, drugs, power, sex or whichever of the seven deadly sins might be our failing. To find a man who is strong through and through, disinterested in easy gratifications, set on what he wants to achieve in life, and caring, is to find a rare and precious jewel. To make an acquaintance of such a man is a rare gift because he does not suffer the company of fools for long. He does not make fast friends of idiots. However, to the degree that he will, in the time he allows himself to entertain acquaintances, we can learn by his example how to build a more rewarding life and live well ourselves. These rare and few men are worthy of our respect and we would do well to aspire to the code by which they act in life.

I had hoped to find sure-handed guides to a life rewarding beyond measure, who were supportive, generous with their knowledge and who possessed unparalleled understanding. It is a necessity that a young man find himself in the presence of good mentoring in order to develop into a fine man with strong moral character and sound judgment. Yet sadly, the men to lead them, men with strength of character, good and decent men of even temperament, generously giving of their time and concern, are just too hard to find these days.

I had hoped to find examples of this mentoring for myself, men who would be happy to lead me to the highest enlightenment, men of prodigious understanding alive and well in the general populace of humanity-at-large. My sincere desire to understand and make sense out of all the ideologies I was taught, from childhood through adult years, left me in a position of having many false illusions. I was certain I could find people with something profound to offer, a man worthy of learning from, who could share with me the knowledge of the right way to live, the direction to go on the path toward a truly rewarding life. I was not disillusioned, rather I was a seeker, looking for the examples of the fruition of traditional teachings, the people who embodied all of it and lived out the rest of their days in the beautiful perfection of the meaning of life well-grasped. Where were these persons? That's the deal right? You dedicate your life to a traditional teaching of some sort and it is supposed to be true. It's supposed to pay off.

Uhhhhh, well? It took me many years to conclude that I needed time, many years, decades in fact, to simply digest all of this hoopla I was taught and this would, quite naturally, all distill down into wisdom and into my becoming a better person. When I tried to find someone who had accomplished this amazing achievement, of becoming a better person, and talk to them, to learn from them, the ones I sought were the easiest ones to gain access to, the ones who advertise their services publicly, the ones who had books out in the market. God forbid, the published authors, the ones with best sellers. These were the ones with many followers, fans and a lot of people who are willing to pay to see them. Wow! These must be exceptional people.

However, I found them to be highly insulated, worshipped deities, sort-of-celebrities with special organizations who were responsible for keeping them inaccessible to an average guy like me. I had to join a community, cough up cash, become a member of something in order to one day maybe chance an opportunity to receive a "special invitation" to (pay a special fee in addition to) sit in the same room as the "spiritual celebrity", with a thousand other people, to listen to that highly-admired person give a general talk about really abstract shit and maybe do a short question and answer period.

These highly admired, spiritual celebrity people had a brand, a logo, printed materials, books out, several different programs you could buy. They had their own minion people who dealt with the public on their behalf, so they could focus on just being an enlightened genius. These are the clean-cut, well-dressed, friendly people who greet you like an old friend at the door. These minor minion people are the one's who have ascended in the ranks, who volunteer to teach the classes on how to be a better person, the way the celebrity person taught them personally, to become the better person they are today, like a super, really good better person. These minor minion people are the ones who come around looking for you, if paying your tithe happened to slip your mind. They also have a sordid habit of gaining extra credit by netting up meandering pretty young girls and ushering them right in to the celebrity better person, for personal tutelage.

If I took a lot of expensive classes and weekend workshops on how to be a better person, who knows, maybe someone who is a better person will talk to me and I'll finally find someone who is everything I'd hoped a good and decent man, or woman, should be. As it so happens, the people who learned from someone special, the students of the guy who is a fully realized better person, are themselves very anxious to help you. I found a lot of students of "a fully-realized better person" who wanted me to know how much better they were than me and how awesome it was to be a better person than me, and how glamorous it has made them to have close personal relationship with the "celebrity better person." They were quick to take me under their wing and show me the ropes. They were certified and authorized to charge $85 per session for counseling and services in the ways of the sacred brand logo. They let me know that if I wanted to be a better person, all I needed to do was to learn from them, the minor minion person.

Such is the way these communities work. All of them.

To Glamorize By Association

When a newcomer begins entering the sphere of influence surrounding a spiritual cult leader, a religious community or a set of teachings of some kind… (whether corporate, spiritual, financial, self-help or whatever the field of endeavor) and sadly, I have entered into many, it is automatically assumed that, simply because you are a newcomer, there is something wrong with you. You're not yet worthy of heaven, success, enlightenment or the highest state of being. Even if you had already achieved the highest realization of oneness with all the love in the universe and meditated in the presence of the light shining through the God Window within your own heart, they don't know you, so they assume you are an ignorant beginner. Somehow, they all agree... and they will convince you of it, because there is still something left you need to do first. It usually involves giving someone money.

You are not yet an enlightened man of knowledge, or whatever the term they reserve for their esoteric inner-few is. You're not yet clear, purified, transformed, or any number of states they want you to believe you can only attain if you pay them, for all the many levels of their training program. The "organization" has a given set of reasons why you are not enlightened, why you are merely a piece of shit, street-level character and need to change. They will list their complaints against, not only you, but the general public as a whole and the world. You will dutifully study their argument and agree that, "Yes, I am a piece of shit and I do need to change." Or, "I must be delusional, if I think I am somehow further along in my spiritual growth than these people."

What you are seeking is validation from outside yourself that you are indeed a good and decent human being, worthy of being loved by others, worthy of feeling self-empowered. You are looking for someone outside of yourself to give you permission to take control of your own life, to show you how to master your own self and become the master of your own mind and behavior patterns.

If you are knocking on the door of a cult, the things you will need to change usually take the form of numerous spiritual diseases like impure thought and bad behavioral habits, things the newcomer needs to get rid of, like property and possessions. That stuff is nasty shit. You'll need to sign those over and give all that stuff away, preferably to the organization which is telling you this. You have sin because you have thought and acted wrongly. You are separated from the divine; you are too attached to these worldly possessions. You are weak. You are worldly. We need to isolate you from the world, from those ordinary people in your life who actually care about you and will talk sense to you.

These organizations will tell you that you are not ready to receive, you need to clear your runway, you are not yet worthy of the highest state because there is something deeply wrong with you. You are not yet ready to be who you always already are because you are habitually trying to be something you're not! The organization will have all the solutions for all of these diseases and they will sell them to you, in the form of instructional videos and books, yoga panties, sacred underwear and karma burning candles, for a healthy fee. And you will buy them. You will, literally, buy your way to enlightenment, to gain acceptance by the organization, by the people you wish impress. Then, you'll glamorize yourself with by association with them. So you do everything they say and attend all the events, so you can be seen as an upstanding member of the community.

You want a reputation that commands respect and you believe that associating with this group of people will offer you this. You will want the next generations of newcomers to admire you because you have paid your money and gone through the Level II or Level III training. People start to know who you are and you make a bunch of new friends and you all blow smoke up each other's asses in the main lobby, in the courtyard, during the breaks between workshop sessions. You will buy the training programs and the special level II yoga panties; then experience a new feeling of confidence and empowerment because you are tired of being a lowly piece of shit, because you are exactly the type of person these organizations have been developed to feed on. You are beginning to aspire to a better life but you don't know what it is yet. So you keep buying your way along. This makes you an excellent candidate for the grand old art form of *Being Taken Advantage Of*.

The Spellbinder

Carlos Castaneda wrote and taught about an ancient Toltec path of knowledge he called the warrior's way. He earned his anthropology degrees from UCLA based on his thesis and fieldwork studying an indigenous shaman of the Sonoran desert named don Juan Matus. He developed an intricate body of work relating the teachings of this man's shamanic knowledge. Castaneda alleged he was involuntarily selected by don Juan, or more correctly, by omens and phenomena don Juan perceived, to become his apprentice. Don Juan was purported to be descended from twenty-seven generations of ancient Toltec seers, who themselves each had sorcerer-apprentice relationships. Castaneda said he dutifully recorded everything he was told and everything he saw during his time in don Juan's world. His books were alleged to be an accurate record of this sorcery apprenticeship to don Juan Matus.

By the time I came into direct contact with Castaneda, he was as old as don Juan was, when he alleged to have met him. I met Castaneda by attending his workshops in the mid 1990's. I had been studying his work and practicing it in my own life for almost 15 years by then. As it turns out, after all this time, I've still had no personal interaction with him, or any of his inner-circle, whatsoever outside of that arena. The closest I ever got to this "celebrity better person" was that of being a general attendee at a workshop with a thousand or more people present. In his world, they had a name for people like me, I would be known as a solitary warrior, a solitary bird but I am sure Castaneda's circle had far more derogatory names. Though I had many friends who were as similarly involved as I was, none of us had any relationship with any of Castaneda's people or him. Carlos was as insulated, protected and inaccessible as anyone could possibly be. He came out when he wanted to come out, and he controlled everything about what you saw of him and when. Being inaccessible was a feature of his knowledge and he devoted an entire chapter to it in his third book *Journey to Ixtlan*

We spent dozens of mornings, afternoons and formal evenings with him, within the structure of this highly controlled format. No tape recorders, no cameras, no recording devices of any kind, and we were individually searched and metal detected before we could go in. Every single time. There was no way you were smuggling anything in there. And yet, every opportunity to see him was a highly-anticipated event. We all waited eagerly for him to finally appear, then we would all applaud loudly and become like little schoolgirls at a boy band concert. He would give informal talks, or pop-in during the day while we were learning Tensegrity movements, to clarify details he wanted us to pay special attention to.

The workshops were usually broken up into morning, afternoon and evening sessions. His formal evening lectures were to die for. These were elegant, celebrated evenings when we men would don our most impeccably tailored suits and the ladies would elevate to the nines in their finest evening dresses and we would spend the close of each day taking in lectures by Carlos and his female cohorts, affectionately known as The Witches. They would give delightful talks before the large crowds and leave everyone breathless at the end of the evening, inspired and in awe, walking out three feet off the ground. What Castaneda had created was nothing short of a masterpiece and all of his cohorts, and us too, knew his work inside and out and could articulate for hours, wondrous conversations about his reportage of the magical people and nature of ancient Mexico.

These workshops and lectures were fabulous events. From weeklong trainings at the Pauley Pavilion on the UCLA campus to auditoriums all over the country, in Mexico City and Barcelona, Spain, the settings were always stunning. They were supremely delightful to attend. Everyone would be in the highest of spirits after having worked-out all day learning the Tensegrity movements. Whenever he appeared, we would all be at our best and Castaneda's sense of humor knew no boundaries, nothing was sacred. All manner of subjects and affairs could be turned perverse and utterly absurd or divinely sublime. His peerless intellect combined with his professorial lecturing and storytelling mastery always set us back and made us realize we were in the presence of a truly great mind and a man of great achievement.

Castaneda could hold an audience in the palm of his hand and keep them utterly spellbound by his tales of the furthest reaching mysteries of being alive. He would give us new information that was only for us, only for the ones who made the effort to be there that night. He would always tell us new stories, additional details that weren't in his books. His stories took the form of further details to events we'd read about, his relationships with the characters, the culmination of his personal experiences as a sorcerer's apprentice, all manner of the mayhem we had been reading about for decades in his published work. He had a natural ability to poke the funny bone, provoke our sense of wonder and awe, to transport his audience, his students, far off into his stories and return them safely back again with laughter and amazement.

Like a virtuoso musician could perform a song, lending such masterful touches that leave the audience with goose bumps, Carlos had that same mastery as a raconteur and as an orator. He could make an entire auditorium howl with laughter until our sides would be bursting and then lift our hearts out of our chests, breathless, into the mystical realms of the sublime, referring to inexplicable bonds of affection we all shared for those who were forever joined in a singular purpose. These events were heavenly, purely divinely inspired. Everyone would leave with a romantic sense of wonder and an unshakeable awe for the mystery of the human condition. We would walk off with a galvanized sense of purpose and a mindset that we were indefinable and undefeatable.

Castaneda was the leader of an world-wide community of well-intentioned people who hung on his every word. We all wanted to be like him. He was utterly intoxicating to be around. We wanted to have the experiences he wrote about in his books and make the journeys he had made into the inconceivable worlds of the ancient Toltec seers. We believed he possessed a superior state of energy gained through the practice of an ancient knowledge and he could help us get there, too. He promised he would help us, if we simply followed his instruction and had unbending intent. He, expressly told us over and over again that we could do the same as he was doing, the same as don Juan, the same as all of the ancient Toltec seers had done. He confirmed in each of us, the possibility that we could make our own flight to freedom, we could learn from him how to become navigators on an infinite sea of awareness and fly someday to freedom.

Though I had been to peyote ceremony and had flown on my wings of perception, experienced oneness with all the love in the universe and come to know the natural power within the unbroken circles of the medicine people. I was convinced there must somehow be more to human spirituality. I was convinced earthly life had an ultimate life-long purpose, which we had yet to understand more clearly. It had to do with what was actually meant by going to heaven and living in eternity. I needed to explore Castaneda's teachings further because they held out this prospect that the purpose of life was to master the physical plane, the ordinary self, and move off into what we currently know as dreaming, which was being put forth as if it were actually a doorway to the spiritual plane of existence. Moreover, this path defined a possibility of leaving the physical world, once and for all, and permanently venturing off into this unknowable plane of existence, at the end of our time on Earth. I simply had to resolve, for myself, if this was truly possible or not, I needed to know for sure. I couldn't just let that one slide by in my life unresolved.

He told us the only thing we needed was to live our lives with purpose and we could claim the gift of total freedom for ourselves. So we took him up on it. We paid the fees to go to all the workshops and we practiced everything he taught us, both in his books, and in person. His teachings, along with being steeped in the traditional Catholic imagery of Mexico, ran in very close parallel to much of what I learned from the medicine people, so I was hopeful for the future of my spiritual quest. We were the faithful, the serious practitioners of his teachings. If there was ever anybody who was going to make it happen, who was going to will it into existence, it was going to be us. We were dedicated to this way with everything we had in us.

The basis of taking him up on his offer of acquiring his knowledge, don Juan's knowledge, the knowledge of the toltec seers of ancient Mexico, required committing one's life to the daily practice of the warrior's way and everything it involved, as he described it throughout his anthropology work. The hinge on which the door swung open, leading one to the path of the ancient Toltec seers, was the idea of having purpose. The way he spelled out this purpose, for me, was what set Castaneda's work apart from all the other spiritual teachings I had ever come into contact with.

What Castaneda was offering his students was the opportunity for their lives to have an extremely clear purpose to achieve a very well-defined goal. The goal was to gain enough personal power over the course of an impeccably lived lifetime to attain command of the totality of the self. Then, at the end of our lifetimes, we might have a chance to align all the energy within the totality of the self with the emanations of energy at-large in the universe. This prodigious alignment was also referred to as total awareness or total freedom.

If you go back to Crowbear telling me about overcoming my little self, so the big self could take over and guide my perception through the rest of the ceremony, then, extend this concept one order of magnitude greater. Castaneda was advancing the idea to the next level, where the little and big self together began accessing an inconceivable abstraction of consciousness beyond the human condition. Becoming an impeccable warrior, with the little self was the prerequisite to accessing the big self, becoming a man of knowledge. The ability to act intentionally with the big self required a lifetime of hard, disciplined effort spent willfully, performing prodigious acts of power within the Sorcerer's World, or in other words, mastering the art of dreaming. Only after the little self and the big self were brought into complete alignment, made singular, would the warrior become capable of accessing the universal dimension beyond self and disappear forever from the world we know.

Some scholars refer to this as an emanationist view of the universe with all energy emanating from a universal source and the goal was to align the self and become one, moving on to higher emanating bands of energy. For Castaneda, this was an all-encompassing way of life that required the commitment of an entire lifetime, with no guarantee of success. We were young and we were down with it. Bring it on. Let's roll the dice. We were totally committed. What the hell did we have to lose?

Castaneda took the idea of an afterlife, complete with his supernatural being from hell, which he called the Eagle, and he delivered a tangible practice, so you could to give the Eagle what it wanted, and if you could pull it off, it would let you go free. In order to claim the Eagle's Gift of total freedom, we had to live with purpose, like high-altitude mountain climbers striving for a summit, our summit existed within heightened states of awareness that could be grabbed by the sheer force of *will* and claimed for oneself with unbending intent.

He was flipping the bird to the all the gravity in the universe, by living a lifetime of unwavering purpose, in an all-out-war to destroy every weakness in ourselves, every tie, every bond and attachment we have to the world, in order to elevate a regenerative lifestyle into a super-regenerative state from which a warrior could command of the totality-of-the-self, so as to plant the ice axe of freedom onto the summit of heightened awareness, the summit of the total alignment of the totality of the self. It takes a lot of totals to totally total up to the big totality. We would will ourselves to the highest evolutionary state of the human potential and claim it, as if to capture the flag of total freedom.

This is what Castaneda promised us was possible. He said, the ancient seers demonstrated that it was humanly possible and that he witnessed don Juan's moment of leaving the world himself. He told us he was present at the place and time when the previous generation of sorcerers all joined hands, becoming pure awareness and crossing over into total awareness, lighting up like human suns and flashing over into the next plane of existence. By fulfilling the purpose of the warrior's way, we could follow them. For some reason, I just had to find out if that was really true or not. Like staring down the LED light on my little tape recorder, in order to find whatever lay on the other side of unwavering attention, there was no way I could go through life without resolving this for myself, no matter the cost to myself. Like a warrior going off to fight a foreign war in some god-forsaken land, I was going to fight through to the heart of the matter, or die trying.

If one was to follow such a path in life, it would require the tightening up your whole self and really having your shit together in every sense of the word, in every wavering of attention, distraction of thought or sensation of being. This wasn't a way of life for losers or self-indulgent lazy people who were thinking of laying around tripping out on psychedelics. This was about aspiring to the ultimate state of human development. This was about finding out for ourselves what the highest human potential actually is, or is not.

Having come from a meditation background and with all you hear about the great masters, I had a clear idea of what might be involved in pursuing *attention* to a purely mechanical straightening and total alignment. It made sense to me based on my past experience in handling attention and having amazing things happen, the more powerfully one fixated it. I just didn't know if it was really possible, or not, to go all the way to *The Fire From Within*, the title of Castaneda's seventh book. Many people, many traditions said it was and contained some similar allusions, especially Christianity, where Christ is said to have done precisely this, ascending into heaven as light. Maybe this is what they knew?

Castaneda was talking about making a career out of, and foregoing retirement from, the fine art of being completely and totally shit-together: all the way down to one's most singular thought and sensation of feeling. To become a warrior is to accept the kinds of vows monks take. This is the same life-practice they do, only without the monastery attached. This is monastic life out in the open air of the ordinary world. It was hardcore meditation perfected, made active and turning into a professional major league sport. And there was nothing more right up my alley than that. Now, we were in my wheelhouse and I genuinely had to see it through to its natural end.

The tasks of initiates were similar to those who seriously practiced esoteric stages of the yoga meditations and asanas. There were disciplines of thought, mind and attention, then there were body movements, which it was alleged, the ancient seers of Mexico had designed and could be likened to flowing yoga routines, whereupon the mastery of it became more like a dance. They were intended to keep the body lithe and physically tuned. The handling of attention itself to the point of extreme was also key, and I had already done this, practiced it, nearly mastered it, if it weren't for my kundalini crash, crisis and subsequent psychiatric meltdown. Even though I crashed and burned that time, I still walked away from the accident. I did have to be hospitalized, start over from scratch and this is what I was trying like hell to do. I wanted back in the race. Indeed, I had already gotten off several more laps in recent years. I really had my heart set on being a warrior of total-freedom. I believed there was a chance that I could still go the distance.

By making the body strong and lean, getting every aspect of my whole-self straightened out, the handling of attention would not become so unwieldy, making my mind unstable, as it had for me in those horrible days around my twentieth birthday. I felt the universe itself was my creator and because it was, it knew me as it's own and was leading toward the life it wanted me to realize on its own behalf. I just needed to mature and I needed to reign in all of the daily behaviors which made loose ends of my attention, bring everything together in a way that supported the disciplined practice of high-energy containment within the self. I needed to let go of my anxieties and subtle unwillingness to feel the sensations of being who I am.

I needed to be completely willing to feel everything that came with not-doing anything other than being pure awareness. Basically, I needed to not do anything fun or immediately gratifying for long periods of time without driving myself batshit crazy in order to imbue my attention with penetrating power I would need to employ during meditative practices. I needed for my personal energy to become a regenerative circle of power, *The Second Ring of Power*, as was explained in Carlos's fifth book was titled. I had to find peace in the power of the big self. I needed to get back to my practice of quietly and patiently scaling the mountain of attention. I had to get back to the land and set my soul free.

In the course of my life, aside from religion and the meditations with Howard, the knowledge I was seeking began with a bang when my aunt introduced me to the sport of the handling of attention for the sake of out-of-body experience. What I did next was to tap into the real power of attention in meditative practices and find it came natural to me, but not without paying the price of admission. So, I had studied yogic traditional practices and began to practice it on my own, seeking out teachers. Now I was paying the price of admission to summit the mountain. I felt like the universe had me on a path toward something truly great and powerful. There is only one human anatomy, the one we actually have. I was guessing attention had to be the same for yoga practitioners, the same for Christ, as it was for the sorcerers of ancient Mexico.

* * *

The prerequisite for handling attention, the way it was said a Toltec man of knowledge could, was to develop the ability to enter into total inner-silence for sustained durations. In Yoga, there is something very similar to stopping the world called *Samyama*. It contains three components, the first is *concentration*. The second is the ability for this concentration to be held for a *sustained duration*. These two together, *sustained concentration* are also known as *meditation*. When concentration is held for a sustained duration, it leads to *absorption*. So the three together would be *concentration, duration* and *absorption*. This is *Samyama* as it is taught in yogic traditions.

However, in both Yoga and in Castaneda's writing, there is a baseline requirement, which must be met before we can enter into a state of total inner-silence, or samyama. The requirement would be the long term leading of a very clean, tight, well-balanced life, where the practitioner develops a sophisticated sense of human decency, kindness and deep consideration. We have to become capable of impeccable behavior in all of our daily affairs. There is the unbreakable law of energetic conservation, regeneration, the circular flow we see in Native American ceremony. This leaves both warriors and yogis strong, clear-minded, emotionally present in all that they do, keeping them ever ready to enter into the state of total inner-silence and to, in turn, stop the world, or as in yoga practice, enter the state of samyama.

Total inner-silence, on the other hand, being nearly identical, was the baseline requirement for what the ancient Toltec warriors called *stopping the world*. So here we have Castaneda's version of samyama, another three-component idea: *handling attention* (concentration), *total inner-silence* (meditation), and *stopping the world* (absorption). To *stop the world* was to enter the *sorcerer's world*, (breaking the seal on entering states of *heightened states of awareness*.) Entering the *sorcerer's world* was where the actual sport of it all begins. In Castaneda's world there were places to go, things to see and people to remember you had somehow known before. In yoga meditation, one sits still in meditation, which is considered *action through non-action* or one becomes active through yoga poses or asanas.

In yoga, to enter samyama is to begin to experience more energized states known as *samadhi*, or in other words, to enter into *cosmic consciousness*, states culminating in progressive levels of *intensity*. I now had come to understand two different ways of describing the same thing. What differs is the purpose. Yoga is practiced for the purpose of health and well-being, to become disciplined and self-aware, to realize the highest state of cosmic consciousness, oneness with the source of all life. For those yoga practitioners who believe in reincarnation, the highest state of consciousness frees them from the wheel of earthly life, the endless cycle of births and deaths, and lifts them into the unknowable, the next higher plane of existence. This sounds indistinguishable from Castaneda's Toltec description. Two descriptions of the same thing.

For me, this could only mean one thing. I had unearthed two sets of labels for one actual universal anatomy. I had corroboration and agreement. In my mind, this meant hard evidence. I was on the trail. I was on the case. I was doing a little detective work trying to track down the way life actually is. I was fast on the trail of absolute proof of the meaning of life.

To Answer A Higher Calling

Castaneda used to say his warrior lineage was very similar to the life monks lead, but without the confinement. He went so far as to tell us the warriors of his lineage had great affinity for those who chose the monastic life and that some of the ancient warriors during the conquest would hide among the monastic orders, to hide from conquerors hell-bent on eradicating the sorcerers from the earth. He told us that it was not our fate live in the relative safety of monasteries The Toltec way required we face ourselves in the world of everyday life, this was our battleground. To face ourselves in confinement would be tantamount to becoming paper warriors, unable to face the rigors outside an ideal environment. To live and work impeccably in the ordinary world, yet stand apart from it in every respect, to deal with insanity and yet be unfazed by it, to live among ordinary people while living an extraordinary life, this was our challenge.

For Castaneda, his work stated the ancient Toltec were involved in a lifelong business of mastering shifts into heightened states of awareness for the purpose of learning and teaching how to handle attention. They worked in traditional sorcerer-apprentice relationships, according to Castaneda's written work, up until it was time for the sorcerers of the previous generation to make their viaje definitivo, or their definitive journey.

Once the old generation was gone, the apprentices of the by-gone sorcerers were left alone in the ordinary world. It would take them many years until they were able to remember the totality of themselves and take command of it. Once they had achieved this inconceivable feat, they had to wait for the right omens to point out new students, then hook them the way they had been hooked and start the cycle over.

The significant feature of the Toltec path was that the greater portion of sorcery lessons were taught to apprentices while in states of heightened awareness, which students would be unable to remember during their years as apprentices. The sorcerers, who were also seers, would shift their apprentice's assemblage points. Castaneda described this assemblage point as a small glowing spot of human awareness, about the size of a baseball, within our total field of energy; think of the idea of having an aura surrounding your body. The assemblage point would reside at a location within us where the self assembles our perception of our external world. Everyone in the ordinary world has their assemblage points in the same location. We all share the same perception of the same world because of this position, according to Castaneda. The small glow of the assemblage point is located within the total volume of a luminous egg-shaped field of energy surrounding a person's body. Got that? That field of energy surrounding the body is in the domain of the *second attention, the sorcerer's world*. Castaneda called it a luminous egg, or luminous cocoon.

The luminous egg, or *energy body*, contained vast regions of dormant emanations, and the seers would shift the apprentice's assemblage point into these regions to align alternative worlds of perception, dreaming worlds. Then, the sorcerers would teach them really scary stuff, which they would be unable to handle in their ordinary state of awareness. This involved the simultaneous activation of both dreaming and waking consciousness. This is the kind of state that puts people in psychiatric wards. The apprentices would be taught about taking command of the totality of the self and stuff like that. Then, the sorcerers would safely shift 'em back to their ordinary state of awareness without the apprentice realizing anything had happened at all. All memory of dreaming-awake while in a state of heightened awareness would no longer be accessible to their conscious mind. It all would seem to them no different than having a dream while sleeping and not being able to remember it when they woke up. Only scant fragments of out of context trace images would remain, enough of a deficit for them to completely disregard it.

These two sides of the self were said to be the ordinary awareness, or the first attention, and the *dreaming* awareness, or *second attention*. Castaneda described ordinary awareness as being sealed off from the vastness of the second attention due to lack of knowledge and discipline to stop the world. Once the apprentices became adept at the basics of the teachings, maturing in their practice, the seal would eventually give way and they would be able to shift the assemblage point, or the glow of awareness, into dormant areas of the luminous cocoon. They would break the seal, releasing a flood of memories containing everything the Sorcerers taught them in heightened awareness. Now, by aligning the perception of other total worlds, and reclaiming their forgotten knowledge, they could begin to develop the totality of the self into a functioning whole. To dream while awake and control the dream was an act of power only a man of knowledge could perform, after having broken the seal, and doing so without finding it necessary to check himself into a psychiatric ward.

This life-long process is what Castaneda described to the world as remembering the totality of the self. They would finally succeed in breaking the barrier between waking and dreaming by entering into states of heightened awareness during the day and by practicing conscious dreaming at night. The net result would be unifying and taking command of the totality of the self. At this point, absolutely everything was a clear, unified whole self. Breaking the seal between our ordinary awareness and the dreaming states made a warrior into a man of knowledge. It made an apprentice into a sorcerer and an ordinary man into a *seer* of energy as it flows in the universe.

The act of *remembering* the totality of the self was said to be like having the ability to remember all of your dreams with coherence and clarity. It was an extremely prodigious feat by any standards. Such a possibility rendered me dumbstruck because I had stood at that very intersection several times by this stage on my life and I had to say, I did not realize there was so much beyond this threshold, which could be made into controllable territory. The thought of opening up to these states and being in the presence of mind to gain complete control of them was deeply humbling, for me. I had firsthand knowledge of just how powerful this territory is. It can be terrifying stuff.

This meant there was a lot of work to be done to open that territory in myself (which I had broken into the night I was taken to the psych ward) and venture back into it. I understood that if I lived like a warrior, I might have the strength, stability of will and clarity of purpose to render it all somehow comprehensible and not feel the need to check myself back into the loony bin. It seemed like a daunting task, a life-long task. But Castaneda had us all convinced that the ancient Toltec had discovered that is the way life actually is. This is the purpose of life on earth, to explore these vast regions of dormant emanation in the luminous cocoon, to align them, little by little through the years that lie ahead, so hopefully one day, maybe we could develop the discipline to align them all at once, in one fell swoop. Sounds like a total rush, if you ask me. This is why they demanded the full price of admission be paid up front, because you weren't going to receive the full shipment until long after they were gone. You had to go for years on faith alone, or else it wouldn't work. (The truth is, it was never going to work, because it was all imaginary.)

Castaneda professed to have uncovered a lineage of people who possessed the secret knowledge of how the universe was actually designed and how to act in ways that allowed them the opportunity to explore more of the universe than was previously imagined to be humanly possible. Come to find out, eternal life, the whole shebang, it's all in there. It's a great way to sell a lot of books and get through life without having to work very hard, if you're the author. It's great work, if you can get it.

To command the utmost discipline required to make oneself energetically whole, as Castaneda described, implies a man would have to become, not just a disciplined man, but an impeccable man, in all of his doings. He would be a man with an impeccable warrior spirit. He would have to become a really, really good person and yet maintain the ruthlessness of a trained killer. This is not merely an abstract idea. This has a very practical daily application. When Castaneda wrote and spoke about being a warrior he meant the kind of person who ruthlessly attacks his own weaknesses and safeguards his strength for the high purpose of achieving freedom. This is just what really, really good people do.

A good and decent man must sometimes be a hunter, with a killer instinct, just to survive day-to-day. It doesn't make a man indecent or amoral to kill in order to feed his family. Quite the contrary, it is an act of nobility. This is the way the universe was designed, even if it all happened randomly through pure physics, we don't know. We are animals and we kill and eat each other in order to continue living. No man is immune to survival of the fittest. It's the way the universe is. It's not wrong in any spiritual sense to hunt, if to take a life is solely for the purpose of sustaining one's own and to feed a family. But the warrior in Castaneda's world hunted for power. Not power over other men, per se, but power to stop the world of everyday life, the power to enter the sorcerer's world and the power to become a man of knowledge, unifying the totality of the self.

While I had approached the gates of Castaneda's sorcery world a few times on my own, I was able to travel further in under the guidance of Chief Crowbear in the protection of his medicine circle. I was able to glimpse the possibility of turning the first and second attention into a singular functioning unit. Castaneda's teachings said it was possible to actually enter into dreaming together, consciously exploring dreams at night and each participant would be able recall the events the next day. The warrior's way offered a chance to open up into the state of dreaming awake and still maintain a calm cool composure, to handle the business at hand and deal with the sheer intensity of it. I was staggered and could only shake my head that such a thing was even possible. So, while I found the path of the warrior to be my true calling, I stood in awe of it and was deeply humbled, doubting I could ever succeed. The task appeared to be far greater than my strength. But I accepted the challenge anyway, knowing I may not have what it takes.

I went on believing that what I was doing was for the benefit of mankind, that good and decent men must sometimes go to war. So, I was called and I would go. This was my calling. As any honorable man or woman in the armed services of any military, men of knowledge are said to be warriors. They go to knowledge as any armed freedom fighter would, as any true warrior would go to war, as tight and disciplined men, with all their wits intact. They go to war ready to fight against all that would undo them. They go to war ready to kill. They go to war and stand ready to die, today. And yet, these good and decent men do not go in anger. They go to war in answer to a higher calling, to serve others, to protect those who are unable to protect themselves and they will never cower in the face of duty. They can only walk in awe of having the power to remain alive another day.

They do not know what will confront them, or when, so they stand armed, at the ready. As warriors, they hold reverence for the fact that each day they are alive may be their final day of life on this earth. Without fail, they go bravely into the horrifying face of total war. They go reluctantly, but they serve honorably, with a deep sense of humanity. They would rather lay down their lives in the field of battle, as so many great warriors have before them, than live in a world where enemies gain power over them. To pay the ultimate price, by laying down their lives on the field of battle, they have lived with honor, they have lived as warriors, and dying the warrior's death, in the afternoon, beneath an endless sky, under a universe of stars, they have died in service of the only purpose in life worth living for.

According to Castaneda, his path of knowledge was that serious, that sublime, and that deeply meaningful.

The Incorruptible Man

Castaneda told us emphatically, over and over again, "I do not lead a double-life. I am as you see me. I am everything I have written about myself in my work. I do not say one thing publicly and go home to live some other way. I live the warrior's way and no other." He must have told us this, in one way or another, at least a thousand times. Carlos loved to beat you over the head with it. He would tell us the same thing over and over again, until it became absolutely hilarious and he was convinced his point was made.

His position as the leader of a party of sorcerers was known as The Nagual. The word was said to be from ancient times, something to do with the ancient Nahuatl language. The Nagual selected for the newest cycle of apprentices was called the new nagual. The new nagual was meant to rally all of his knowledge and take the leadership role in directing his generation of sorcerers to total freedom. It's a tall order. Total freedom could only be attained once the ancient knowledge was securely planted in a new generation of apprentices. Carlos was once the new nagual.

Now, in light of all of us gathering around, wanting to get in on the action, he was now considered the old nagual and preparing himself to leave the world forever, fully aware of the fact that his knowledge, the knowledge of the entire lineage, was securely planted for the next generation. I coined the nickname, The Old Nag, because he would nag us incessantly about every little detail of the warrior's way. He never stopped, he just harped on detail after detail of everything he felt we needed to know, what we needed to be practicing, how we needed to act, everything we should and shouldn't do. There was no end. He would go on for three full hours. Nag. Nag. Nag-nag, nag.

Even though he was an old nag, we believed Castaneda was the epitome of a good and decent man. We believed he was touching the face of the highest human potential and turning back, momentarily, to leave us with the secret to how the universe actually is, how anyone with enough guts and determination could go forth and follow him. We believed in don Juan's linage of Toltec men and women sorcerers. We were convinced they were living out the realization of the highest possible human potential. We believed it because, in light of everything we had been taught, about Christ, about the realizations of master yogi's and mystics throughout the course of human history, it might be possible. We were eager to find out if it was true. We would never know unless we did everything within our power to follow them.

He asked us to give him the benefit of the doubt and we did because we believed it would be worth it. We were always taught we *had* to believe, up front, and that believing, having faith in the system of thought was the only chance we had for the magic of the unseen worlds to come to life for us, to change our lives, to break us free. I had been prepared to accept this idea since I was old enough to drink out of a Dixie cup. So, I accepted it.

I just had to know, was this a practical new version of what so many holy figures throughout the history of mankind tried to teach. I had always wondered if those great historical figures were all simply misunderstood by the masses and I wondered what they really knew. Historic figures had lived in such a way, to show humanity a way to eternal life, or the next plane of existence, but they were only able to show us so much. Maybe men like Christ had it all wired and we just didn't understand the way the universe and human consciousness actually are yet. Maybe this is another teaching for modern times that gets the job done this time? I had to know for certain if it was or wasn't. We all felt like we were getting in on the ground floor of something really big, as if it were going to take off and turn us all into angels of pure energy.

Why not? If you follow my story from child being taught to believe in the unseen, through divorce and the violent death of a childhood friend, torn between parents and homes, trained in psychic meditations and yoga mediations, incomprehensible experiences and the long road to resolving all the mystery that comes with simply being alive, day-to-day, then why not? All I ever wanted was to become a good and decent man by doing everything right and learning from everything they told me good and decent men know. I just wanted to find that missing piece of the puzzle that is going to make it all work, make my life fit together and make it all rewarding, joyous, worthwhile. I was just doing what everyone around me was telling was the right way to live. It was a blessing, it was an honor, it was an opportunity of a lifetime, one-in-a-million.

It's possible Castaneda set foot on the same path of knowledge and found he had a natural proclivity for following the mystical teaching to the letter, the whole way, all the way down the line and never wavered. I just wanted to know if my meditation practice of straightening and fixating attention, the way I had done it, if I kept going for a lifetime, would it lead to higher orders of magnitude in the experiencing the power he wrote about and what others were writing books about? It seems possible from that point of view. Doesn't it? It seemed worth footing the bill for a thorough investigation.

And here he is. He did it. He's a great man, a best selling author and a doctor of anthropology. He's a famous celebrity of a man. He has wealth. He has people. He has the admiration of thousands and a body of work unlike anything the world has ever seen. Here's your example, young Vince. Here's the man. Here is your role model. Here is the guy you can look up to, even though he's only maybe 5'1", and aspire to be like. Here is a truly good and decent man. Here is the man who is good, through and through, with not one single skeleton in his closet, an honest man. "A 100% incorruptible human being," we were told by the Witches. I felt relieved that good, decent people actually exist. There was hope that maybe, one day, I could be more like him.

"Don't throw the baby out with the bathwater, Vin," he cautioned me. *"You're still going to walk away from this with some seriously valuable spiritual lessons here. You don't want to disregard that."*

Chapter Eleven
DANCING IN THE WORLD OF MAKE-BELIEVE

Once Castaneda returned to public teaching in the mid 1990's, over the period of a few years, there was a time of honeymoon. Everyone was overjoyed that he was back again, coming out of private life to teach publicly. And he came bearing gifts, wonderful little workshops we could all attend and a whole community of people, new friends we could join with, in our journey to the unknown. There was a huge demand. A thousand people at a time came like cattle, to learn Tensegrity movements and hear the wondrous stories.

Eventually, a few years into this wonderful new time, we came to find we were swallowed whole by the stories. We had always been such huge fans, traveling to places far and wide, being tantalized by the farthest-reaching mysteries of being alive. We found ourselves living inside the Castaneda books, for real. It felt like a magical dream come true. We were now part of the story's continuation. We were all being enveloped in the farthest-reaching mysteries in the evolution of mankind. The universe was sweeping us along in a mystery and we were being taken on a journey into the sorcerer's world. We were the inheritors of the ancient Toltec path of knowledge, the next generation of Toltec spiritual warriors. Now we were all forever part of don Juan's ancient lineage, on our way to total freedom, total awareness, total alignment.

Then Carlos died.

The End.

I heard it on the television news. It was being reported months after his actual death. It happened sometime after the Oakland I & II workshops, which I attended. Carlos was at his finest at all of those workshops and even gave an impromptu, 3-hour lecture standing on the floor of the gymnasium that final Sunday morning, in addition to his formal lectures in the auditorium at night. He spent extra time with us. We admired him and loved being in his company.

I did not know then, standing only a few feet from him, right next to him, listening to him talk, that he was going to go home and die; that I would never see him again in this life. He had spoken so often of his own death. He mocked it so hilariously. One of my fondest memories are of him clutching his heart, while pausing to clear his throat during his evening lecture at Oakland the night before, "My Respirator!!" he yelled. His ability to cast the spell, to keep an audience spellbound by story, through the weaving of tales is simply one of the most delightfully entertaining things I've ever experienced. He could make seasoned actors seem weak by comparison and he was just telling stories off the cuff, improvising.

He made you feel so inexplicably wonderful, so empowered, like anything was possible for you. He made you believe in your own highest state of personal excellence. He made you believe in yourself, that you were worthy of human evolution's highest achievement and nothing less in life was worth living for. He made you believe, in the most romantic way, that you could accomplish anything, that earthly goals were challenging but possible, attainable. You could get two Ph.D.'s if you wanted to. However, becoming a spiritual warrior of total freedom was the only thing in life worth dying for. The only reason he stood on that stage was to help each of us understand that we could reach for the highest possibility and claim it for ourselves with unwavering intent.

And you would do it, you would go for it, you would commit your entire life because he made you believe in him. He made all of us believe in ourselves, that anything was possible. He made us believe there was no higher cause than to fight a spiritual war against all human weakness. The rewards of success were about gradually developing the kind of strength required to enter into the next plane of existence of one's own volition. This was the journey we were on. It was a journey to power, of acquiring inner-strength and the ability to will incomprehensible feats of perception.

Eventually, after a few more workshops in different cities, without him, news of his death finally came out. It was liver cancer. I had trouble reconciling the notion with my system of thought, the system of thought he had given me and painstakingly cultivated, developed in me over my entire adult lifetime. The two didn't really fit together without some serious incongruence. I have to admit, I had a serious philosophical and intellectual crisis on my hands. One minute we lived in the state of total war against all that would weaken us, the next our leader had fallen dead at his house in Los Angeles. So, unable to reconcile it in my mind, I dutifully remained a true-believer, no matter what the news said, until the crack between the two worlds began to appear.

It took a few months, up to a year, once Castaneda passed, until some of the truth of what was happening behind the scenes began leaking out. From the inner circle, to the serious practitioners, the information about who he really was, who the ladies in his inner circle actually were and what they were really doing was leaked, and started reaching the light of day. After a while a steady stream of facts started emerging which Castaneda would have never allowed to see the light of day, while he were living. Over-my-dead-body kind of stuff. All of his skeletons started coming out of the closet and wandering around, through what has now become social media but was once just called the Internet. They were now free to roam about the internet.

Gradually, over that time, the realization slowly dawned on me there was ample evidence to suggest that Castaneda and his cohorts were indeed leading double lives. I had kind of suspected it, since the Pauley Pavilion workshops at UCLA. Something opened the door in my mind one night that Carlos could actually be bluffing. Of course, I dismissed the thought but there was no doubt it occurred to me, large as life. As it happens, I am also a writer. I had written my own book, one that was never published. I wrote about what Carlos wrote about: big idea non-fiction. He was my idol and I was young. I wanted to be just like him and do what he did. So I would try. I wrote my ass off. I wrote my own book about my own experience and tried to make it sound great, like his amazing best sellers, but I was only an amateur, a nobody. But most importantly, my experiences weren't as miraculous as his. Mine were more ordinary and occurred inside me. I didn't have any great teacher, except Phil. How could I make my inner revelations sound as fantastic as the stories he wrote about during his interactions with these extraordinary people he met?

In my writing, I could be become anything I wanted to become. I completed my book. I knew what it was like to slam a project shut and call it finished. I knew what it took to typeset and proofread and put a finished project in the can. It's a really big deal and it requires years of focused effort. It's not easy to put a finished masterpiece on the shelf, ready for the world. I learned something by doing that. I learned from working so hard and having it not be a masterpiece. I learned something a lot of people, who haven't done it, don't know. What I learned cracked the door open a bit wider for me and offered a little peek inside Castaneda's world that others may never guess. That lesson guided my eye to see something in Castaneda that I saw within myself while writing my own book.

In writing, I could be anyone I wanted to say that I was. It was that easy. All I had to do was put it all into words. I discovered on my own, during the writing of my earliest book, what writers call, writing over your head. It is a phenomena where an author can go to a place only defined as The Zone and write from a place far beyond himself, make statements which sound as if they were channelled from another plane. A writer can elevate. We can go anywhere, do anything, become a conduit for the highest, most sublime universal self, say whatever we want, whatever we can imagine the highest universal self might say, and we put it into words. I discovered, as a student of spirituality, I could write from the point of view of the master and say things the master might say, the low self could write from the point of view of the high self. Whatever it was possible to imagine, as a writer, I could make the most sublime and inconceivable flight of thought appear as though it could be real. But would I? Would I tell my autobiographical story and embellish? Is that even honest to write things that aren't exactly true just because they occur to us while working, because they sound fantastic?

Something in the way Carlos would always say, "And don Juan said. . ." then launch into some amazingly brilliant statement allegedly told to him by his teacher, told me he was reaching into that place. Sitting in front of the stage inside the Pauley Pavilion that night, something told me, Carlos was drawing on this ability to reach over his head. My instincts told me don Juan was nothing more than Carlos writing from his most elevated self. It was something in the tilt of his head and the shift of his eyes as he spoke. I had seen him lecture so many times, it was like I knew it was coming before he said it. He would rare back on his heals as if he were about to knock one out of the park. I could see it the look on his face, the way his eyes changed and I saw it. It was like my aunt Marina's ability to give a psychic reading. Sitting feet away from him, I was reading Carlos. I could see what was written all over his face. Then it struck me. Carlos was writing over his head like no one on earth! He made a career of it. He could even lecture over his head! He mastered the craft long ago and was it even possible? All of his stories are fiction?

It struck me, that all the noise I had been tuning out all these years, might not be noise, maybe it was true. Could Carlos be making it all up as he went along? Improvising over a tune he himself had written? The thought was mind-bending. I couldn't even conceive of it. How much of an asshole would someone have to be, to do such a thing, for so many years, to so many people. I just couldn't accept how anyone could be so fucked, to do something like that to people who genuinely loved you, adored you, supported you and gave you everything you had. We practically worshipped the ground he walked on. Everything he sold, we bought.

Now, after his death, so many incongruities, the possibility came glaring front and center, that Carlos had not been who he had said he always was all these years. We would come to find out he did not live in accordance with the warrior's way and no other, the way he had always taught us he had. Coming to that realization was like trying to choke back from a terrible episode of an inevitable vomiting. The resistance you feel just before as you refuse to accept the possibility. It was something everything in you wants to avoid doing until there is simply no other choice. It's the last thing in the world anyone would ever want to have to do, so you keep trying not to, but eventually, you have to accept the pain and surrender to the horrifying fact that it is overwhelming you. It was a deeply, unavoidably painful, yet cathartic experience of anguish.

Those who were critical of him from the beginning were finally winning out as a large body of documents was made public presenting evidence that conflicted with Castaneda's published story. The most stinging part for me, personally, was the fact that it was now certainly a closed case that don Juan was a fictional character, and no matter how bad it looked on the people at UCLA, who awarded him his Ph.D., all of his books were completely fiction. Carlos had dreamed it all up. This was the hardest part for me to choke down, that my entire spiritual life was imaginary, pretend, and worse still, there was no way out, no path to total-freedom, as promised. There was never such a thing as total-freedom and that I had been led to believe there was made me feel like the biggest idiot in the world.

The possibility of crossing over to the next higher plane of existence by practicing these teachings only existed for a time in a world of make-believe. The highest state of human evolution, our goal, our purpose appeared to be some kind of hoax. This was the part I resisted through to the bitter end. I had truly suspended disbelief all those years and I held out faith that if I fulfilled every step of the way, the path of knowledge led to total-alignment of the body, mind and spirit with the limitlessness of the third-attention. I desperately wanted to believe that all the characters in those books were real people. I desperately wanted to believe they were the living proof that I could perfect the path of sustained concentration and through the alignment of attention, claim the summit of the human potential.

❋ ❋ ❋

The universe was never designed as he promised us the toltecs seers had said it was. His entire body of work appears to be completely fabricated. There was no path to total-freedom as offered in his teachings, no cause worthy of the very best in us and nothing less. There never was. There was no don Genaro, no don Juan, none of those self-realizing, highly-empowering characters were actual. They never were. There was never any alignment of the first, second and third attention the way his teachings suggested. No egg-shaped cocoon of luminosity surrounding us, no energy body to galvanize, thus there was no opening in this world through which to go, no darting past the eagle to be free.

Our purpose, the stunning core of the teaching driving every action of our lives, was in itself, nothing more than an imaginary phantom traveller, an apparition along the road to Ixtlan, like those Castaneda so stunningly wrote of in his thesis for his master's degree. We found ourselves to be fellow travelers on the road to fictionland and the world of sorcerers was not real, no matter who we were with or how much we wanted it to be real. Carlos promised us a way out of the world without dying an ordinary death was a possibility. Even if I never realized it myself, even that it was a possibility was a new idea, a completely amazing discovery. But it was all simply pie in the sky. We were doomed. It was worse than the worst day I had ever come to in my life. I had been ripped off in the very core of my soul. I had been violated for years, by a charlatan who led me to believe his visions of life's true purpose were authentic, and they weren't. It was pure fiction.

But why the sad face, Buckaroo? Was there really any harm in it? Had I really been violated, like a common altar boy, in the rectory basement after a catholic service? I had only imagined Castaneda's stories were real, while countless other people I had known, along with millions of others, who had all read the books and simply dismissed them as any other oddity, regardless of whether they were non-fiction or not. All my hopes and dreams were finally, one day, shattered in an instant of being deeply honest with myself about all I now knew. It was worse than the day I realized Santa Clause was imaginary. Now don Juan, too?

FUUUUCK!

At first, I tried to ignore it and just keep trudging on, but it was my colleagues, my fellow practitioners, the serious Castaneda devotees, the ones to whom I had shown my Tensegrity brand yoga panties during the breaks at workshops, who finally took me aside and said, "Vin! Stop!" Like I was missing a big part of the story. "You've got to look at all of this. You've got to see these documents for yourself. Then decide for yourself based on everything you know."

What I needed to see was everything Rich Jennings had discovered, compiled and placed on a timeline for the world to scrutinize. Then, those who studied the information could make up their own minds and come to a reasonable conclusion on the matter. This was very simple and direct.

At some point, while all of the workshops were busily happening, Jennings, one of the serious practitioners, slowly found himself being drawn into the fold, the inner circle surrounding Castaneda. It was his skills as an attorney, which caught the eye of the Cleargreen staff and led them to seek his council. They probably wanted to take advantage of his generosity in some way or other, to get cheap or free legal services out of him. Once within the organization, Rich started to notice glaring inconsistencies in both the way Cleargreen did business and in Carlos' entire story. In other words, something made him, too, raise an eyebrow and wonder what was really going on.

Rich was as dedicated and as loyal of as any one of us ever were, he believed as whole-heartedly as all of us did, but he was the first of the more advanced practitioners to begin having doubts based on information he came in contact with, through his association with the Cleargreen staff. Because he was highly-practical and close enough to the group, he began uncovering a different story about who Castaneda was and what he was really doing all these years, privately, as well as publicly. Rich was honest with himself, he was an honest person, and he had to admit to himself that maybe he was wrong about this whole thing. His instincts told him he may be getting duped and if he was getting duped, so were the general public. He felt he needed to act, to try to discover what was wrong.

Using everything he had in him, he rallied all of his knowledge, everything he had been taught by Castaneda about applying ruthless self-examination, everything he had learned about investigation from becoming an attorney and everything that came from years and years of being an impeccable warrior. He decided to begin his own full-scale investigation of Carlos Castaneda and his little friends, too.

He began tenaciously searching through public records in Los Angeles County, unearthing documents, tracing where they led, placing everything he discovered onto a timeline which he compared to the chronology of events depicted in Castaneda's published work, which are meticulously dated throughout. As he did this, an entirely different picture of Castaneda's lifetime began to emerge, one of a normal man living a normal life in Los

Angeles, not Mexico. All the documents he discovered in public records contained conflicting dates to those in the recorded dates published throughout his anthropology work.

Jennings collected and amassed an entirely new body of data about Castaneda, an entirely different picture from the one he had always maintained was true in his case. When taken in tandem with the body of documents he uncovered on the true identity of each of the witches and each of the women in Castaneda's inner circle, along with the newly leaked information about their daily lives, alleging mental and verbal abuse as well as rumors of Carlos's long term promiscuous sexual behavior with young students, it was conclusive. It was damning.

These official documents on public record from throughout Castaneda's life, took on a life of their own, from his birth certificate, to his first entering the country, through his multiple marriages, offspring, to his various addresses and the dates. The dates. There were so many conflicts arising from the weight of the evidence. It was hard, cold evidence which suggested the unthinkable. It proved the opposite, for me, in my own mind and that was all I needed for my world to come crashing down.

I was now convinced Castaneda had lied about all of it. He had been, in fact, living a double-life the entire time. It wasn't even really a double-life, it was a single life, just not the warrior one he'd published. He was living only an ordinary life and never living the austere life he professed to live as a leader on the warrior's way. Public records proved there was no way he could have been in two places at once, living opposite lifestyles. There was too much there that ran counter to his published work and not one shred of evidence in favor.

And be that as it may, this sort of conclusion had long been suspected, something he had been accused of all along, faking it all. So for most, this was really not news at all. It was just a public confirmation of common knowledge among those who knew him. And the public never even gave a shit. It was all ancient history by then anyway. Castaneda was dead. Nobody cared anymore. So no one ever cried foul in the media or reported on any of it. It was when Rich began turning his investigation skills onto the members of Castaneda's inner circle, what he found were the real identities of average people, not the lives of extraordinary sorcerer's living secretive lives in Mexico, as we had been continuously led to believe in the workshops.

It is beyond the scope of this work to examine this evidence in all its damning detail and lead the reader to the unalterable conclusion, which led to the collapse of Castaneda's life's work. There have been several books published since his death sharing information and juicy gossip of the lives of those close to him. I am not a court of law, in this regard for anyone but myself. I can only defer, at this point, to a whole body of work by several other authors who participated in Castaneda's unfortunate madness much more deeply than I. Also the site where Jennings first made public all of his chronologies and evidence, remains intact to this day at sustainedaction.org. Through all of their accounts, these authors, as participants in this bizarre story, sort through all the lies and deceit and wreckage to build a very compelling case against the entire body of Castaneda's life's work. For those of us who were there and lived through it, it was just sad that it all came to naught.

Of Metaphor And Make-Believe

I was fortunate to enjoy a visit from my dear friend Tom Hess during this dismal period of my life. He came through Portland, Oregon with his wife and stopped in for a visit and we all went out to dinner at McMenamins, Edgefield. As we ate dinner in The Power Station, of all places, it was then when he asked the logical question. Tom is a man who had found his rightful path to spiritual understanding and went his own way long ago. He marched steadily throughout those very same years on his own journey along the path of knowledge, which he believed was right for him. He reached his destination, when after traveling back-and-forth to India for many years, he became a fully-trained and certified Iyengar Yoga instructor. So, he wouldn't hesitate to ask me, his life-long buddy, the hard question about my chosen road, to state the obvious.

Tom had read much of Castaneda's work, yet he was never as caught up in all of it as I was. He found it interesting, fascinating, as anyone would but it wasn't for him. It wasn't his path. He was more levelheaded, stable and practical than I was. He was always a man who stood on his own two feet, who did not need to lean on others to make his own way in life. He was always a strong, direct and capable young man. I was secretly envious of his sound judgment and well-chosen path in life. It had obviously been extremely rewarding for him. He had opened his own yoga school in Chico, California and was enjoying success in every area of his life.

His question to me was, "Yes Vin, but isn't it true that, when we take everything he wrote about metaphorically, there is still great wisdom and value to be taken away from his work? The path with a heart, the power of internal silence, the wings of perception, the second attention?" He threw up his hands as if to say ,"C'mon, dude, really?" he looked at me bewildered, as if I were best explained away as a personality type who would flip from one extreme view to an opposite, a like a militant ex-smoker. How could I just turn my back on spirituality entirely? "There is so much there to come away with. Isn't there?" he asked me.

I just looked at him like, "What?"

Of course. Yes. It is true, kinda. In the hustle and bustle of the restaurant, I couldn't explain to him all I knew about Castaneda the author. But for the record, my point of contention had always been this: the work was sold as non-fiction. It was never the intent of the work to be taken metaphorically. If it was the intent to take it metaphorically the entire story falls apart, Castaneda's entire career falls apart. His Ph.D. would have been earned through fraud. Worst of all, our path to total freedom, our purpose, was a metaphor for what? I felt as if it were simply a metaphor for my own stupidity.

I wouldn't be afforded the opportunity to defend my position so Tom could see my point-of-view, the dinner table with our families simply wasn't the time or place for it. If I could have, what raged through my mind, were all of the sticking points I could not make him aware of. First off, Castaneda accepted several academic degrees based on the information given to him by a living informant, not a fictional character. They don't give university degrees for information dispensed by fictional characters whenever a student decides to fabricate one. Secondly, Castaneda went on to many well-paid professional teaching positions based on the credentials he earned from UCLA.

If you take away his degrees, he was never qualified to hold those teaching positions. He won awards based on the truthfulness and authenticity of his contribution to anthropological science. Imagine a scientist making a great discovery based on false evidence? Castaneda claimed the events he reported were factual accounts depicting real people. He said many times his results, entering the sorcerer's world, achieving total freedom, were a reproducible science, independently verifiable by those who were willing to participate in a lifetime of struggle.

I resent listening to him tell us the stories over and over that were simply not true. I felt that he was lying to me, personally, and I felt stupid. He never won a Pulitzer Prize. He never had an audience with the Pope, as he had so hysterically alleged he had. In my opinion, he could have only been a psychopathic liar, an extreme case, if ever a diagnosis could have been made. That is my only, and was my only beef. The fakery, the moral wrongness of being dishonest and lying to the entire world. It makes a mockery of an entire field of science, of UCLA, of me and everyone.

And it was the ever-present potential for fakery that amused Tom to no end, as he puckered his lips and scratched his nose to hide a growing smile. Having known me since the early days, my brother-warrior on the path of knowledge, he seemed thoroughly amused with how the whole story finally resolved itself. As a close friend, he had long known of the story of the man on the bus who spoke to me about Castaneda as the ultimate trickster. I think in Tom's mind, Castaneda's work was always metaphorical, so he was relatively indifferent to it, immune from Carlos's literary fraud. For him, seeing his friend become deeply involved with Castaneda's work was no different than if I had decided to practice Judaism, Islam or Buddhism. I chose to follow a path of belief and faith, as billions often do. He felt the value was personal, just as how beauty is in the eye of the beholder.

While he's not wrong, I asserted it was the work of a cheating student who, once caught up in the phenomena of a big hit bestseller, could not go back on his statement and instead pushed it all forward to the height of the ultimate absurdity. Which now that I look back, was truly his wheelhouse anyway, pushing everything past the point of absurdity, all for the sake of a good laugh. That was Carlos. I hate to admit it, but I think he just enjoyed a good laugh.

Tom expressed his feeling that, "If it pointed to the mystery and the wonder of being alive, then, like any religious or new age teaching, all is forgiven, right? I mean, even Dan's book, *The Way of the Peaceful Warrior*, and many others you enjoyed so much, are all novels. Lobsang Rampa, Richard Bach and Jane Roberts, you had no problem knowing that was all fiction. What about J.R.R Tolkien? As fiction, Castaneda is no less fascinating than Lord Of The Rings. Maybe more so, because it speaks directly to today's counterculture."

"Don't get me started on Lobsang Rampa," I warned him. "He's another big time faker who turned up dirty."

Tom showed genuine surprise, "Oh, I didn't know? Is that true?" he laughed, "All of this is news to me. I have just been off doing own thing. I didn't realize all this drama was unfolding."

I told him the story of Rampa, whose autobiographical work depicted his childhood growing up in a Tibetan monastic order, in the city of Lhasa. Eventually, he was discovered to be some fat, old white guy in Ohio who had never even been to Tibet. He claimed, once he'd been discovered, that he'd had an accident and been killed by a knock on the head. It was then when Lobsang Rampa's soul *transmigrated* into his body and wrote all the books," I explained.

Why couldn't he just say Rampa was his noms de plume and simply be the novelist he actually was? Why did he have to lie to the public and say he was writing his autobiography? Twenty, or more, books and I read every one. Loved them! I even shared them with my friends who also loved them. How many misrepresented books have I read in my life now, and believed to be authentic? The field is ripe for the picking when suckers like me are born every minute.

"Yes, but even so, Vin. You loved those books more than anyone I've known. Please, you have to look past the sour grapes and see the beauty in it. Sure, you're upset now. But one day, you'll move on. It's only a matter of time." Tom spoke to me with such love and compassion. He was making perfect sense. I had taken a big hit and needed time to work through the damage, which my worldview has sustained. I still needed time to let the chips fall, to pick up all the pieces of my shattered journey and move on. So much make-believe had been sold to me as fact, and I bought it all. I was more jaded and cynical than I had ever been.

I had to admit there *are* so many great fables throughout history, wonderful examples of metaphor, myth and legend, which do have deep lasting value for mankind. It didn't bother him that they weren't factual accounts, and he wanted me to not disregard everything I'd learned from those years.

"Don't throw the baby out with the bathwater, Vin," he cautioned me. "You're still going to walk away from this with some seriously valuable spiritual lessons here. You don't want to disregard that. I mean, just because Carlos turned out to be the Coyote Trickster, right?" He paused and waited for his reference to register. "You were warned," he laughed, pointing his fork at me while eating his meal, "Many times."

I was so embarrassed. I felt like such an idiot. It was far worse than I can describe, how deep my dismay with myself ran. I had definitely become bitter but it was more complex than that. My inability to make sense of human spirituality was so complete that I just had to dismiss the subject entirely from my life. I didn't want anything to do with any of it anymore and for the next 15 years, I vehemently renounced all of it. I was done with being a spiritual seeker. And I was done with magical thinking.

For me, the real take away has been about exposing how grown adults use imagination and the world of make-believe to take advantage of their fellow man. From my fifteen years in Castaneda's world, what did I get for my time and trouble? What separated the baby from the bathwater? What gifts of knowledge and understanding had I received, from the point when I was a child in church at St. John's, to the day I first met Phil King, to the moment Rich Jennings drove that final nail into Castaneda's coffin?

For me, Castaneda did teach me some very valuable lessons. Not unlike the lessons he professed to have learned from his teacher don Juan Matus, they were, not at all, the lessons I thought they would be. But they were lessons, none-the-less. These were like the lessons one learns from suffering a nasty divorce, or surviving a tragic accident, from losing everything, some horrific event one could only wish had never happened.

And if the lessons he intended to teach were the lessons I actually walked away with, then he was, indeed, far more brilliant than I will ever be able to give him credit for. You really have to be able to step outside all the boundaries of human decency and morality to deliver, or even be the one who has to swallow these lessons whole. I admit it, I stepped outside. And I got clobbered. I thought I was so clever that I could learn to hot-wire reality, because of reading some authors who were saying they knew how. I went down the dark back alley because I was curious. I wanted to find out where Castaneda's intoxicating journey led to. And I found out.

In the end, I wanted to know the way life actually is. I would rather it be this way, even getting hurt, than to have gone through life believing Castaneda was for real, never having known for sure, because I never had the guts to go straight to the source, to pursue it all to its natural end. I know the truth now and the matter is completely resolved, in my case. This much I am truly grateful for.

My first loyalty has always been to the universe, to life, to know what it has to teach me about itself, not what any man has to say about it. The universe itself is the only spiritual authority, life itself, not man. Carlos proved I can not trust any man's opinion, or perceived authority, in regards to learning about the way life actually is. I can only learn about the way life actually is, by seeing how life actually is, for myself.

I had to be willing to throw away the polite descriptions of humanity as a divinely-descended, child-species and regurgitate the stock depictions of human spirituality written from the point of view of man's arrogance. I had to turn the whole idea on its head and not see myself looking out, through my own eyes at the universe, but from the perspective of the universe looking down to see what is actually here. When we no longer see ourselves as something separate, looking out at the Milky Way galaxy, we see ourselves as if we *are* the Milky Way galaxy. Each person is as much a part of the Milky Way galaxy as the solar system itself, as much as any object anywhere in the system. We are as much a part of the whole system as any other part of the system. Whatever our worldview is, whatever we might believe we are, once this supposed definition is destroyed, the only thing left is what actually is. When belief is destroyed all that remains is pure perception in the state of being. There is only being.

His lesson was about being taken advantage of by the very nature of belief itself. Taking that long hard look in the mirror to see the collectively imagined for what it is: apparitions, concatenations of the human mind, mythical fiction, structures designed and built out of pure thought and nothing more. As I wrote in the opening of this book:

> ...imagination and make-believe, aren't actually real because they are merely made of thought, which has no corporeal reality. We cannot touch imagination, nor can we consider anything that is make-believe to be real. Since all of our thoughts are simply imaginary, theoretically, they don't exist. And in this sense, they are nothing.

He broke me and I had to admit that, once belief is defeated it was clear to me, mankind is, by and large, enraptured under the spell of his own imagination, living in the world of make-believe regarding far more than simply human spirituality. Now, I could see how imagination and the world of make-believe are interwoven throughout the fabric of human relations, to much greater degree than I realized. The human ability to imagine and form beliefs about everything affects us all far more broadly than we would dare to admit to ourselves. Fascinatingly, there are countless people who have already recognized this quite naturally, or were never susceptible to magical thinking and mythical belief. They simply understand what is made of mind and what is made of matter and never had a problem distinguishing between the two.

Imagination and the world of make-believe are the glue holding the interactive realm of human doings together, holding all of our intricate systems of thought, under it's spell. And if it were not for the power this spell holds over us, the whole of humanity would come apart at the seams and descend into chaos, we would become unknown to ourselves and to each other. It is precisely this spell which Castaneda highjacked and made use of for his own ends. What is imagined runs through everything we are and far deeper than any of us might be willing to admit could be the case.

Castaneda taught me exactly the way the guy on the bus in West Los Angeles told me he would. By being a trickster coyote, he put himself in a position to become the ruthless destroyer of my deeply held illusions, making himself wealthy in the process. And I can hear Carlos laughing all the way to his grave. He got me a good one. I was taken advantage of by the very nature of my own belief. It was all a big practical joke for the sake of a good laugh. But I didn't find it so funny.

Castaneda's final lesson, which he did not deliver to me until after his death, in grand fashion, was *don't believe everything people tell you.* (Sadly, it was the same lesson my Dad taught me repeatedly as a kid. Go figure.) My Dad told me over and over again, his own adaptation of an Edgar Allen Poe quote, "Don't believe anything you hear, half of what you see, maybe a little bit of what you read and you'll do okay in this life."

If anything, Castaneda did more to point to the mystery of being alive than anyone I ever knew. He gave us another convincing version of what the mystery of being alive might be, and showed me that no matter how elaborate, or spellbinding, or beautiful, a creation story might seem, it is all still a glossary of terms, a handful of labels and a fictional story, a concatenation of the human mind. It's only a description, puffs of air, a little choo-choo train of words running through the head of a mindless ape. It only exists in the human imagination in the end, and nowhere else in all of time or space.

Down The Rabbit Hole

The further I have chased this imaginary rabbit down the hole of make-believe, the more astonished I have become by how far down this rabbit actually runs. Imagination is all-powerful and can completely consume the human mind in worlds of make-believe, until not a trace of common sense remains. It is so powerful that others can use it to convince us of nearly anything and we'll be absolutely certain that it's true.

Everyone who participated in Castaneda's strange fictional story got something out of it, but for others the price was simply far too high, the damage from the cost of entry into his world, the price of admission, was far too great. I was young enough still, that once I made it out and went through the painful process of cultic deprogramming, I could pick up the pieces of my life and build something out of it. Others were not so fortunate. A lot of people, and even myself to some degree, had their lives permanently damaged by devoting themselves so totally to these teachings of a false prophet. Many had left their families too late and stayed isolated too long. Their loved ones died while they were away and they were robbed of the richness of relationships with the people they loved most in this life. They were stung by regret for mistaking their loyalties. Many had foregone having children, choosing instead to dedicate their entire lives to the pursuit of these teachings. I was nearly one of them.

Others I was close to, were simply too far removed from the world to ever make it back completely and still wander around, from cult to cult, looking for something new to latch onto, something wonderful to become apart of again. As sad as it seems, they still want the magic. They want to find someone to love again, the way they loved Carlos and his many wonderful stories. Sadly, for many, it was too late to pick up the pieces and return to a normal life, too many years got behind them and the brainwashing was so powerful that even with all the cult deprogramming work in the world, there is a residue it leaves on your soul which you can never quite shake.

When I followed Castaneda, I unknowingly travelled with him into the world of make-believe. As I joined in his various workshops, I unwittingly entered into collective group imaginings within the shared world of adult make-believe. To the degree we acted in the world of everyday life, discussing his books, joining in the Tensegrity movements, we danced together in the world of make-believe. For me then, it was one of the most beautiful experiences I'd ever had. And if dancing together were all that it was, then fine. It was a wonderful evening. I had a marvelous time with my elegant, glamorous friends. It was many, many wonderful evenings and glorious afternoons spent dancing with my warrior brothers and sisters in the world of make-believe.

Imagination can be used to mislead us, both innocently, by those who love us and intentionally by those who seek to take advantage of us for money, sex or power. We hear the wonderful story being told to us and we choose to believe it, we give-in to the suspension of disbelief as we do when watching a Hollywood movie. There are people who keep repeating what they want us to believe, even though they know it's not true. They are entirely convinced that if they say it enough times, and with enough confidence and conviction, they can make us believe whatever they want us to, because it is all just make-believe. They make you... believe.

The Suicide Pact: Five Missing Women

For some, it has been alleged there was a criminal act woven into the teachings of Carlos Castaneda, hidden within the romanticism of acquiring the most noble of human attributes. Moreover, it may have been some twisted long-form style of murder, which Castaneda himself may have committed. It is possible he was no different than Charlie Musslewhite, Jim Jones and David Koresh, leading some of his followers to intentionally take their own lives in order fulfill a pact, some suicidal clause, an intoxicatingly romanticized aspect of his teachings.

At the time of Castaneda's death there were rumors circulating that Carlos had succeeded in reaching total freedom and when he left he world, he took some of the warrior party with him, not all. Since he did not have sufficient energy, he only took those his energy could afford. The rest were left to find their freedom at a later time. Being perceived as leaving the world in the way his teachings describe it can be done, would make him look like a hero and cement his story within a mystery of biblical proportions for all time. This may have been the motivation for Castaneda to develop a plan to make it appear as if his teachings really did prove out in the end. As well, it would keep the cash cow rolling for Cleargreen, Inc.

I believe Castaneda truly wanted the world to believe his stories were true, so he could go down in history as a figure of mythic proportions. I am convinced he would do anything, go to any lengths and tell anyone anything, in an attempt to give future generations the impression that he was a historic figure the likes of Buddha, Confucius, or even Jesus Christ. I believe his megalomania knew no boundaries. Having suffered from the psychiatric disorder myself, with the way people around him worshipped him, his wealth and fame, he was in a much greater position of risk than I ever was, for the condition to overwhelm him completely.

Some have also hypothesized that Castaneda somehow came to believe in his whole story himself, that what was emerging from his stories, for him, came from a reality all its own, not just from him. He may have started to believe that his stories were the account of how the sorcerers were actually contacting him in a separate reality and entering his world this way, to teach him, to teach the world through his stories. So he made the sorcerer's world a physical story about him going to Mexico, because whether it happened in physical reality, or make-believe reality, what the hell's the difference, if you decide that any conceivable sense of reality is all a form of the dreamed anyway. He didn't need to go to Mexico, he was being taken, by beings who were capable of doing that kind of stuff. Whether from one dream or the next, if he could imagine it, then it was all coming to him as if from a supernatural reality, one that he was now being called to report to the world about.

He may have started to believe that his famous stories were not the product of his own imagination, but the sorcerers were using him as a conduit for their knowledge to reach the world. So, like he told us in his published work, he faithfully recorded it all and reported it through his anthropological work. In this sense, it was real to him, because it all existed in *A Separate Reality*. If he believed this, then it would account for how vehemently he defended the authenticity of his work to his death.

With all the religious teachings in the world, the notion of being contacted through supernatural means, is not rare. For example, the stories of how Joseph Smith, Jr., who as a fifteen year-old boy, was contacted by the angel Moroni, and given the gold plates, which no one ever saw but him, touched off the Mormon religion. Since Castaneda's stories were so rich and powerful, and his fame so great as a result, he may have started to believe his books were evidence that he had been taken by the sorcerers, captured in some way and hauled off into a separate reality where he became an apprentice to the art of sorcery. He became convinced he was interacting with the sorcerers through an unseen dreaming reality. Since the world itself had become so fascinated by his stories, his face making the cover of Time Magazine, the media frenzy which came to him from these stories, it may have gone to his head in some inconceivable way. As a young undergraduate, he may have been caught up in his own hype and started to believe in it all by some twist of reality, one he had a rationale for in his own mind.

The next step, which Carlos reinforced to us over and over throughout his workshops, was that his make-believe world could also become real for anyone who would simply join him in believing in it. He constantly harped on us about the suspension of disbelief being the hinge on which the door into the world of the sorcerers of ancient Mexico would swing open for us. Like any children playing a make-believe game, Carlos set up the rules of the game, in his books, further elaborated and changed them in the workshops, then he convinced everyone that if we all believed in it completely, the whole thing could work, possibly. It could become a separate reality which could be inhabited only by those who believed. (Sound familiar?) He honestly admitted, many times, the odds were stacked against it. It was the warrior's way to fight in the face of inconceivable odds. If we all made the life-long commitment to reach for the goal, to live with a singular purpose, to live out the warrior's dream, there was a possibility we could succeed in joining the sorcerers of ancient Mexico in a separate reality somewhere, someday. And this is how he got us. This is how he got so many girls! The women loved it! And so did everybody else. So, he kept it up.

And from being there with him on so many occasions, I can tell you, this is exactly the way he liked to put it across, that only if you believed in it, only through suspension of disbelief could anyone become capable of witnessing the separate reality he had made a career out of reporting on. For him, don Juan was real, because he had built-out this elaborately intricate description of a tantalizing universal mystery, somehow this meant mankind actually had the potential to align the total-self and burn with the fire from within, escaping death to fly off to the next plane of existence. The only problem with this is, a little issue some would call the laws of physics.

I believe he knew he was making it up and putting one over on everyone. If we follow this line of reasoning then, in his mind he could have been thinking, "How could what I am doing be any different from any other religion or belief system that is alive and well on planet earth in the modern day. And what about people like L. Ron Hubbard? If he could develop Scientology, than why not me? Why shouldn't I deliver *The Teachings of Don Juan*? The public is hungry for it. So, I am giving it to them." Hook, line and sinker.

All too often, the public never realizes, until after the fact, how harmful something actually was. Maybe Carlos felt he was another L. Ron Hubbard, a Joseph Smith, Jr. and so what?

Well, how about this for so what? At the time of his death, five women went missing and have never been seen or heard from again. Kylie Lundahl, Patricia Lee Partin, Talia Bey, Florinda Donner-Grau and Taisha Abelar have not been seen or heard from in over 20 years and are all believed dead. The remains of one of the women, Patricia Lee Partin, has since been found in one of the most remote areas of Death Valley and identified through DNA testing. The other four have never been seen or heard from since. The fact that Partin's remains were found in such a remote location reinforces the notion that her intention was to never be found, to make it look like she could have, indeed, left the world with Carlos.

There have been plenty of articles exploring the details of what may have happened to them and the details of these five women's sad story can all be found there. What I want to bring to light is how and why this happened. I have no doubt they all took their own lives and I will explain why. To understand why, you have to understand how a woman feels and why she feels that way. You want to look at what she believed and what those beliefs meant to her. You need to have, at some point in your own life, felt the incomprehensibly powerful magic of romantic seduction, to even begin to comprehend what may have led these beautiful souls to kill themselves for Carlos.

The Story of Kylie Lundahl

I was present on more than one occasion, in Seattle, Oakland and again in Pasadena and Anaheim, where Kylie professed what I can only refer to as some strange warrior's code of self-determination. She told the attendees that if ever all was lost, and there was no way to "go with Carlos" or claim total-freedom, if it were to be her fate to be left behind, her final act as a warrior would be to take a gun and leave this world by her own hand, rather than allow anything other her own unbending intent deal her final fate. She did not come up with any of these ideas on her own. Everything was taught to her by Carlos. I was also present when Carlos first raised the idea of suicide as a warrior, by one's own hand, as being superior to *being assassinated from afar*, dying the insulting, impudent death of an ordinary fool who failed to reach total-freedom. Claiming total freedom was a deliberate act. If one's leaving the world meant the deliberate act of aligning the totality of the self, then even in failure, one's leaving the world through a deliberate act of dying a warrior's death must still be so.

Kylie believed, as Carlos described to us, that only the Nagual Man could lead her to freedom. She needed him to take her with him or all would be lost. Somehow, if she was left behind, all hope was lost and that was it, this was final. To be taken by a lesser death, was suddenly now, not a part of the warrior's code of self-determination, I was learning. It was being cheated of the right to choose for oneself the day and time of leaving the world. There was a romanticism that Carlos invoked in dying. He summoned the mystique of the Samurai with his air of finality, likening the path of his teachings to the sense of nobility warriors take in dying. With this romantic magic, he would wrap a woman in its sweet embrace and she would be defenseless, swooning in it, seduced by this, by his wealth and his celebrity, and she would be willing to do anything he asked, willing to die to keep such a powerful romantic magic alive to the final moment. She would gladly go to her grave, considering it her highest virtue to make her own ultimate sacrifice, to keep the spell unbroken. This romantic seduction of the warrior's death becomes the most meaningful action she could ever take, her final act on this earth, which proved she truly meant it all, that she was deeply sincere, to the very core of her heart. Only this warrior death would forever keep the romantic flame, of her total commitment, of her warrior's heart, alive to the final moment.

Somehow, the appeal of this magical romance story also had to do with its creepiness and how Carlos could use the creepy to paint himself as their shield from the terror of a sorcerer's world. The women, enflamed by primal fear, would cling to Carlos. He told them he alone could show them how to save themselves from the creepy crawly creatures, which meant to do them harm. He cemented himself as their protector this way. Kylie was absolutely convinced everything Carlos was teaching her was the whole truth, that he was an incorruptible man of unquestionable sincerity, whose leadership was imperative.

We were all told this on many occasions. It had long-been common knowledge that only the Nagual man could hold open the portal to infinity just long enough for his party to slip through. No sorcerer's party could make it without the leader of the party, the Nagual man, guiding them. She believed, like many cults do, including Heaven's Gate, that she needed her leader, she needed Carlos to take her with him when he left this world forever. He was her spaceship behind the Hale-Bopp comet. Carlos was her Kool-Aid and only through him could she drink her way to the other side of infinity and be romantically whisked off her feet forever. She believed, and stated on several occasions in my presence, she would either go with Carlos and live forever when he left the world, or she would die by her own hand.

Most notably, in Seattle, she stopped the Tensegrity exercises, in mid-session, to do what Carlos and the Witches would do, give a spellbinding and inspiring talk to the crowd of participants. She gave the same intensely passion-infused, romantic speech her mentors had given us on so many occasions. She said she was encouraged by them to do so, since only her and her two counterparts, Renny and Nye, the Chacmools, were presenting this event. Kylie spoke with the same romantically charged passion about the purpose of Castaneda's work. She was maturing in her understanding and practice of the teachings and was capable of delivering a speech with the same level of power as her masters. It was all-or-nothing for her, and she drove the point home that they were not even remotely fucking around in their pursuit of total freedom.

She made it very clear at that workshop that if Carlos did not take her with him she would take a gun and go off somewhere, where she could never be found, and take her own life. She romanticized the idea of how it would be better to die than to live without him, to live without hope of freedom. She asserted that the only true statement of a warrior's spirit was that if they had to die, then the warrior alone, should chose the day and hour of their own death. No other force, should tell a warrior when it was time to die.

Journey To Ixtlan is filled with references to a warrior's death. Carlos relied heavily on references to death, throughout his work, to create an atmosphere of romance between warriors and the presence of their own deaths, as a literary device to tug at the heartstrings of the reader. But nowhere in any of his written work does it insinuate that a warrior would take his own life in any circumstance. It was quite the opposite. The quest for total freedom was a fight for life, to live, to conquer death, not give in to it. If you're still alive it's because your death hasn't touched you yet, and you're not going to allow it to touch you.

The idea of the warrior dancing to his death, that death would wait, while a warrior continued to dance, was one of the most beautiful things I have ever read. The fight, the whole warrior ethos, was a battle to go on living, to live for freedom. If you weren't dead, this meant you were still alive to keep on fighting for freedom, to live another day, and no force in the universe, other than a warrior's own will to live, could determine how far one could go on the path of knowledge. Yes, a warrior accepts that today is a good day to die, that this could be their final day alive on the earth, but they never throw in the towel, ever. The idea of accepting death was more about accepting it as an inevitable risk in hunting power, in cracking open the self and entering into the world of apocalyptic visions. That's dangerous territory, the world of psychiatric patients. They would give themselves completely to attempting these daring acts of power, and if they died in the process of making their bid for power, than so be it. Warrior's were brave and daring in pursuing the totality of the self, but never suicidal.

It's odd that the original idea in the books, how a warrior will never give himself to death, was suddenly being contradicted. In the workshops, he contradicted his books, fairly often, changed his mind, made a different argument. When I first heard Carlos deliver the idea, in October of 1995 at the Culver City workshop, I was perplexed by how he had gone from the original statement of a warrior never giving himself to death, to now we are to interpret this to mean that warrior would kill himself rather than die naturally of old age or if freedom was no longer possible. If you died trying, that's not the same as taking your own life. It seemed so morbid. It was hard to accept and I shook my head every time I heard the subject breached. All four of them spoke of it in their lectures, Carlos, Taisha, Florinda and Kylie.

I believe, as do many others who were also present, that when Kylie went missing immediately upon Castaneda's ordinary death, she did exactly as she told us she would do in Seattle and mentioned at several other workshops. She did what Carlos said he would do, what we should all do, if we were truly warriors of total freedom and all hope of freedom was lost. She went off somewhere where no one would ever find her remains and she took her own life. There is a lot of circumstantial evidence to support this. She was never seen again, shortly after Carlos died. She stated on several occasions she would take her own life if certain conditions came to exist. Those conditions did, in fact, come to exist and immediately when they did, she went missing, as did all five of these women.

I find it strange that all five women showed more balls than Carlos. He died the death of an ordinary man. He was a coward in his own professed context, in that when he learned he had liver cancer, if he lived to his own standards of warriorhood, he would have immediately gone somewhere and taken his own life, instead of dying from cancer. But he was a Jackass, so he told all five ladies go take their own lives, while he died like a coward, in his comfy bed, with all his young girls tending to him. From a fighting warrior's perspective, he was never a warrior, he was a disgrace to the uniform. That he spent his life and career making reference to the greatness of the warrior, claiming to live the life of the warrior, teaching the way to others, only makes him a poser, an embarrassment to himself and all those who associated with him, myself included.

Kylie possessed a very strong personality. She was extremely forceful and definite. Her words were final, absolute statements of her total commitment to this way of life. She had to be the most disciplined practitioner out of everyone. There was no one more dedicated to embodying the teachings than her. She was the shining example of everything Castaneda taught us the warrior's spirit should be. So, if she said she was going to do something, I am convinced she would even go to her own death, in a heartbeat, to keep her sense of warrior's honor intact. Even if, in her mind, it meant taking her own life, her reasons were sound. It was more than romance, it was more than passion, it was honor, bravery and valor. To her, it was her proof to the universe that she meant it.

It saddens me deeply because she was one of the finest, most exceptional women I have ever met. I would liken her to the elite warriors, like meeting a heroic Navy SEAL or an Army Ranger, a highly trained individual who was fully prepared to give their life on the battlefield and consider it their highest honor. She was woven of the same material as any combat-ready freedom warrior on the planet. She went to the state of total war, ready to die, for all the same reasons, for all the right reasons, she was a good and decent human being who lived an impeccable and honorable way, whose heart was in the right place but like so many who fight and die, she fought for the glory of commanders who were flying a losing flag. She was a brainwashed victim of Carlos Castaneda's propaganda of lies. She died for all the right reasons, with complete honor, nobility and valor but for no purpose other than to serve a megalomaniacs ego-driven false glory. And it's not like she was the first person in history to ever do that. What we are seeing in this case has played out millions of times throughout the course of human history. She died for a belief system that taught her it was honorable to do what she did.

If she had been serving her country, she would have died for it in the line of duty, and been worthy of the Medal of Honor, but since she lived in the service of a madman, she died in a line of duty no less honorably. Her valor as a warrior remains forever intact. The banner of belief under which she gave her life is of little consequence at this point. Only that she became a martyr in the line of duty remains. The only thing that mattered to her was that she had lived and died as a warrior. For her, there was no more dignified way to have lived, no calling more worthy of dying for. That she called-in a strike on her own position, to uphold the honor of her leader, to serve his mission, was proof of her bravery and valor.

Whatever imaginary power of propaganda led her to her appointment with the infinite it would, by no means, tarnish her own impeccable warrior spirit. Throughout human history people have only needed a context in which to live for their own highest calling. Kylie did that. She lived her life in alignment with her highest possible attainment of personal excellence. It is no fault of her own that her cause was in vane, imagined, make-believe. Her nobility was clear, pure and inviolate. Though her cause was imaginary, her answer to her highest calling was sincere. She had the heart of a true warrior.

Her family has been searching the world over since she went missing, pleading with the public for any information as to her whereabouts, to no avail. Their intense sadness and grief, must surely know no boundaries. Like the family of Fred Gomez, they are left with a totally merciless lack of closure and the bewilderment of an unanswerable why.

Florinda and Taisha

At the time of Castaneda's death, Florida Donner-Grau and Taisha Abelar also went missing. Abelar and Donner-Grau, both authors, whose books attempted to parallel and support the authenticity of Castaneda's story, have never been found. They are believed to have been in on Castaneda's hoax, since public records have yielded marriage certificates with dates conflicting with timeline of Castaneda's published work. They could have been in on the hoax or, if not, he led them to believe he was the leader of a party of sorcerers from the beginning. Having been around them many times and listening to the ladies talk, it appears Castaneda did draw-in all the women in his life under the auspices of romantic claims that he was the sorcerer he said he was in his books.

If so, it is believed the ladies took their own lives shortly after the time of his death and just have not been found. All of them were certainly smart enough to leave no trace and never be found, if this was their instruction. If Florinda and Taisha were in on the hoax, as the authoring of their own books about their apprenticeships to a fictional don Juan Matus might suggest, then it is thought they simply took the money and fled the country. Since nothing has ever been found of them, it is possible they were more like the younger female apprentices and under the spell of this master storyteller and manipulator.

By my own admission, I believe it is quite possible they also took their own lives. Like Kylie, Patricia and Talia Bey, they were simply following the directive driven into them by Castaneda. I have personally heard both Florinda and Taisha speak publicly in the workshops about taking their own lives, preferring to die like a warrior, if they discovered all was lost on the warrior path and they failed to attain total-freedom. Using this language in their lectures is how they would ratchet up the power of their presentations. It was all a life or death proposal. They sought to enflame the passions of their audiences as much as possible by parading the idea of death around for dramatic impact. Death sells. Death gets headlines. Castaneda had a romantic obsession with how death gives to life this ultimate touch of poignant beauty.

For a while after his death, Cleargreen was issuing the story that Castaneda had actually done what he set out to achieve in his books. They issued a statement telling everyone that he basically achieved total-alignment and crossed over into the third attention with the missing women in tow. Cleargreen attempted to make Castaneda's death look like the final proof that he was not bullshitting and that his written work was, in fact, genuine. To me, by making this statement, it appears reasonable to suppose this implies the possibility of collusion on the part of Castaneda's remaining members, that they knew these five women were meant to die and knowingly conspired in the process. It was stated by Cleargreen that Florinda, Taisha, Kylie and Patricia Partin, (a.k.a. The Blue Scout) were all in the warrior's party that left the world with Carlos and have forever travelled into the unknowable. We were supposed to celebrate their success in achieving total-freedom and therefore, claiming a conditional form of eternal life, and here is the most chilling part, until the day we could all join them.

"It appears as if time is some incomprehensible mirage and even memories are tenuous, at best. The here and now, Square One, is really the only place worth living. And that voice in our heads is made purely of imaginary thought. I learned to let it go, pause it, barely listen."

Chapter Twelve
WHEN ALL IS LOST

PORTLAND, OREGON, IN the winter, is wet, cold, gloomy and gray, a fitting and dismal location to have landed only to bottom out spiritually and call it quits. No longer on a spiritual quest for total freedom, no longer seeing myself as a warrior fighting to gain control of the totality of the self, I put down my dreaming diary and my Tensegrity balls and finally just looked at the world as an ordinary person, all spiritual bullshit aside. I took a long, hard, honest look at myself in the mirror and could only shake my head in disgust. For the first time in my life, I looked at the world as a purely physical place. It was still a wondrous mystery and this was the singular point I have never let myself lose sight of in my long, painful recovery from this horrible accident.

No longer a warrior on the path toward some ridiculous infinity, I looked up into the stars and felt the hard finality of a cold, black and very finite universe, a finite life and I was growing old. Everything was still an open-ended mystery, but none of it was what I thought it might be. None of it was what I had been taught to believe it was. The world is only what it is and has never been anything more all along. This whole, long, strange trip has been nothing more than my own mind trying to come to terms with this simple fact. It was no longer the kind of mystery I could imagine myself having gained any insight into, what so ever.

I was so amazed to find that after fifteen years of studying the mystery of existence, I knew jack fucking shit more than I did the day I first set foot on the path of knowledge. What was worse is that I actually knew far less. I knew nothing. I actually knew absolutely nothing with any real degree of certainty except that I was a total idiot and a real-life loser who hadn't accomplished anything meaningful in life. I had let my life come to the most unrewarding place imaginable. I had nothing, I knew nothing of any value and I had just spent thirty-five years going absolutely nowhere. Talk about lamenting one's misspent youth. This was where I landed at this point in my life.

I was now a few more failed relationships down the line and about to start-in working on my second wife. Fortunately, for me, she turned out to be a far better person than I, and took pity on me during these bitter and bewildering years. I was the (extremely good-looking) train wreck of a man, which she had found and scraped up off the side of the information superhighway one day, on a matchmaking site, taking me home to nurture back to good health. I felt fortunate, as if dodging a bullet, to still be young and able enough to find a nice girl to marry, to settle down with and have children of our own. Although it was now later in life, I still had this last-train-out-of-Dodge opportunity to start a family and carry on with my life. How fortunate was I, at the age of thirty-five, to make the acquaintance of a single, childless beauty in her thirties, who was now ready to settle down and start a family?

For now, what my life had come to bewildered me to no end. Up to this point, everything about me was fake. Everything I had ever said to myself in my most sincere moments was all narcissistic self-reflection. I began to question my longstanding denial of the bi-polar diagnosis and considered the explanation that kundalini might be nothing more than superstitious belief in the supernatural. I began to question the true state of my mental health. If a man were truly crazy, a lunatic, how would he know it by looking outward, seriously inquiring from within himself? I had a lot of shit I needed to work out with myself. And that's all it was, just shit. I needed to take a long, hard look at my life and get my shit together.

I was dead wrong on so many levels in making the most important life-decisions about the direction that would be best for my own future. The subjects I studied and the decisions I made in pursuing useful knowledge, marketable skills and what I believed would lead to a highly-rewarding future, came crashing down to the complete opposite. The subjects I felt passionate about, the fields of knowledge I trusted would deliver the most rewarding discoveries, betrayed my trust. I was now living the most unrewarding life imaginable. I had failed miserably in choosing my life's path because everything I believed was true, once I ran it down and pursued it to its natural end, through over a decade of effort and expense, proved to be nothing more than imagination, like chasing a pot of gold at the end of a rainbow. I did that over and over again in my life. How could I ever even learn to trust myself again?

I realized my confidence had taken on damage to the point where I'd lost the ability to even trust my own judgment. Even while I had been so confident and self-assured, the most physically fit and agile I had ever been,

I lost all respect for myself and wallowed in self-loathing. It was a sad place to be. I was devastated but I took responsibility for my decisions and tried to keep a stiff upper lip in looking forward. I would have to remake myself into something new. As the seasons of my lifetime would have it, starting a family and becoming a father to two lovely little girls was going be the door that was now opening for me.

All I ever wanted was to filter out the confusion and conflicting beliefs and understand what actually *is* and only what *is*. As Carl Sagan said, "What the universe has to teach us about itself." All the human believing in the world isn't going to change the way life actually *is*. Evidently, I believed the universe was going to teach me, what I believed it had to teach me, but what I believed was not at all what the universe had to teach. And I was still struggling with that. What does the universe have to teach *me*? What am I going to understand once I began to see life the way it actually is?

This is the only reason I became a seeker and explored everything I did, why I'd tried everything I tried, why I followed the paths I followed. I was thirsting for truth about the way life actually is, like a drowning man desperately gasps for a breath of air. I went everywhere, turned over every stone trying to get to the bottom of it. Now, here I was at rock bottom. What was it I needed to learn? Something about everything I had been taught wasn't working, so I was always looking for that next thing which would bring me into a state of deep inner-peace and satisfy my longing to feel like I belonged where I stood. But I finally came to realize, I had allowed myself to be misled all this time and it was nobody's fault but mine.

It occurred to me that the sum total of all of the circumstances of my earlier life had contributed to this susceptibility to be influenced by creeps who take advantage of the beliefs of others. I was somehow an incomplete and needy person in my core. The seeking was all about how to put a salve on that sore spot. Trying to unravel the mysteries of the universe was a nice distraction from the wounded core of who I am, which needed to find some tangible form of peace and well-being. I was always only seeking to make myself whole, find my own completeness, come home to the place where I belonged. I never understood what I needed most was simply a place to call home and people who would always be there for me, who never would abandon ship and leave me alone. I came to find that beyond this crash would follow a new beginning.

Without a foundation for my life, my personal growth could not take root. I had been cut off at the roots long ago, and had been wandering around lost, trying to find fertile soil ever since. I was only ever seeking repair the warmth and power of my own sacred unbroken circle, so the natural cycles of my life could one day come to their own fruition. Everything else I tried to build my life around was just an empty attempt to arrive at a place I could call home, to live the rest of my life in peace with the people I love and most want to be with.

Early in my life, all my core beliefs had been radically and emotionally disrupted and my inner-self had become a place of upheaval which left me vulnerable to those who take advantage of others under the banner of self-completion, wholeness and inner-peace. Having met my wife Yolanda, this changed my personal circumstances completely in regard to this vulnerability, without my even realizing it. I have always known my personality needs a stable environment to thrive, structure, a firm foundation. I needed to belong to a warm, healthy family and I was consistently drawn to that throughout the course of my life. But it had never been my fate to find such lasting belonging. So I continued perpetually looking for my answer.

I know now that I was always searching for something I desperately needed to feel whole. I felt like I was missing a huge part of who I was. I had lost my center and was searching for it in everything but myself. This is what led me to seeking. These were my footsteps in the dark, something Cat Stevens had written about, something I couldn't completely understand. But I had now given up on the spiritual quest and renounced any sense of seeking. Letting go all my self-concern, I was finally about to come home.

Chasing Rainbows In The World Of Make-Believe

Now that I am older and can look back, having, quite haphazardly, found wholeness and completeness in my own nuclear family unit, in the absence of seeking and in being who I always already am. It now appears obvious that I was a vulnerable and ready candidate for falling prey to any group or cult that would help me feel like I belonged to something emotionally rewarding. The problem I found is that we can't fake emotionally rewarding. What we invest our precious life energy in has to be authentic, genuine and true to the inmost self. We have to pursue meaningful ends and, to the degree we are able, enjoy the rewarding satisfactions which we painstakingly cultivate in the process. There has to be a pay off. We can't just keep getting ripped off and remain emotionally healthy.

I always thought I was on the right path but, time and time again, I kept pulling up in dead ends. It was the result of my neediness and my inability to feel whole on my own. While I had touched on this understanding of wholeness many times, and intellectually grasped its significance, the deepest part of myself still needed to have it all hit home once and for all. Until this actually took place for me, I would latch on to the next thing that was going to pay off quick with the emotional reward I so desperately craved. I would invest and reinvest, my energy, time, money, commitment, heart and soul into the endeavors I have outlined in this book only to trace them back and realize it was an apparition, a mirage, an empty placeholder for what I actually needed. None of it had led me to the place where I needed to be, the place where I was always meant to be.

But when I met my wife Yolanda all of this changed. The moment we met, I found a stillness and wholeness in just being together. It was entirely involuntary and I recognized this difference in how I felt immediately. She was different from all the rest. She was going to play an important role in my life. She is the one who would never leave me. The moment I met her, a voice inside me said, "This woman is the mother of your children." It wouldn't have mattered if I had trusted that voice or not because, in time, it most certainly proved to be true. My goose was cooked and it had probably always had been, since the moment the world was first written into the stars. The horrible emptiness and loneliness, the neediness and deep emotional vulnerability I had been carrying around for decades just vanished the moment I met her and now, 20 years later, has still never returned.

When I met my wife, I had returned to college full-time and was also working full-time. She was living alone and doing the same. I reached the end of my spiritual path shortly after we began living together, within a matter of weeks. Castaneda had already died and not long after I'd come to Portland, the truth started coming to light and I went into a period of cult deprogramming. She'd had a similar disillusionment in her life, with organized religion, years before, something in her past had deeply ripped her off, taken advantage of her trusting nature under the banner of faith, but she never spoke of it. She is a quiet woman and there are many things she keeps to herself. What happened to cause her to stop going to church, is one of these intensely personal things I never imposed on.

I only learned the details by happenstance, years later, from a stranger who happened to know the whole story because he lived nearby. The incident was all over the papers at the time. Similar to the man on the bus who told me about the UCLA Trickster, a coworker I knew very briefly, explained to me, one night when we were working late, what happened to a church community outside of Sandy, Oregon in the early 90's. He had long lived in that same area of Sandy, a largely white, rural farming community and once I had described my wife's family and the house they all would visit outside of Sandy. He was well aware of who they were and all that happened to them. He told me a story that shed light on the events of that terrible time and what turned my wife's heart away from religion.

It was another case of a well-meaning congregation starting out with the best of intentions. Before long, they found themselves being led by an overzealous control freak. The church community was gradually overtaken by a black militant leadership and began descending into a intensely chaotic period. This new leadership began blending religious motivations with militant ideology in order to take advantage of financial resources and control the congregation for purposes the charter members never originally intended. This all culminated in some unsolved murders, in the now infamous house, and a spotlight of unwanted media attention on a bunch of folks who were just trying to build a nice little church in the Oregon countryside.

Yolanda was in her late teens, early twenties at the time and has never spoken of it to me. The whole debacle disturbed and frightened her at a very deep level. The only thing she did say about it to me, after I'd learned of it, was that she felt she, and the rest of the congregation, were taken advantage of in the name of organized religion. When she went to find another church after, she could only see, lesser but varying degrees of, the same underlying self-motivations running beneath the surface of the established authority wherever she went. She lost faith in her fellow man, in regards to religious authority. The idea of a perceived authority is what she found to be the most deeply abused influence employed in taking advantage of others. She just couldn't stomach it anymore.

In some quiet way, we helped each other work through the difficulties these tragic events created in our lives and we simply moved on into our future together. After all we'd been through, evolution just made more sense, for us anyway.

When I came to Portland, Oregon to live with her in her tiny one-bedroom apartment, I was juggling an impossible load, at thirty-five years old, a full-time job and carrying fifteen units of college courses each semester. With the mindset of a warrior of total freedom, nothing seemed impossible. The cult mindset I was now crashing out of, contained a feature that knowledge is power and it was possible to tap into infinite energy. I was a 100% true believer in that. I had tapped into it before. Academic success, advanced degrees were considered commonplace in the crowd I had been running with. Ph.Ds. were like a hobby one would do in their spare time. The real pursuit was that of unraveling the mystery of existence, the knowledge of what life actually is.

I witnessed first hand, how important mindset and believing in yourself is, while reaching toward successfully tackling life's biggest challenges. One minute, I felt a winning confidence that I had a truly brilliant mind capable of university success by sheer will alone; I could work hard and study with confidence and certainty. I believed I could easily attain an advanced degree in the field of my choosing, even if I did have to work forty hours a week. I was well on my way. I could break through my limitations and reach for my highest calling. I had no inner whiney baby. I just did it. However, the next minute, I was embarrassed, exposed, failing by lack of any internal motivation what so ever. My academic life, all my hopes and dreams, all my visions of enlightenment and my identity as a man collapsed into a pit of disbelief, like the question I posed in my poem from earlier in the book, was it all just an imaginary thing? Being predisposed toward rapid cycling bi-polar manic depression, with zero treatment, was no help either.

The death of Castaneda and the subsequent emergence of the truth about him had a devastating impact on my mindset, initially. It was a big blow to my confidence in myself, to my self-image. I nearly drown in the shame, the humiliating sting of being horribly wrong in regard to my life's work. The most central effort of my life, everything I had poured all of myself into for fifteen years proved out to be nothing more than a fool's game. I became despondent and morose. I couldn't see any reason to keep pushing into eighteen-hour days of classes, a graveyard job and piles homework, midterms and finals. I honestly tried for several months to keep going and finish what I started. As a warrior, I could shine through it. I could excel and thrive in the rich intellectual landscape of being challenged by knowledge. But as an idiot fool, I saw only hopelessness and a man in the mirror who was so lost, gullible, idiotic. Black and white thinking in its finest hour.

While others had the common sense to pursue in life what others normally pursued, I went after lofty and useless idealities and came up empty-handed. I had wasted fifteen years chasing rainbows in the world of make-believe. It was not just fifteen wasted years but the most productive and valuable fifteen years of my life. From age twenty to thirty five were such crucial years in setting up a life's work and I had wasted them chasing my own tail. That was the real collateral damage for me: a life of promise, which would go unrealized. The things I had put my whole self into for so long, now seemed to me like self-serving forms of narcissism, the consequence of a broad spectrum of personality disorders.

At least these ordinary folks at school were coming away with credentials with which they could then use to go out into the professional world and build nice careers and rewarding lives. I had painstakingly earned multiple Ph.D.'s in Jack Shit. I had written a thousand songs, which amounted to nothing, and a book that was trash. I was broke and had nothing to show for my pursuits into human spirituality, no degrees, nothing of any real value. My intellectual pot of gold was purely and completely imagined and worthless. What I thought would be my brilliant and super-rewarding life's work was nothing more than a game of pretend, which I had been playing in the world of make-believe. Coming to this realization was like a punch in the stomach.

Did I fail or was I merely still within the learning phase? Was everything about my life, my future, my career said and done and is this the result or am I still in the process of learning what the universe has to teach me? Is my life's work over, ended in a flaming failure or am I still in the research phase and everything has taken turns I never expected? Of course, I tried several paths toward enlightenment and they have all come to naught but have I ever tried simply living? Do I need specific training to merely *be*? Was I put on this earth to have everything make sense? What's wrong with simply being who I always already am and not knowing the rest?

Outside The Church

I neglected to teach my children about religion. I let them find their own way without ever mentioning it. When the subject came up, I just told them we believed in evolution. That was as much as I ever said about it and it seemed to be plenty for them. I think it was just that I didn't trust my own judgment in regards to defining the world for them, or for anyone else, at that point. When my daughters asked me, I would simply defer to their mother, in cowardly fashion. Though we both came from a devoutly Christian backgrounds, my wife stood behind me 100% in raising our children outside the church. I did not want to burden my girls with additional falsehoods beyond Santa and the Easter Bunny. Those two were hard enough. I took a lot of shit off those little girls for the crime of lying about Santa and the Easter Bunny. I didn't want to sin against Jesus by lying about him, too, and saying he was real. They'd never forgive me for that.

When my oldest daughter Pepper, was about four, we were sitting at the table having lunch. Her mom and I were talking about people at work and something came up about nationality and I asked if the person in question was Muslim or Christian or something other.

Pepper chimed right in, "What's Muslim?" she asked innocently while she nibbled on her peanut butter and saltine crackers.

I said, "Muslim is like a religion, honey." I told her, "People who are Muslim believe in Allah. Christian people, like Grandma, they believe in God and Jesus and stuff."

"What do you believe in?" She casually slid the question out there, so innocently, still studying her cracker as she drove it deeply a pile of peanut butter. I had to think about it for a second.

"Your mommy and I believe in evolution." I told her. She looked at me. Her reaction was hilarious and said a lot about the nature of human belief.

Her eyes widened and she seemed to explode in joy. "I believe in evolution, too!" she proclaimed loudly and suddenly. Leaving her cracker stuck in the peanut butter, her hands and legs and went flailing in every direction as if she were cheering a grand slam home run at the world series of baseball.

We all laughed with her because she seemed so happy to be the same as what mommy and daddy are.

"Oh, wow!" I teased her, "You believe in evolution, too? That's an awfully profound statement for a four-year old."

"Yeah!" She grinned, as she casually returned to her cracker. Then, once she'd thought about it for a second, she looked at me with a question on her face. "What's evolution?"

Her mother and I just about died laughing. Children want to believe what their parents believe because they want to please them. As children we want to receive the pleasure of their acceptance, not the disapproval going against them yields. I might have been able to tell her I believed in monsters but I think she would have known I was pulling her leg.

I told her, "It's kinda like growing up, honey." I explained, "You were once a little baby and now you're a little girl." I explained, "Evolution is kinda like that. Everything changes a little bit over a long time."

She accepted that and returned to her peanut butter and crackers.

On another day, when she was maybe five years old, we were getting her bundled up to go outside in the cold weather, I happened to say the word God in front of her and she immediately asked me in her childlike way,

"Who's God?"

Before I could put my brain in gear, I heard the words, "Just some weirdo," come falling from my mouth.

My wife looked at me like, "What the hell... are you..." and before I could stop myself.

"Just some weirdo, trying to sell us something." I heard myself saying.

"... telling our children now?" her mouth fell open with a look of bewilderment on her face.

I could only shrug my shoulders and walk away.

"Oops!" I thought. "My bad..."

Later, my wife's family members would take my daughters to church but we found they were naturally immune. Fortunately, we had raised them to be honest and they could only exclaim of how boring everything was, even Sunday school was boring them to tears. Then, one day, I had a very enlightening conversation with my daughters while driving them home from school. When my youngest was about five or six, she told me about her friend, whose family believed in a strict religious upbringing, and went to church almost every day.

Her friend's family did not allow their children to celebrate their birthdays, to accept gifts, nor did they allow the children to celebrate any holidays, even while their elders could drink wine and enjoy special bread on such days. This is what she told me and it bothered her deeply that her friend could never enjoy her birthday. This is coming from a girl who starts counting the days until her next August birthday, starting in September, and keeps continually redefining her wishlist, on a bi-weekly basis, until it arrives.

My daughter had been preached to by her friend and asked me what she should do, or say, when being confronted by people who tell her she's doing wrong by not praying over her lunch or not going to church every other day. These are the same two little girls who figured out the whole Santa thing very early in life. They were probably 4 and 8 respectively, when they started balking at the idea of where all the awesome gifts were actually coming from. I was surprised how early the youngest put the kibosh on Santa. I think she started hearing things from the older kids in our cul-de-sac.

I asked them if they believed SpongeBob SquarePants was real. They laughed at the absurdity. "SpongeBob is a cartoon, silly. He's not a really real person," my youngest responded.

"Right!" I said, "But how do you know for sure? "

They looked at each other, genuinely puzzled at the question and my youngest, Sienna, ever the argumentative one replied, "Because he's... not...

real. Hello?"

"So, you watch the whole cartoon and you enjoy it, but you don't make-believe it's more than a cartoon, right?" I asked. "And you have all the t-shirts, the plushy toys, the books, the DVDs, the bath towels, the SpongeBob aquarium decorations, and all the SpongeBob toys in the world and yet, you have never lost sight of the fact that SpongeBob is a cartoon, an imaginary thing." We all laughed. They were having a lot of fun with this.

"For example," I tried to bring it closer to home, "your grandmother for instance, is deeply Christian. She reads her Bible, prays and goes to church every Sunday. She even says grace over every meal. A lot of grown ups believe that things we can't see are real. So they naturally want to convince others to believe what they believe, too. Like, Pepper's imaginary friend, Linda. She knows Linda is imaginary, but she still enjoys playing with her sometimes.

"Adults have imaginary friends, too, sometimes," I told them. "Think of Jesus as an imaginary friend who a lot of adults like to play with together. The dangerous thing about adults though, is that they are taught, by other adults, to believe the imaginary, but just this particular kind of imaginary, like religion, is real... and they get really, really mad if you tell them it's not.

"When we're around Grandma, we never say anything bad about church or Jesus Christ. We don't say 'God damn it,' and we don't say, 'Awww, Jesus Christ!'" we laughed. "We just smile and say grace at dinner, whenever the whole family is here. It's just a traditional thing to do," I told them. "We have no problem playing Jesus with the family. But it's not just play; this is what I want you to understand. It's *serious!*" I told them. "If we don't play along, it will hurt their feelings really bad, they might even get really mad at us. They would probably call us bad names and wouldn't love us anymore, and that would be really sad." We all had a good look at each other, a serious look, a look of bewilderment. We all naturally had a moment of silence just thinking about how horrible something like this would be, if it happened. They honestly understood, fully, the gravity of these types of situations in our lives.

"So, if you think about it," I told them, "Jesus is kinda like SpongeBob, but for adults. The only problem is, a lot of adults still believe Jesus is real, that he lives in the sky with his father. It's like Santa, at the North Pole, or the Easter Bunny, but for adults. Some adults, a lot of adults, actually, still believe in things that aren't real. And, because it would hurt their feelings, all the other adults aren't allowed to say anything any different to them. It's kind of a strange thing grown-ups do. Grown adults let each other believe in Santa-like things, if they want to and we aren't allowed to say anything bad about it. So always remember this," I advised them. "Just like it's very wrong to tell a child Santa isn't real, it's considered even more wrong to tell adults, and children, too, for that matter, that their religious beliefs are imaginary."

I seriously admonished them, a second time, so they would never forget. "Never say to your grandmother that Jesus is like SpongeBob, or you will upset her very badly." They easily understood it all. We all seem to have an inborn instinct for letting grandma think we are all little angels.

"Just like little kids who still believe in Santa Clause, there are countless adults who hold imaginary beliefs about how life on earth got started. They are called Creation Stories." I told them.

"Creation stories?" they said in unison, "What's that?" they asked.

"It's just stories! Like the ones in all the books you have, like evolution. It's just a story we tell ourselves about how the world first began." I laughed, "Because we don't know. Nobody knows exactly for sure," I explained. A lot of people think scientists are starting to figure some of it out. So, since nobody knows for sure, everybody makes stuff up and tries to get everybody else believe their story is real because they can get money for it, if others think it's real. They can pass the offering basket and that's how they get around having to get a real job and working for a living, the way mommy and daddy have to work for our money. We don't want to take people's money for make-believe. We don't feel right about taking advantage of people like that, so we just have regular jobs.

"But everything is a story, honey," I told them. I wanted to make this learning opportunity hit home. "Stories are part of everything we do! They are what make everything about living so wonderful. Everything is a story! Some stories are true and some aren't. A lot of times we don't know which stories are true and which aren't. So we have to be careful what we let ourselves believe. We have to be really, really honest with ourselves about what we actually know and don't know. Sometimes that can be hard.

"People can say anything they want when they tell a story," I told them. "The story is what makes Christmas seem so beautiful. Christmas would not even exist if it were not for imagination and the world of make-believe. The only reason we have Christmas is the same reason we have Santa. Everyone wants to believe in the Spirit of Christmas. I love Christmas!"

Oh, man! That got a rise out of them. "I love Christmas, too! I do, too!!" they both shouted. "Christmas is awesome!" my little one said.

"Christmas is something people made up and now everyone thinks it's real. In other parts of the world they don't even celebrate Christmas. They believe in something else. And we all know Christmas is imaginary but it's such a beautiful time of year, we would never admit it, even to ourselves, because we love the magic that believing in it brings! And that's why adults like to believe in things that aren't real. Because it makes us feel good. Sometimes believing in things makes life magical and we all need a little magic in our lives sometimes," I conceded to them.

"Christmas is a story we keep repeating to ourselves, like a favorite book we love to read over and over again because it makes us feel so good to hear the story again. Stories and books would not exist if adults didn't like to play with imagination and the world of make-believe, "I explained, "and you know how much you guys love your books!"

Their eyes grew so wide. I said, "How would we live in a world without books? Without stories? Can you imagine a world without stories?"

"NO!!!" They laughed. "Are you kidding?"

"See? Stories are part of everything we do as people. Everything we do has a story. SpongeBob is a story. Each episode is a whole new story all its own. Your friend's religion and the reason she can't have any birthday presents is all a big long story they tell each other," I explained to my two little passengers.

"I went to the store and something happened. You went to school and something happened. What? What? Tell us! What happened? Well, let me tell you the story. Right?" I laughed, "Mommy comes home from work and what does she do? She tells us how her day went. How does she tell us? She tells us the stories! Huh? Everybody has a story to tell!"

Once we stopped laughing, having so much fun talking about how life is, I said, "A lot of adults still believe in religion. They never really examine the story, they just choose to believe it. When we do this, we don't distinguish between imagination and reality. A lot of adults don't even care. They just assume what they believe is real. Adults like to disregard the difference between faith and facts, so it would be very impolite, even hurtful, to say anything to upset them. Just like it's really uncool to out Santa to little kids. Same/Same." Their eyes grew very wide and they looked at each other and shook their heads in agreement. "Let them believe it until they are ready to come out of it on their own. If they never do, like Grandma, that's okay, too. We love her anyway."

We have to give our children credit for being as intuitive and instinctual as any full-grown person, maybe even more so. Children have a way of apprehending life directly because, unlike adults they are used to not knowing everything. If their sense of trust in themselves isn't somehow interfered with, they'll figure quite a lot out for themselves. They'll hear people out, listen to what everyone has to say and then decide for themselves. In this instance, I was trying to prevent my daughters from being drawn into the world of make-believe without being conscious of it, by their friend who was suggesting they were being ignorant of a supernatural law dictating what you need to say to yourself before you can eat your lunch in good conscience.

I have always taught them to think for themselves with their own mind and not let others, even myself and their mother, draw their conclusions for them. I have taught them to take everything anyone tells them and think it through for themselves and decide how they feel about it. If they honestly feel differently after they've thought it through, I've tried to teach them that they should never be afraid to express how they really feel about the issues that matter to them, especially, in regards to the election cycles and the evening news.

I have emphatically tried to guide them toward thinking for themselves and never blindly believing the way the news media might try to make things appear. "Always think with your own mind, not someone else's," I have said to them many times. I never try to convince them one candidate or party, which I might prefer, is better than another or how to feel about news stories. I have always wanted them to look for the source information in each story, for the raw, unfiltered information and decide for themselves how they feel about what actually happened, what was actually said. I have always tried to help them understand the difference between facts and spin.

I'm suggesting that we have the ability to come out of the world of make-believe, wherever we still maintain our fortresses and join completely in the natural world, the world we all share together. I'm not asking anyone to blindly accept anything I have put forth in this book. I could never suggest that my words are a replacement for the way life actually is, but I would simply ask that you keep an open mind in regards examining your ability to distinguish imaginary things from the actual world. I am hoping to initiate a deeper awareness of what is imagined and what actually exists. I have quite honestly been deeply surprised, in my inquiries, how far down the hole the imaginary rabbit actually runs.

Being There

Once my life came crashing down and I had successfully made my way through the process of cult deprogramming, I just sat at home and shook my head for a long time. My true home would eventually become Yolanda and my two beautiful daughters. Wherever she was, wherever they were, became the only place I would ever want to be. If she was at work, then I would just go our place of residence and wait for her there. If our place of residence changed then I would go there and wait until all of us had come home. If we were on the road, wherever Yolanda was, we would figure out where to meet up and that's where we would go to be together, that was home for me. Home is us together. It doesn't matter if it's in a hotel, a motel, a car moving down the interstate, a restaurant, the waiting room at the ER, wherever she happened to be, that's where I'd go to find her waiting for me. Then, together we'd decide what to do next. I think we are pretty much still doing that, last time I checked. About twenty years have gone by now and not much has changed in this regard.

Once we were married, our children arrived and we bought our first home. The years just went zooming by and I forgot all about any spiritual quest, or whatever it was I was seeking. The core of my identity morphed into the man I turned into today. I ate, I slept and I went to work. We struggled with normal issues of raising children and having to work full-time. We struggled with childcare, paying the mortgage, keeping the cars running. We lost our jobs. We found new jobs. We got behind on the bills and really stressed out. We got ahead on the bills and took the kids to Disneyland. We went to weddings, funerals, baby showers, dinners, concerts, movies, parties. We planned for retirement. Maybe I wasn't going to be a glorified rock star or an artistic spiritual genius but maybe it was enough to accept it as my duty to be the Daddy of two little girls.

All my hopes and dreams came falling back down to earth. At every major junction in our family life I always tried to place my selfishness aside and give each of them the quality life and sense of security I wish I would have never lost. Along the way, I had to face all the same issues my parents faced and learn my way through all the same lessons. Some of those lessons were far more difficult than I ever could have possibly imagined. In the end, it felt like I had to solve issues which weren't exactly my own. Sometimes, I felt as if I were resolving multigenerational dysfunctions, that if I didn't get past it, my daughters would have the same issues to deal with. I felt like I had to hand my children a clean slate, so their lives could be emotionally better than mine was, more productive, more rewarding. My mission has always been to provide a stable and warm family home for my children, where they never feel threatened or exposed to the nightmares I experienced.

The imaginary, the inaccurate conclusions I had come to about the world, dancing in the world of make-believe, was it all a part of growing up?

Like the thousands of imaginary tea parties I would attend with my daughters over the years to come, and then one day to attend not one more. Even time itself began to appear as if it were some kind of bizarre mirage. As if to hold her tiny hand in mine to cross the street, only to one day feel her tug her hand away and realize only years later that this had been the final time, that I would never hold her hand that way again? The years went surging by me and I never stopped to recognize the joy that was slipping away even as it was happening. I tried to savor every instant of the finer years and the special moments of being alive. The more I savored them, the more sweetly I tried to embrace them and deeply enjoy them, the greater was the sting of my despair upon realizing, at once, they were forever gone and could never be recaptured. And my, my, my. . . How quickly they went by.

How soon my daughters grew too old to hold my hand, to climb to the top of Daddy Mountain while I sat on the couch, to sing the SpongeBob SquarePants song at the top of our lungs at the beginning of every episode. I knew I didn't want to miss it. I never knew it was coming until it was almost gone. What simple joy we took in living out the moments. It was nothing more than our being together. *Being there* was everything. The more suburban our being together could be, became the very essence of what made it all so significant and vitally beautiful. Driving my daughter to soccer practice or simply sitting in the park, one sunny morning watching them play, couldn't have been more perfect. There was never any other thing you could possibly ever *be* but *there*.

And now it all lives only in my memory, and barely even there at that anymore. It appears as if time is some incomprehensible mirage and even memories are tenuous, at best. The here and now, Square One, is really the only place worth living. And that voice in our heads is made purely of imaginary thought. I learned to let it go, pause it, barely listen. I finally found my completeness and contentment, once I had built it for myself, through being honest, putting in the effort of maintaining my integrity and doing a lot of good, old-fashioned, hard work.

I had carefully formed relationships with quality people and built a world where there was no other place I would rather be than in my own here and now. It took a lifetime of struggling to find, to weed out the toxic relationships, to let go of the maladaptive daydreamer and all the bad habits, but one day I would look up only to realize I had done it. Together we had built ourselves a place in the sun. We had sealed our family within a sacred, unbroken circle of daily self-renewal and each new season naturally empowered continually regenerative harvests of personal growth, healthy relationships and contentment. There was nowhere else on earth I'd rather be.

"One of the most potent fertilizers of abuse, is the power we give up when we look upon others with the perception of authority. By virtue of perceived authority, ordinary folks often give away inconceivable amounts of their own power for reasons which are entirely imagined."

Chapter Thirteen
IMAGINARY UMBRELLAS

AFTER I'D HAD time, perhaps another fifteen years, to let the dust settle, it began to become apparent what the universe had to teach me about itself. Like my friend Tom Hess had suggested long before, not to "throw the baby out with the bathwater," that I would "still come away with some seriously valuable spiritual lessons" from it all. Eventually, it occurred to me that maybe it hadn't all come to naught. Maybe there were some *lessons that stuck*, for lack of a better phrase, after the dust and debris all fell back to earth. What were the lessons that stuck and which ones were "seriously valuable?"

First of all, I dropped the idea of spirituality from my life. It didn't work for me in its present context, after years of trying to make it work. I, in no way, think of myself as Atheist, someone who denies the validity of all theology. I had spent too many years developing a love of scripture and creation stories to consider myself an agnostic, but if that's what I don't know means, then sign me up. However, if what I do know can't be put into words that would satisfy a rational definition, then that's something else entirely, a space between, a world without words, a non-religious, incomprehensible physical mystery. Moreover, I came to a baseline state as a passive observer of the human condition. Spirituality is too amorphous and magical of a concept, so I had to let it go. When I did, there was obviously a residue left in its place. Over that next fifteen to twenty years, I would sit in the presence of this burned down building and try to instinctively intuit what this area of life is, which had consumed so many years of my lifetime trying to understand. All I could do was sit there and shake my damn head, for many years.

Spirituality, works as a metaphor, as in lifting someone's spirits when their down, as a description of attitude, such as being in good spirits. In this sense, I acknowledge the value of spiritual guides and the need for faith in our lives, because I also work to lift the spirits of those who are down, suffering from madness and just generally being miserable. If one could imagine a non-religious spirituality, regarding the health of the human spirit, the bonds of trust we need to nurture between us and the inconceivable mystery of being alive, only in this sense, does spirituality make any sense to me anymore.

They say there is an exception to every rule and the exception here is this idea of body, mind and spirit. I have come to approach this idea as "body, mind and ?" However, as a literary device I am not so certain "?" is as appealing to the reader as the more romantic idea of the nobility of human spirit and the ideal of an eternal soul. To have spirit, in the traditional use of the word, we have to venture back into belief in the unseen again, and as I've said, I am cautious and guarded in how I regard belief of this nature. Nevertheless, the unseen is a vast domain of human experience and through it all, this entire book is a platform for addressing the "?" in body, mind and ?

So, how do we refer to spirit? It's a quagmire to adequately define the word spirit here. For the sake of this present work, I'll say it's the indefinable part of ourselves while, at the same time, I offer the reader an olive branch. At this point, I am left to define for the reader my bare bones worldview, which is all I have left, once I had scraped up the measly little pieces of my shattered dreams and gave up on ever trying to make sense of everything.

To address this subject of body, mind and spirit more accurately, after all this time and effort, spirit and spirituality are domains riddled with I don't knows, for me. If someone asked me to identify whether I am a Buddhist, or an Atheist, or a Somethingist, I have come to the conclusion that I am an Idon'tknowist. Knowing that I don't know many things, and being okay with not knowing, is one of the seriously valuable lessons that stuck. Accepting not knowing dismissed all the mental grinding, imaginary conceptualizing and intellectual arrogance that had robbed me of an extraordinary amount of open space within my being. It was in this newly opened space where I would come to sit each day, to humbly lick my wounds and without talking to myself about all the things I didn't know, simply be, getting in touch with who I always already am.

I found my worldview opened up and some concepts came along to the new view and many were abandon because they didn't carry their own weight, or betrayed my trust in them. I don't have enough time left in my life to be burdened hauling around a bunch of dead weight, lugging the heaviest concepts of unraveling the mysteries of life. I travel lean now. I travel light. I simply am. I eventually landed firmly in the center of Square One and I never looked back. The lessons that stuck are about the essence of life, not about spiritual life, these are lessons the universe had to teach me about itself, the lessons which brought about a definite result I could feel, I could measure, a reward for getting it right, a sense of clarity and aha!

I have had to overhaul the entire subject of human spirituality in my own understanding, based on what worked for me and what didn't, based on what my study of imagination and the world of make-believe has brought to light, and based on what appears to actually exist, to the best of my knowledge and experience. In experiencing all that I have in the course of my lifetime, I have naturally come to new conclusions. I'll begin to elaborate these conclusions I have come to now, and explain my stripped-down world view in the coming pages. The lessons that stuck will be self-evident and if you find anything "seriously valuable" then I hope it serves you well in keeping all you hold sacred in life, safely regenerating, within the daily self-renewal of unbroken circles.

The sacred circle, I hope you noticed, that's one of the lessons that stuck.

Imaginary Umbrellas

> *Imagination and make-believe aren't actually real because they are merely made of thought, which has no corporeal reality. We cannot touch imagination, nor can we consider anything that is make-believe to be real. Since all of our thoughts are simply imaginary, theoretically, they don't exist. And in this sense, they are nothing.*

Revisiting the statement at the beginning of this book, that this is an imaginary book about nothing, we have made our way through a work in-process and here we are at the other end of the book. I have been diligently plugging away at the keyboard for a year and a half now and because I have put forth the slow, focused, methodical and sustained effort of work, arranging all the little symbols we call letterforms into words, suddenly, the little choo-choo train of thought is out chugging along the tracks, and what was once an imaginary book about nothing is now an actual book about the power of the human imagination. It's now making its way around the bend to where you are.

It is no longer an imaginary book; it is an actual book that anyone can read. In its present state, it is only for humans who speak the English language. As a reader scans these pages, my ideas are merely springing to life within the confines of the human imagination and nowhere else. The deep meaning I am presenting is leaping off the page, rummaging around in some mysterious way through the brain and into your consciousness. We are two mysterious beings, you and I, communicating through the wonders of our symbolic forms, these invisible boxes filled with magical meanings. Through language we are enjoying the fruition of this long, slow, painful evolution the human brain has made from primal man, to behavioral modernity. We are now coming into our own as who we are today. We find ourselves in this very human condition we are in. And you have a book in your hands.

My thoughts are now doing what we said thoughts would do, during the earlier portions of this book. They are being shared and through the wonders of language, becoming part of the collective human imagination. If the ideas in this book went viral, through the power of our shared imagination, they could influence the way a lot of people think about life, change the way mankind behaves and thus change the world.

We have now looked at how primal man first began to evolve from the first nascent signs of greater cognitive capacity, as the human brain grew larger in his head. We have considered how religion, faith and marriage all are so central to who we are, how we develop and draw our intensely personal identity. We have contemplated the meaning of life through considering all that we believe, even though these may be nothing more than variables to which the human imagination assigns a given value, then like a function, spits out a conclusion. We looked at the rule of law and jurisdiction, geopolitical borders, nations, corporate entities and how these are human inventions as well, not existing in nature of their own. All of these individual systems of thought, these incredibly powerful guides for human behavior, are nothing more than make-believe umbrellas and yet, beneath them the power of the human imagination somehow naturally draws us together to operate purposefully, under a single ideology, delivering the unimaginable power of our highly-focused collective action.

As adults, we have developed a powerful need for all of these conceptual playthings, to stay sane as individuals, keep the peace as a civilization and live well together, safe in our communities. All of these imaginary systems of thought exist because we've needed them to, our lives demanded them. We have looked at how each and every thing in the man made world has been derived from the seed of an imaginary idea, then built-out using our ability to do careful work together. Through planning and construction, manufacturing and production, we unite beneath the form of our imaginary umbrellas, these systems of thought we have carefully derived to facilitate thousands, millions, and more, performing together in a singular, orchestrated effort. We have examined how work itself is as magical as the stuff of imagination is made out of. Work is a form of practical sorcery in which human beings have become especially adept. Work breathes the imagination to life, building out all the man-made wonders that make our lives so richly rewarding.

Imaginary umbrellas are present wherever we gather together with purpose, especially to work and to accomplish meaningful goals. We gather beneath the umbrella of our alma mater, our school in education, the logo of a company in a business enterprise, as a community in civic duty, in our churches, marketplaces or even sports leagues, a larger umbrella under which teams are smaller umbrellas. An imaginary umbrella has a central idea, a purpose for being and many spokes which all function as a unit, to support and expand on the main endeavor. Wherever we gather, the purpose that binds us together is like an imaginary umbrella under which the collective efforts of many join into agreements and mesh together to initiate planned action in the world.

One of the central elements of an imaginary umbrella is the binding force the idea of perceived authority holds. We are drawn together collectively, to work in concert for our mutual interests, around the sensation that there is someone *in charge*, an individual or group of individuals who hold the reigns of control over the situation at hand. Whether this is an individual investing his own money and needs help to start a business, or an elected official we entrust to handle our community efforts, or a little league coach, there is someone in charge, a person or group with the responsibility of keeping the umbrella's purpose functioning.

For whatever reasons we choose to do so, we grant this perceived authority the over-arching rights of a specialized form of control, which the rest of us beneath the imaginary umbrella won't have. We give this power away when we come under any given umbrella. Whoever this central figure is, takes control away from the others and becomes the collector of power at the center of a vortex where all parts of the umbrella meet. For example, a homeowner's association, a little league coach or the president of a charity organization, each becomes the perceived authority under the context of their umbrella. The perceived authority has the power granted to it, by everyone else, to make decisions, make changes and control the procession of whatever happens according to their own will, generally based on a set of rules, while everyone else beneath the umbrella carries out their part of the agreements made beneath this banner. It works beautifully, when it works, and it works well most of the time. Imaginary umbrellas are everywhere. They are big, small and every size in between. Children, adults and people of every age form them. They are as natural to human life as trees are to the natural world.

Sometimes our part of the agreements made beneath an imaginary umbrella are simply to buy a ticket, take our seat at a particular time and listen to a perceived authority give a lecture about his or her area of expertise, sing us a song, or teach us how to do something in a new and better way. We agree to be respectful, keep quiet and only applaud when it's appropriate.

You may see where I am going with this. The imaginary umbrella can be where we are employed and the perceived authority may be a supervisor, management or executive administrator. It's not rare to find individuals in these positions corrupted by the notion of perceived authority, who exhibit a tendency to abuse the idea of perceived authority and become tyrannical. The name Jack, my mother's second husband, comes to mind here, for some strange reason. Corruption and tyranny exist all throughout human societies. One of the most potent fertilizers of abuse, bullying and subjugation, in the absence of brute force and military action, is the power we give up when we look upon others with the perception of authority. By virtue of perceived authority, ordinary folks often give away inconceivable amounts of their own power for reasons which are entirely imagined. And the other party is more than happy to receive it from them.

Legitimate authority and perceived authority are two different ways of looking at the same imaginary idea. In legitimizing an authority, we have all agreed to respect a person or representative body, and give away some of our own power under the umbrella idea that this will be in the best interests of everyone, for the common good. It will make life better, if we all agree to entrust our power to the newly empowered legitimate authority. The keyword here is trust. When we issue authority to an individual or body, we do so out of public trust. When abuse of perceived authority occurs, the trust is broken.

A sacred trust is no different than the natural law of the unbroken circle we learned from the medicine people. The reason family bonds are able to grow stronger is because all the family members grow to trust each other very deeply, they feel emotionally safe together and stay committed to holding this trust sacred. Everyone involved, does everything they can, to ensure the trust in each other is maintained. Hey don't hurt each other. They don't wound each other. They nurture each other's soundness of mind and personal growth. They place a very high importance on maintaining this sacred trust between them. Being together takes precedence over other options, often enough to keep the bonds from weakening or breaking.

These rare individuals and groups have developed an emotional intelligence to feel which way their relationships are moving and take responsible action to keep things right between themselves. They don't neglect the difficult work relationships sometimes require to stay healthy. Quality of life, whether in a relationship, in a family, in a community and in a society is a matter of nurturing trust. The larger the numbers, the more difficult it becomes to maintain the trust between the people and those given authority. The authority needs to be transparent, honest and concerned. The people need to keep their side of the agreement, as well, being mindful and caring about the difficulties of positions of authority. When trust breaks down, only openness and honesty on all sides can heal a broken circle of public trust, and the same holds true at the interpersonal level for individuals. In today's world, we're witnessing tremendous breakdowns of public trust nearly every night on the evening news.

Through the pain and anguish of my life, I've come to this conclusion, the hard way. The virtues of being open and honest, while delivering the greatest rewards life has to offer, in our family circles, in our business interactions and in our communities, have been the most painful and hard-won lesson of my lifetime. I can only hope the lesson stuck well enough so I never have to repeat the process. Take it from me and learn to be tactfully honest and open with everyone in your life about everything. This simple change alone, frees more vast territory within us, which can be made available for lasting personal growth in every area of our lives.

By the same token, once we each get a handle on how to shut down the imagination and stop everything that flows forth from it, the idea of authority is going to be reduced down to simple laws of physics and matters of the heart. However, from this point of view, if the police came to my door, guns drawn, I am not going to go out there to challenge their authority, whether I feel it's legitimate or not. But this is exactly what all kinds of idiots do every day. They stop believing in the perceived authority of the legitimate officials. Next thing you know, they are out on the front lawn with a gun, challenging the living hell out of a couple dozen nervous cops, none of whom want to take a stray bullet home with them today.

What makes this guy able to act like such an idiot? Well, authority, for the most part, exists only in the world of make-believe. The man on the lawn waving a gun in the air doesn't want to play this make-believe anymore and he's going primal. If all men were created equal, then we just have a bunch of average, everyday hominids standing out there waving guns around. But when we throw in the idea of perceived authority and the imaginary umbrella, one of these hairless apes is vastly outnumbered. We have to return to the notion of a well-armed idea reaching out of the world of make-believe to issue a real-life beating. Serious consequences are about to flow out from the power of the human imagination into the world, through action.

Like King Hammurabi before them, when there is work to be done, the cops are getting ready to lay down the law. And when it comes to collectively organizing human actions beneath the power of imaginary umbrellas, size matters. Now imagine the guy on his lawn has two hundred militia buddies who start gathering around to present themselves behind him, armed to the teeth with assault rifles and rocket launchers?

Imaginary umbrellas. They are very powerful things.

If the alpha male challenges you, do you back down because he is the legitimate authority, created by nature? Or is the alpha male the one with the most confidence and self-belief? Is he merely a perceived authority? The structure of our social order can be a very complex study. In some families the man is in charge and rules the family with fear and intimidation. In other houses, the man cowers whenever the woman raises her voice and she is the true head of the house. Interpersonal roles, being imaginary, can be difficult to think about. The point I want to make is that our roles may not be as hard and fast as we might believe. Often, the tables can be turned on bullies, tyrants and corrupt authorities when we refuse to play the mind game of perceived authority. We gain a freedom to decide our own destiny and choose our own future when we refuse to empower a perceived authority in our own lives. We can choose not to be taken advantage of.

Often it works best if we let perceived authorities play their game and believe we are playing it too. Nevertheless, by not playing it and acting like we are, we gain latitude to secretly lay better plans and, when the moment is right, take control of our own situation. We deliberately take charge and move out from under the imaginary umbrella, or take the whole thing down entirely, destroying the fake umbrella of perceived authority. Whether taking down an abusive husband, a human trafficker, a corrupt politician or a rogue nation, understanding that perceived authority exists only in imagination and the world of make-believe offers us the opportunity to see, where in our own lives, we are giving away our valuable power to others. Just because someone might be extremely dangerous does not give them the right to impose their will on the less dangerous, nor does it mean they can't be taken down.

Giving away our power to others under the banner of perceived authority is an all-too-common abuse of the power of imagination and the world of make-believe. We can lead self-determined lives, even in the face of those who are screaming that we absolutely cannot. The need to distinguish between what is imagined and what actually is, becomes the deciding factor of whether you will be defeated or succeed in becoming the one who is in control of your own life. Corrupt individuals may believe they are able to control us to get what they want. Let them think whatever they want, until the opportunity presents itself for you to demonstrate, with complete finality, that they cannot.

We have considered the paradox of how imagination *is*, but it isn't. It's real, but it's not. Imagination is one of those things that we know we do and yet, we don't know why. The ability to imagine, runs full-time, and most of us never consider the possibility that it doesn't need to, that it's not mentally healthy or particularly hygienic to be encapsulated in make-believe imagery twenty-four seven. As well, it can often amount to a huge waste of valuable energy. Imagine how much better each of us might feel if we saved this valuable energy, took time to pause and do some inner-cleansing work each day. We need to wash and deeply cleanse the mind with the clean, fresh waters of a universal peace and stillness. This might sound like an airy fairy notion I am expressing here but I want to be clear, however I might sound in describing the practice, underneath my words is an open space which affords us the opportunity to experience the true substance of who we are. I am merely trying to draw the attention to one of those seriously valuable underlying themes I came to find worthwhile. Many of these themes I speak of are wordless experiences of an indescribable nature.

Our imaginary activity can be paused a while each day, so the mind can be refreshed, completely cleared. This allows the whole mind to return to its natural state where it can ring true, like the clear tone of a singular bell, intoning on a well-tuned frequency, acting as a harmonically-balanced amplifier of internal silence, of universal bliss, peace and wisdom. But you don't have to take my word for it. Give it a try and see if you are capable of being one with your whole self. I'm convinced everyone is capable of tuning out the distractions and getting in touch with more of who they always already are.

When we spend sustained durations of time simply being in the present moment, the mind becomes clear and present, mentally healthy and hygienically wholesome again. How would that feel, to tune out everything that is not immediately present where you stand? How would it feel to enjoy our whole being in good health and vibrant again, full of energy and revitalized? The mind can experience a regenerative self-renewal in each day, when we set aside a time and space for health and well-being to flow into us. We never seem to consider the possibility of what would happen to our health if we cleared out all the noise and self-concern, opened up a space, a period of time in our lives for pause, to simply ride along into this time in a state of simply being. Our own automatic imaginative theater leads to an enormous amount of personal madness, as much as clearing it leads to the beauty of a life made sweeter by the wisdom of our years. Whichever one we choose, both require the same amount of effort, either way.

It is the purpose of this writing to show how the imagination is responsible for both the great magicianry of human invention and a vast number of very great dangers in our world today. Many of the problems we all lament on the evening news and wish we could find answers for, are the product of human thought. We always think someone else should be the one to fix it, to solve the problems. Isn't this what we have entrusted authorities for? We dismiss the possibility that we can be the one who lights the match that starts the fire, which might blaze through human consciousness and ignite a planetary explosion of universal calm.

The Presence of the Whole Self

Throughout this book I have referred to the imagination as both good and bad. It functions to serve many of the most fundamental needs in our lives and in our world. But many times in the preceding chapters I have referred to how imagination can work against us, even becoming a formidable barrier to our most important needs of all, the need to develop and to feel complete and whole.

Imagination has become a place of refuge for mankind, a place to hide from the harsh realities of life and all we'd rather not face. It is easier to retreat into a fantasy, to live in denial and act as if all we believe is sufficient to advance our world into the future. But we are at the edge of a new age for mankind and many of our religious beliefs are still arcane, purely imagined and lagging behind the rest of human development. The rate of scientific discovery in the last hundred years has accelerated human evolution at a rate we've never seen before. Not only can we now walk erect but suddenly we can fly, we can travel in outer space. We have the ability to reach a level of understanding about ourselves greater than ever before in human history. We stand at the threshold of being able to turn our reality into something far more rewarding than anything imaginary could possibly be. For this reason, I want to raise the idea that imagination can act as a formidable barrier to one of the most rewarding but hard-won satisfactions in life, the presence of the whole self.

As conscientious adults, we run scenarios in the theater of imagination where we are having make-believe arguments, altercations, physically and mentally stressing-out, worrying and getting worked up by things that have not even happened and most likely never will. We can get drawn in, either on our own, or by others, into looking forward with anxiety or into the past with regret. By doing so, we lose sight of our actual place in the present moment. From here, it's a stone's throw to where the emotions get out of control and everything can get the best of us. A lot of bad things can happen when we enter these states of instability.

There is a way we can avoid this kind of thing entirely from now on. All this worrying and mental tail chasing is how we avoid our responsibility for personal growth, the uphill push of our own personal development. We live in denial of simply being in the presence of everything we feel because, sometimes, it can be uncomfortable and unpleasant, or too intense. We would have to stop what we are doing, pause for a moment, and clear our minds. This is an interruption. It's a change. We would need to consciously sit in silence, spend some time and attention in the present moment, until we had a chance to neutralize the charge of our own static cling. Because this takes a little time, many of us are too impatient. We don't want to pause and take care of ourselves this deeply. Like exercise, we have to decide for ourselves why we need this kind of self-care in our lives, why it's necessary. Once we get up and get going, it feels really good to break through the inertia and get our bodies moving. It also brings good health and fitness. The same is true for getting in touch with who we are, feeling through our own barriers, entering the space we've cleared in our daily lives, caring enough about ourselves enough to really find out who we are. It is in this space where we come to wait for the presence of the whole self to return to us.

I am presenting the idea that mankind has yet to fully mature into his more developed faculties. All things considered, we have not yet emerged from behind the veil of our own self-reflection. Grown men and women, adults still remain lingering in childlike state of imagination and make-believe. This half-cocked state drives the actions of madmen and terrorists the world over, affecting the outcomes of our lives and possibly our fate as a species. This is fast becoming a hindrance to our own evolution and an imposition upon all the creatures of the earth. There is a mass-extinction taking place all across the planetary surface and it would behoove us to awaken from the negative side of our imaginary pursuits, lest we may prematurely fall as a species into the history of the fossil record.

Over and over, throughout this book, I keep returning to the idea of being able to pause the imagination and return to a place I call Square One, the name I have given to the state where attention is fixated in the present moment and all mental verbalizing and visualizing activity is paused. This state is immediately on the other side of a barrier of distraction, one held in place by imagination and the world of make-believe. There is a great wealth for each of us and for the future of mankind beyond this barrier.

To become present in this state beyond the barrier opens the space necessary for the basic physical sensations of the body to become a part of our conscious experience. The conscious mind and body blend into a singular, integrated whole within the larger world. This is a more intense place to dwell and the intensity is why we often tend to avoid it. It takes intention and practice to turn the mind outward away from self-absorption, bringing it into harmony with the silent and wordless hum of the natural world. Nevertheless, it is personally rewarding to successfully venture into this open space within our own experience and feel the self-empowerment of being more in touch with who we actually are and what the world actually is.

To actively embrace this abstract idea of an alignment between the body and mind with the higher self, we need to first consider living our daily lives in a way which is healthy and regenerative, incorporating quiet time and meditative practices for personal growth, health and well-being. This is our starting point. Let's give this regenerative lifestyle a name to make it easier to process. Let's call it the right way to live.

When our subconscious tendencies of the body are consciously tempered by practicing the right way to live, they are brought into alignment, integrated with all we experience consciously in the mind. We release a lot of *resistance* we feel toward our real life sensations in feeling. We begin to experience more of an alignment between body and mind. This is very healthy and can cure many medical issues if approached correctly. For this to occur we need to clear a little time in our lives, even if it's only a matter of minutes, it's a start. We have to open a space to experience what it feels like to be who we are.

The pangs and cravings, the sensations of the animal self rise into our conscious mind and make us crazy. They make us do crazy things to alleviate the discomfort these urges bring. They make us have imaginary arguments with ourselves, play make-believe movies of how we are going to seriously deal with our boss at work, once and for all. We eat all kinds of bad stuff, we drink liquor, we smoke whatever looks smokable, we howl at the moon, we do any number of things on a list a mile long to avoid getting in touch with all these countless sensations which are pieces of who we actually are. These countless sensations are very basic to us, therefore I refer to them as coming from the basic self. This is a term which originally comes from the ancient Huna teachings of the three selves.

For the Huna, the three selves are represented by unconscious, conscious and higher conscious selves. The basic, conscious and high self, as

I refer to them, are one of those seriously valuable lessons which remained within the remnants of my burned out spirituality, and has stuck with me for a lifetime. This concept remains with me, even in states best explained to the reader as the absence of all words. I have found, these are accurate descriptions of the subtle sensations of human experience common to everyone. I like these terms because they are the clearest way, I've found, to articulate a deeper understanding of the realm of perceptible sensation and what it feels like to be human.

When the imagination is no longer dominating our ordinary day-to-day self, and the verbal mind is paused for a time, their is a direct apprehension of the natural world around us, without the filter of verbal interpretation and visual imaginings. Halting the imagination halts the automatic machinery of the verbal self entirely. This creates a vast open space within us and leaves only the presence of an observer standing in its place. Only the being who lives in the present moment in the natural world remains. In this state, we are now being lived by *something greater than ourselves* in the present tense.

We experience ourselves as being part of a greater system of life. We transcend the individual and approach a more universal state. In this state, who we are and the world around us, can be felt directly, allowing everything to become what it actually is. And when the little self gets out of the way, the big self has the space to take over, the presence of who we are and the presence of the world around us tends to blend out into one continuous field of being. Gone is the intermediary wall of imaginary boxes filled with interpreted meaning. When we break through our own walls, we apprehend life directly and our personal growth begins naturally advancing with each passing season. As the seasons pass and we grow in our ability to become more conscious, more whole. We grow more adept at aligning our individual presence with the universal calm.

We have to come completely down to earth in order to make contact with presence of the whole self. I learned during my time with the medicine people that in order to soar with the eagles into the rarified air of dreaming awake, the little self has to have it's feet firmly planted in the solid ground of the here and now. I found the more engaged my presence of mind became, the more awake in the physical moment, the clearer and more capable I was of reaching further into the dream of universal wholeness, the higher I could fly on the wings of my perception. The earth is the mother of our species, the mother of all life as we know it, and by being present where we stand on the earth, our roots grow down as much as our spirits learn to rise and eventually to fly. This is only a way of speaking in metaphor, because I am talking about states of being.

There is no way to imagine what actually is or to make-believe anything about the present moment. What actually is, is merely so. To become the presence of the whole self is to become totally present where you stand and to be unafraid of feeling everything you already are, in every situation all throughout your day. To tear down the walls and allow the whole self to return to us is a process of letting go, opening up and allowing everything we can possibly feel to become present at the same time. To be able to sit still and open up to everything we are capable of feeling is one of those seriously valuable lessons.

It's not about emotional self-indulgence, quite the opposite; it is a willingness to be in the same space with everything we are and work through the issues until there are no more. When we are suffering cravings while on a diet, breaking a powerful addiction, feeling impatient or annoyed, overcoming the loss of a loved one, the turbulence of a lifetime lived out of balance, if we are able to honestly open up, *without resistance*, to everything we are feeling in the present moment, we come to understand why it is truly worthwhile and how rewarding the presence of the whole self can be in our lives. There is a calmness we can come to, a quiet place and it's in this place, when we're truly centered and fixated in the here and now, where the wings of perception can open, unfold and we can experience the power of silence, orders of magnitude, states of grace.

When the whole self enters into our presence, body, mind and spirit are all quietly aligning within the present moment. It can happen naturally to anyone, whether they know it or not, in moments of dire consequence, when it's all on the line, when everything they are is there and with complete sincerity they really mean it. Whatever it is that brings us to this state, the basic, conscious and highest sense of ourselves can come together, align to help us meet the greatest challenges we will ever have to face. Moments like these are very rare in our lives. However, they don't have to be.

The state when we are approaching the alignment of the whole self is something which can be nurtured, if we sincerely care enough to make it happen. The high self doesn't stick around long once honesty, sincerity and deep concern for others, for what is right are no longer present. However, when we put it all together… as rare as it is, body, mind and ? become one and this is an extraordinary place to stand.

It is a nearly indescribable state of the presence of everything we are. There is something very heartfelt and transcendent, a connection to the only things that truly matter in the moment. And it's interesting when you talk with people while you are in this state. They feel that you are sincerely present from the center of the earth to the top of the sky and it moves them very deeply. You are emanating a feeling of calm they only wish they could feel and it touches them. Anyone in this state has the power to change the way people around them feel. They walk away from this experience a little different, often with goose bumps, their high self communicated with your highest self and theirs reached down to touch them and it moved them and they probably don't understand what it is. But their high self knows. So, maybe they will be drawn toward it more often. We can only hope.

There is so much about the body we don't know, which remains subconscious. There is so much about spirit we are unable to conceive of. By clearing the conscious mind, we bring ourselves to pause and align everything we are in the present moment. There is nothing between the world and us. Even these words I am using to describe this state are not the *state of being* itself. By looking into the space between the words, between our thoughts and all our imaginings, we can teach ourselves to dwell in the space between. As sure as the seasons pass, we can reach out to others from this state and touch them with the powerful calm of wholeness. To everyone who needs it, we can emanate a state of grace.

*"The path of knowledge I chose to study was
the invisible field of human experience.
It led across the imagination and the world of make-believe
and out to a universe of open space that lay beyond."*

Epilogue:

THE TAKE AWAYS

A DISTANT BELL

Chimes cool the afternoon silence,
The leaves will all be whispering soon
While I wait, on a visitor who never comes,
For a pot of tea,
The movement of a curtain beside an open door
When night crept slowly from the east, consuming the hills
There is love in the remembrance of towns,
    in the shadows of the eves,
        in the warmth of old friends and new faces.

And I will have to move away
From the waterwheel pond within my garden walls
From the place of all I know to somewhere I can't yet remember
And there will be flowers in bloom
Even as the stars are strewn across the fields of the heavens
And the grasses will all be waving
In this afternoon's receding light.
Along the street, an old woman sits in rapt repose
Listening for a distant bell that has no sound.

Her thoughts become invisible boxes filled with nothing
Pouring water over the edge of the infinite
While the curtains dance upon her lonely window frame
I cannot look back.
Even ourselves, fashioned of imaginary nothings,
Untether futile moorings
and overflow into forever.

The Invisible Experience

Imagination and the world of make-believe appear to transect the physical universe as a separate, invisible plane of existence. We cannot say because something is imagined it is not real or has no value. Look around, most of our human experience is created from the power of imagination. It is stunning how much the human imagination is responsible for.

We can imagine anything imaginable but the fact remains we are merely animals who live in the natural world. We have evolved to where we are today because we are a function of the natural world, a product of the natural world's slow, grueling evolution. We, in fact, *are* the natural world. Human life is a fully integrated component in a larger living system, the part of the natural world, which is presently human. Like the cells of our bodies or any vital organ, all parts mysteriously function in concert to maintain the health and vitality of the whole. We are a natural product of the earth as much as forests, or geology, or the weather. Somehow we tend to view ourselves and everything man-made as somehow unnatural, contaminating nature, we separate our species out of nature and think of ourselves as apart from the natural world. Many religions teach that the world and everything in it was created solely to benefit man, that we have divine right and are not of the earth.

We are present in nature, right now. We are as much a part of nature as anything else. Everything mankind makes is as natural as honey, or any given fruit we find on trees. Everything man-made is as natural as the rain forests. It is just a different kind of natural. Much of what we do poisons the environment for all the creatures of the earth. Our waste products will change the chemical composition of the earth until it is no longer suitable for us, then we will die off and something else will evolve, better suited to the environment, as it exists then. The earth will evolve something new. Nevertheless, in our time, we came up from the earth, even if man's world does look like the scar of a volcano eruption, we are no less natural than the scar of a volcano eruption. We may use caustic chemical processes to turn natural resources into our products yet, trees and plants have been performing the same mysterious processes to produce their own flowers, fruits and vegetables for eons. So have volcanoes.

My point is, since imagination is present inside us, as a function of nature, it appears to be a product of the human brain, what we sometimes refer to as grey matter. It must exist in many species to some degree, for all we know. Thus, imagination is based in matter, it's natural and of the earth. It has to be considered a result of what is physically present within the natural world, an extended capability of the natural world itself, a product of evolution, therefore a component of the larger system of life itself. If it is present in us and we are present in the natural world, it must be true that imagination cannot be considered imaginary. Obviously, imagination is a product of physiology. This approach would render this work moot and I am well aware of this fact. But I can justify my reasons for writing this book.

For me, whether or not we regard imagination as neurochemistry and physics, the point of this book remains intact either way. I've set out to carefully examine how the ability to imagine functions in our world, in our lives. In this book, I wanted to examine what the contents of imagination are, what they do, what they cause to happen in the world. By following this line of reasoning through to it's logical conclusion I wanted to suggest that the power of the human imagination is capable of being reinvented and harmonically re-tuned to better serve mankind going forward. To examine imagination in this way, I have had to carefully separate the hardware from the software. I have separated the imagined from the imaginer, the product from the machinery that makes it. I set out to separate the content of the imagined from the content of the natural world. To accomplish this I have had to separate myself from the process, the activity of imagining. Indeed, it was by doing this that I came to rest at Square One.

I wrote this book to better understand the human imagination, but by doing so I came to better understand myself. There is something here that is very rewarding on the individual level, if we take the time to trace it all back to our own state and understand how imagination affects our own inner life. The purpose of this book has been to share what imagination and the world of make-believe are obstructing us from seeing, why it is so valuable to pause and cleanse our conscious experience every so often.

By understanding imagination and the world of make-believe in this a new light, what this present work leaves the reader with is an invisible device to keep in mind, a little software application to run every now and then. Here is a tool that can be applied wherever we go and it can be used whenever we find ourselves at the intersection of here and now. The application of this abstract idea, clearing a space in our lives, to align everything we are with everything that is, can be employed at anytime, anywhere. It only takes a moment to pause, clear a space and open ourselves up to align body, mind and ? Once we have enough practice, this becomes an active meditation we conduct on the fly. It becomes a natural part of who we are. We are now living a new life, beyond the barrier of distraction, flying on the wings of perception at will. We are living a freer, happier, more natural and rewarding life between our ears.

I have made it my life's work to follow the path of knowledge wherever it led me. As you can see it has led me into a lot of places where I wound up looking awfully stupid. I have pursued many forms of knowledge that have turned out to be imaginary nothings, pseudo-knowledge. Nevertheless, I followed through to the end and paid full-price in order to completely resolve each matter for myself, until all I needed to work out with myself was made clear. I have made it my life's work to see the world the way it actually is, to learn what it is the universe had to teach me about itself, not what I believed I should be taught about it. Through the process of being torn completely down, spiritually broken and emotionally laid bare over and over again, through having my most sincere spiritual idealities toyed-with and annihilated in the most bizarre, twisted fashion, my world view was stripped down to nothing. I was left with the task of rebuilding, not only my life, but who I understand myself to be, from scratch.

Imagination and our world of make-believe became the phantasmagorical land I had to journey through in the process of fulfilling my life's work. People think I am an idiot because I have never done anything meaningful with my life. I chased rainbows while everyone who has known me built wonderful lives and look at all they have, careers, money, cars, and houses. Like a monk, I've lived my life in an active quest for a deeper understanding. However, the path of knowledge I chose to study was the invisible field of human experience. It led across the imagination and the world of make-believe and out to a universe of open space that lay beyond. It was there I took stock of everything I am and began to rebuild myself, from the residue and ashes of all that was destroyed and whatever lasting truths I had left, my seriously valuables.

I was honest with myself about everything and learned to be honest with everyone. I worked hard. One day, it occurred to me that although everything had been destroyed, beneath the ashes, I had found my life's work is still intact. My life's work is who I am. For better or for worse, I have come through all of this, lessons in hand, ready to give back to the teacher, to the universe that made me who I am. This is what my life's work has amounted to. It has been a study in imagination and the world of make believe. By traversing its boundaries from beginning-to-end, through it all, I came to know what I now call the presence of the whole self.

Now, I have done what I set out to do and everything is all complete. If I am still an idiot, after all this time, then so be it. My area of specialization has been the silent, invisible experience of being and, of course, this hasn't left me with a lot to show for a lifetime of research. What I have delivered here holds the potential to help anyone feel better about themselves and lead a happier, healthier, more rewarding life, if only we care enough about ourselves to practice the right way to live. What right means for you and how the experience of wholeness develops in your case will be unique to yourself. If there is anything in this present work that can be found meaningful to others, then I hope it serves you well on your journey to where you were always meant to be, in the place where you will meet the person you always already are.

For Further Information
about the author and his work:

Email: info@sargenti.org

Website: www.sargenti.org

www.ingramcontent.com/pod-product-compliance
Lightning Source LLC
Chambersburg PA
CBHW051748040426
42446CB00007B/276